IDEA CITY

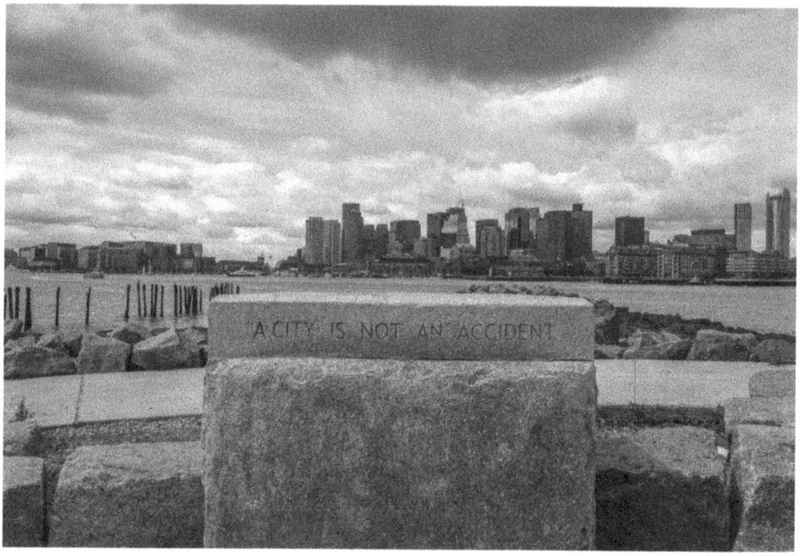

The City of Boston continues to face significant challenges. Intentional, and interdisciplinary urban design and planning will harness our best efforts towards a more prosperous city and metropolitan region. This small monument in East Boston reads, "A city is not an accident . . . but the result of coherent visions and aims." The quote is attributed to architect and urban planner Léon Krier, author of the book *The Architecture of Community*. Image courtesy of Benjamin Cheung Photography.

IDEA CITY

HOW TO MAKE BOSTON MORE LIVABLE, EQUITABLE, AND RESILIENT

EDITED BY
DAVID GAMBLE

UNIVERSITY OF MASSACHUSETTS PRESS
Amherst and Boston

Printed in the United States of America

ISBN 978-1-62534-723-7 (paper); 724-4 (hardcover)

Designed by Sally Nichols
Set in Minion Pro
Printed and bound by Books International, Inc.

Cover design by Sally Nichols
Cover photo by Benjamin Cheung, *"A City Is Not an Accident" East Boston.*
Courtesy of Benjamin Cheung Photography

Library of Congress Cataloging-in-Publication Data

Names: Gamble, David, 1968– editor.
Title: Idea city : how to make Boston more livable, equitable, and resilient / edited by David Gamble, University of Massachusetts Press.
Description: Amherst : University of Massachusetts Press, [2023] | Includes bibliographical references and index.
Identifiers: LCCN 2022045148 (print) | LCCN 2022045149 (ebook) | ISBN 9781625347237 (paperback) | ISBN 9781625347244 (hardcover) | ISBN 9781685750183 (ebook)
Subjects: LCSH: City planning—Massachusetts—Boston. | Equality—Massachusetts—Boston.
Classification: LCC HT168.B6 I54 2023 (print) | LCC HT168.B6 (ebook) | DDC 307.1/2160974461—dc23/eng/20221212
LC record available at https://lccn.loc.gov/2022045148
LC ebook record available at https://lccn.loc.gov/2022045149

British Library Cataloguing-in-Publication Data
A catalog record for this book is available from the British Library.

I DEDICATE THIS BOOK TO ELLE, MY DAUGHTER AND FAVORITE BOSTONIAN

CONTENTS

ILLUSTRATIONS

FIGURES

TABLES

FOREWORD

RENÉE LOTH

Fifty years isn't very long in the life of a city, especially an old one like Boston, fast approaching its four hundredth birthday. But it is long enough to track vast changes in a place and its people, especially when viewed through the lens of a single neighborhood.

When I moved to East Boston in the mid-1970s, the population was 98 percent white.[1] The community's ethnic makeup was overwhelmingly Italian and Irish, mainly first- and second-generation Americans, though a smattering of Jewish merchants continued to run small businesses—a pharmacy, the stationery store—an echo of the days when Eastern European and Russian Jews were the dominant ethnicity in the neighborhood,[2] establishing Boston's first synagogue in 1893. Proudly working-class, East Boston has been a gateway to immigrant families for most of its history, with an immigration station on Marginal Street that processed newcomers—including the notorious swindler Charles Ponzi—arriving by ship.[3] It's no surprise it was sometimes referred to as "Boston's Ellis Island."

Isolated as it is across Boston Harbor from the rest of the neighborhoods, East Boston is today a microcosm of the challenges facing the city as a whole, from housing affordability to climate resiliency to social equity—virtually all of the topics covered in this book. Widening the aperture a bit more, we can see how Eastie's challenges and opportunities are reflected in the entire Greater Boston region: environmental justice in Chelsea, coastal flooding in Quincy and Revere, transit equity along the MBTA's Fairmount Line, and housing pressures even in traditionally affordable gateway cities such as Lawrence and Lynn. As the newly appointed director of the city's planning and development agency told me, "Eastie is all of Boston's issues in one little espresso cup."[4]

East Boston mirrors much of the city, for example, in having been built on landfill. Once a series of five disconnected islands and surrounded on three sides by water, the community is exposed to severe climate threats, including coastal storms and flooding. The city of Boston's interim plan of 2021 reports that "out of all Boston neighborhoods, East Boston has the most population, buildings, and land area at risk from coastal flooding."[5]

The neighborhood's harborfront wharves along Border Street were once the proud home to Donald McKay's shipyard: his *Flying Cloud* clipper ship was the fastest on earth in 1850. But by the time I arrived in the 1970s, many of the creosote-coated piers were rotting into the sea. On hot summer nights, locals teens would dive from the tops of wood pilings into the murky harbor, showing off their jackknifes and cannonballs, suspended for just a second against the twinkling lights of downtown.

East Boston, then as now, was under siege from air and noise pollution generated by a disproportionate share of the city's transportation infrastructure: primarily Logan International Airport, but also two Harbor tunnels that spilled thousands of cars a day onto the local streets;[6] the elevated public transit Blue Line that sliced through the community; and a highway (Route 1A) that served the airport well but contributed only grit and exhaust fumes to neighbors living nearby. In 1973, the Environmental Protection Agency declared air pollution in East Boston a serious concern and proposed a parking freeze and other regulations to discourage car and truck traffic to the airport.[7]

I had come to East Boston to be editor of a scrappy, shoestring neighborhood newspaper called the *East Boston Community News*, founded in 1970 by a small group of conscientious objectors to the Vietnam War who were assigned to a neighborhood antipoverty agency for their alternative service. Aiming to combine traditional newspaper principles with muckraking advocacy for the neighborhood, the sixteen-page tabloid was produced every two weeks by a volunteer staff of local housewives and retirees, aided by "movement types" and earnest journalism students drawn by the promise of published bylines and the cheap beers at Santarpio's Pizza.

We covered school board meetings, budget cuts to city services, and pocketbook issues such as high car insurance rates and home heating assistance, and we even conducted an arson investigation, uncovering disturbing patterns among the fires that were ravaging the wood-frame triple-deckers that comprised the majority of the neighborhood's housing stock. But the bulk of our stories were about land use: expansion threats from the airport, traffic congestion and parking, unsafe abandoned buildings and vacant lots,

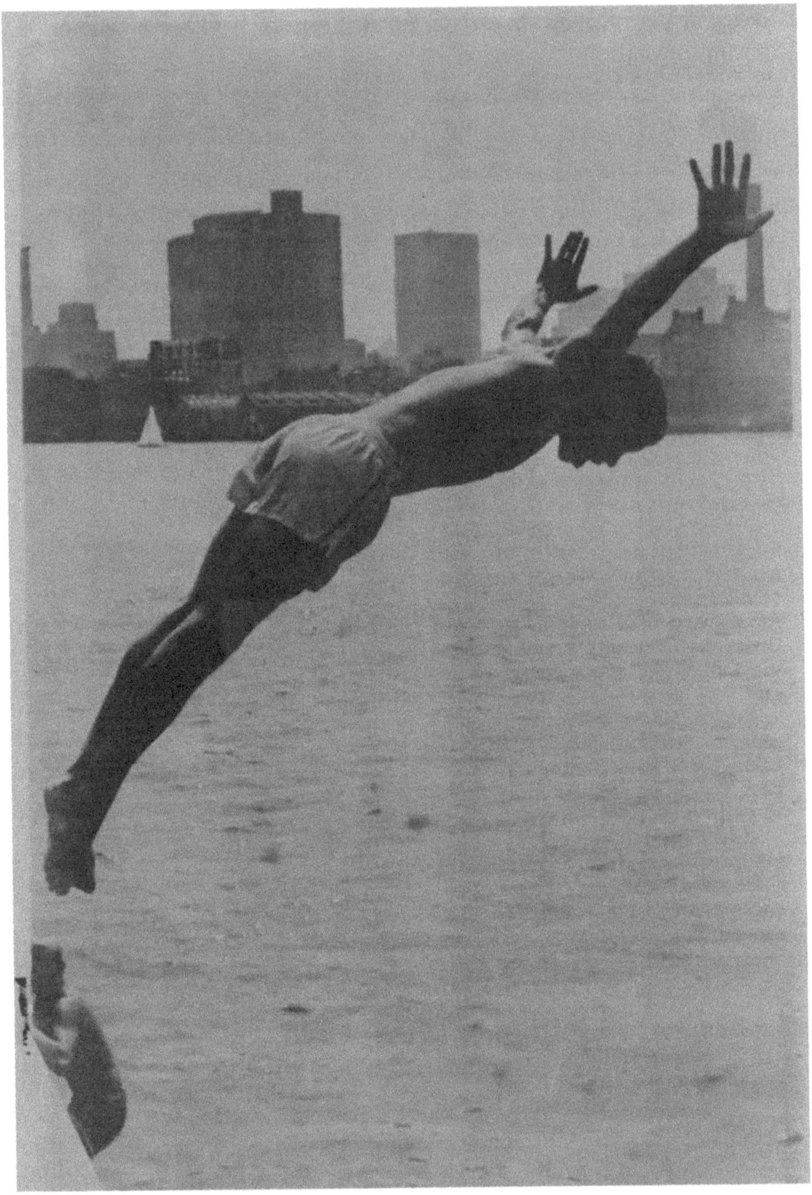

A youth dives off the abandoned piers in East Boston on a hot August night in 1979.
Image courtesy of Mike Rezendes, East Boston Community News, August 7, 1979, edition.

pleas to the city and the Massachusetts Port Authority to get on with developing long-promised waterfront parks.

The term "environmental justice" wouldn't be coined for decades yet, but residents of East Boston knew they were being asked to shoulder more than their fair share of the region's industrial burdens. Especially in the 1960s, as Logan Airport expanded, trucks carrying fill for runways used shortcuts through residential streets;[8] stately elms along Neptune Road were razed for better access to Logan; and in 1969 the beloved forty-six-acre Wood Island Park, designed by Frederick Law Olmsted, was seized by Massport and destroyed to make way for airport expansion.[9] This trauma galvanized the community, compelling residents into lives of intense organizing and vigilance. The late, indominable activist Mary Ellen Welch, whose family lived in East Boston for six generations, told a biographer that the clarion call "Remember Wood Island" became like "a war cry. You don't let it happen again."[10]

I left East Boston in the 1980s and bought a home in another part of the city, but the neighborhood remains in my DNA. I've come back for newspaper reunions, fundraising events, too may funerals, to report the occasional article for the *Boston Globe*, and once, in 2006, to research a profile of the neighborhood for a special issue of *ArchitectureBoston* magazine, published by the Boston Society of Architects. A few years later I became editor of that quarterly magazine, where I met David Gamble, who served on my editorial board. Among his many contributions to the BSA and the magazine was a series of convenings he began in 2017 among some of the city's most creative thinkers on issues related to the built environment, which led to this book. I moderated several of those discussions, and I'm thrilled that they resulted in this permanent record.

In retrospect, the years I lived in East Boston were a time of relative stability, a kind of lull between demographic shifts. But when change came, it came rapidly. In 1970, East Boston had fewer than five hundred Hispanic residents. By 2015 more than half of the population—roughly twenty-three thousand residents—was Hispanic. Today, at least 56 percent of East Boston families hail from El Salvador, Colombia, and other countries in Latin and South America. The former site of the newspaper office is now Los Paisanos Market, a Colombian grocery. New churches have sprung up with names like Iglesia de Dios Fe Salvadora and Iglesia La Luz del Mundo, and even the older, established churches now offer mass in Spanish.

Meanwhile, real estate developers have discovered this neighborhood one subway stop away from downtown, with its colorful vibe and spectacular water views. In what seems an impossibility to many long-time residents, million-dollar condos have replaced the rotting piers on East Boston's harbor. For all the urban ills afflicting the community in the 1970s, gentrification was never an issue. Now East Boston is the subject of academic studies and articles about "green gentrification"—the notion that new parks, climate resilience projects, the Boston Harbor cleanup, and other amenities have so raised the property values of the neighborhood that lower-income residents are being forced out.[11] If the decades of agitating for new housing and waterfront development turn against the very neighbors who fought for these victories, the irony would be cruel indeed.

As Boston was transforming from a sleepy backwater in the 1970s into the brainy, multicultural, and prosperous life sciences hub we know today, its political establishment was more resistant to change. The late mayor Thomas Menino, elected in 1993, was the first non-Irish mayor of Boston in sixty-seven years, and residents joked mordantly that electing an Italian American was Boston's idea of diversity. But in 2021 Michelle Wu—young, Asian-American, forceful progressive, and, perhaps most startling, Chicago native—won more absolute votes for mayor than Menino or any other winning candidate since 1983.[12] A change has surely come.

Among Mayor Wu's first official acts, just two months into her term, was to pause negotiations on a municipal harbor plan for the downtown business district and shift the city's planning focus to East Boston.[13] "We have to get this right on the waterfront and truly plan for equitable access and climate resiliency in these critical areas of our city," she said in a statement. Wu's decision is a significant pivot (or "reset," as she later called it) toward an equity politics that puts neighborhoods at the forefront of city policy, and it isn't just symbolic. At current estimates of sea level rise, 23 percent of East Boston is at risk for flooding by 2030, including most of its major streets and three of its five subway stations.[14]

Wu's harbor plan for East Boston is part of a larger process that will take on other knotty issues in the neighborhood, including affordable housing options, better transportation connectivity, and support for the local economy. That's a good thing, because East Boston is ground zero for nearly every citywide challenge: environmental justice, housing affordability, racial equity, political empowerment, public health—just name it. But even renewed attention from the city's political leadership, welcome as it is, cannot alone protect the neighborhood from forces already set in motion. What saved East Boston from further devastation in the 1970s is what will save it now: sincere, concerted activism by an aroused, awake, informed public. The ideas and inspiration in this book can help residents in East Boston and every neighborhood in the region plot a course to determine their own destinies.

NOTES

1. Boston Planning and Development Agency, "Historical Trends in Boston Neighborhoods since 1950," Boston Planning and Development Agency Research Division, December 2017, http://www.bostonplans.org/getattachment/89e8d5ee-e7a0-43a7-ab86-7f49a943eccb.
2. Rebecca Solovej, "Jews in East Boston," Global Boston, accessed July 20, 2022, https://globalboston.bc.edu/index.php/home/immigrant-places/east-boston/jews-in-east-boston/.
3. On Marginal Street, see Massachusetts Port Authority, "The East Boston Immigration Station: A History," ed. Rita Walsh, February 2012, https://www.massport.com/media/2327/eastbostonimmigrationstation.pdf.
4. Personal interview with BPDA director James Arthur Jemison, June 24, 2022, conducted in Boston City Hall.
5. Boston Planning and Development Agency, "East Boston Today: An Interim Report of PLAN: East Boston," 134, accessed July 20, 2022, https://www.bostonplans.org/getattachment/12076a0b-3a83-4a1a-bb0b-c61b6cb1111b.
6. Herbert S. Levinson, Marvin Golenberg, and Jane Howard, *Callahan Tunnel Capacity Management,* Boston, Massachusetts: Committee on Highway Capacity and Quality of Services, Transportation Research Record 1005, 1983.
7. On the parking freeze, see Massachusetts Port Authority, "A Policy Memorandum," June 2016, https://www.mass.gov/doc/massports-2016-proposal-to-increase-parking-at-logan-airport/download?_ga=2.226423517.615286194.1658366587-1157328597.1657295981.
8. Saritha Ramakrishna, "Land, Sea, and Sky: Environmental Histories and Planning Conflicts in East Boston," Master in City Planning, Massachusetts Institute of Technology, 2019.
9. Dianne Dumanoski, "Parks, Lost and Found—Land&People," Trust for Public Land, *Land&People,* Spring 2001, https://www.tpl.org/magazine/parks-lost-and-found%E2%80%94landpeople.
10. Dr. Regina Marchi, *Legendary Locals of East Boston Massachusetts* (Mount Pleasant, SC: Arcadia Publishing, 2015), 35.
11. Galia Shokry and Isabelle Anguelovski, "Addressing Green and Climate Gentrification in East Boston," in *The Green City and Social Injustice 21 Tales from North America and Europe,* ed. Isabelle Anguelovski and James J. T. Connolly (London: Routledge, 2021).
12. Ari Ofsevit, "Boston Election History," November 3, 2021, https://docs.google.com/spreadsheets/d/1-a9U9JwBdAq3S211HoZpGiQX39mY-FrOCZUvPVz_q6Y/edit#gid=0.
13. City of Boston, "Amendment Process Launched for Downtown Waterfront Municipal Harbor Plan," February 16, 2022, https://www.boston.gov/news/amendment-process-launched-downtown-waterfront-municipal-harbor-plan.
14. Boston Planning and Development Agency, "East Boston Today," 74.

ACKNOWLEDGMENTS

I am so grateful for all of the advice, ideas, and comments on this volume as it has evolved over the years. First of all, thank you to the two dozen authors and contributors. I learned so much from you on this journey. Your critical eyes, compelling ideas, and positive attitudes make me confident that the city and region will, in fact, address its wicked challenges and truly become more livable, equitable, and resilient in the coming generations. One of the most rewarding aspects of living and working in Boston is the engaged citizens and organizations who strive to make it better every day. I am grateful to the Boston Society for Architecture for providing a forum for the initial conversations that led to this book's inspiration.

There are many people that provided timely advice and comments on the many drafts as the project evolved, especially Alex Krieger, Ann Forsyth, David Luberoff, Evan Horowitz, and Kathryn Madden. There were numerous colleagues who worked with me to identify themes and posit future alternatives for Boston, including Kairos Shen, Julie Wormser, James Stevens, Stephanie Berzin, Tiziana Dearing, Diane Davis, Dan D'Oca, Sharon Ron, Anne Hayes, Jill Medvedow, San San Wong, Katie Swenson, Mark Klopfer, Brian Gregory, Antonia Medina Abell, Alexa Usher, and Veronica Eady. Thanks also to Philipp Maue, Alex Batiste, and Miriam Keller for initial research and graphic design support.

This volume would never have materialized but for the publishers at the University of Massachusetts Press. I am indebted to Brian Halley, Rachael DeShano, Joan Shapiro, and Sally Nichols, whose support and keen insights were truly invaluable. Finally, thank you to my best friend and wife, Melissa, for giving me the time and space to engage with these issues in a city we love.

IDEA CITY

CONVERGENCE

INTRODUCTION

PRINCIPLES FOR A GREATER BOSTON REGION

DAVID GAMBLE

This volume began as a conversation amongst friends. Boston considers itself a livable, world-class city, and ranks number one in many categories. It has a thriving digital economy and one of the largest percentage of commuters who walk to work of any major city in the United States. It has distinguished itself with top hospitals and educational institutions. Biotechnology continues to blossom. The region was founded as a culture that places great emphasis on "education, local political control and the pursuit of the 'greater good' of the community."[1] Despite these noble ambitions, there are immense challenges that persist with affordability, congestion, crumbling infrastructure, and increased segregation that thwart our ability to match our high civic aspirations. Boston's historic, tight-knit streets seem to be constantly bottlenecked, public transit is a mess, and our neighborhoods are divided with twentieth-century highways that severed and segregated us. As a coastal city, we are particularly vulnerable to climate change and sea level rise. We asked ourselves, "What can make the city better?"

These initial conversations seemingly began a lifetime ago. They started in 2016, pre-COVID, before the global pandemic uprooted lives and altered (perhaps forever) our live-work balance. They occurred prior to increased political unrest and polarization and before a cultural reckoning of systemic racism and inequality that resulted in more calls for social justice. As time went on, there were critical themes missing and new voices to capture. The list of friends grew.

Idea City presents a range of perspectives on the future of the Greater Boston region. Written by area experts—academics, reflective practitioners, and policymakers—the chapters are organized thematically. The authors describe current conditions of resilience, mobility, affordable housing, social equity, economic equality, zoning, and regionalism. Additional chapters focus on public health, industrial integration, art, and leadership and design excellence. The collection of voices reflects the diversity of the city, and the challenges and opportunities it faces with multiple, overlapping crises profoundly affecting how and where we live.

The themes draw on conditions in Greater Boston, a metropolitan region in a remarkable state of change. From 2010 to 2020, Boston added more housing units than any decade since 1940. That growth is poised to accelerate with over 13,000 housing units permitted in Boston since 2019.[2] With over one hundred major construction projects underway around the city, one sees cranes everywhere, especially downtown. Unfortunately, much of the new growth neither adequately reflects the increasing diversity of the city nor is it spread equally throughout the region. As some places grow, others atrophy and struggle. Finding a more balanced approach to development that leverages our unique assets is necessary for Boston to be a truly equitable place that ensures long-term sustainability. This volume provides strategies to address the challenges at a unique inflection point in Boston's evolution. At the same time, the concepts explored apply to many cities undergoing significant transformation and change. The lessons can be applied elsewhere.

In this regard, at just over forty-eight square miles, Boston's tight geographic footprint aids us; scale matters. Relationships are tighter, and the high concentration of institutions, private sector companies, and not-for-profit organizations offer immense opportunities to address our problems. In order to prevail over our contemporary challenges, we must leverage the relationships we have, strengthen the bonds that exist, and forge new connections where gaps in the system are observed. We must also think more broadly, and beyond the parochial framework of our individual municipalities, to look for solutions that transcend jurisdictions. Enhanced collaboration is needed to overcome the pronounced economic, social, racial, political, and physical barriers.

Individually, the chapters reveal new ways of thinking within one's own disciplinary framework. Collectively, the sections provide insights *across fields*. They expose alternative logics and reveal the complexities and interrelationships between critical issues in urban redevelopment. In this way, an underlying goal of the book is to help readers to not only think differently about their own field but also to draw conclusions from allied disciplines that are involved in urban regeneration. It is the overlapping issues that reveal opportunities, and the intersections that create cohesion and convergence between disciplines and experts who are not often in dialogue with one another. Here then, are examples of such overlap.

GETTING COMFORTABLE WITH DENSITY: REAL ESTATE, REGULATION, AND REGIONALISM

The scale, density, and character of development is largely determined by real estate economics, and what gets built where is highly regulated. In Boston, it is also highly *negotiated*. There are simply few forces that have as direct an impact on the form of our cities as zoning, and this regulatory overlay dictates who can afford to live where. The city is increasingly unaffordable because the value of land—combined with the high cost of construction—requires developers to focus almost exclusively on market rate and luxury units and although the state has an affordable housing law (Chapter 40B), it is not nearly enough to address the affordable housing crisis.[3] Building affordable units at scale necessitates navigating complex local, state, and federal subsidies that require highly specialized expertise. There are firms that do this, but not nearly enough.

Boston is one of the most expensive cities in the United States in which to live, and the disparities between rich and poor are rapidly increasing, crushing an already thinned middle class. With the majority of living expenses for most people going to shelter, we must find ways to make new opportunities to live in a dense, urban context that is both affordable and attractive. Tamara Roy's chapter, "Living Compact," looks at the variables that created a situation in which the vast majority of new housing is tailored toward the well-to-do. As Roy states, an enormous unmet demand exists for units at a moderate-income level, yet the market economy has not been able to deliver them at any scale. Being comfortable in smaller spaces is a way of life for many cultures, but unfortunately Americans associate small homes or apartments with a lack of amenities, or worse, they fear such housing will attract individuals from a lower class. It is not just that people are unsure about living in smaller spaces; in many instances "micro-units" aren't even *allowed*.[4] We must change our mindset about how we value our space. Why is affordable housing so difficult to develop in Boston, and must it continue to be so?

Matthew Kiefer helps to answer this question by clarifying how Boston currently regulates land use. He identifies a new way to approach zoning that limits friction between what we wish to see and how it can get done. The current patchwork system is plagued by a century of fixes that have been gradually grafted onto a set of outmoded rules. In "Zoning 3.0," Kiefer identifies four phenomena that have compromised the effectiveness of zoning, and why it must change. Our needs today are different. If, as he decribes, zoning was all about separation, we must regulate development differently "to produce the complex, lively, even improvised urban places we seek." What would zoning look like if we started from scratch, and how could it serve as incentive for a new form of development?

However, it is not just zoning in the downtown core that needs to change. In "Technology and the Growth of the Boston Metropolitan Region," Andreas Sevtsuk urges more equitable investment in infrastructure that extends beyond the city's core to leverage and better utilize the region's transportation network. He cites emerging economic clusters, such as Assembly Square, North Station, and Union Square, that are easily accessed by public transit, and the need to connect these high-density centers of employment with rail infrastructure to affordable housing around the region. These contemporary employment centers are well connected to public transit and mirror the mid- to late twentieth-century suburban centers of Waltham, Burlington, and Andover, to name just a few. One of the challenges of Boston is that it has both a high concentration of jobs in the urban core and a high concentration of decentralized jobs in the suburbs.[5] Recent legislation for increasing affordable housing near public transit is beginning to take hold, but how can the coupling of housing with transportation policy leverage Boston's transit network and advance walkable, affordable, as-of-right development?

The city may be growing at the fastest rate in decades, but not all cities in the Commonwealth are witnessing the same amount of development. The twenty-six "gateway cities"—Massachusetts' small-to-midsize urban centers—haven't seen the same coordinated investments as Metro Boston. But the core's future is intrinsically tied to the economic performance of its region, and those cities, without strong connections, will suffer. A more robust regional transportation strategy with greater funding for the MBTA will better link surrounding municipalities and foster greater opportunities for growth.[6] Without strong spokes, the hub won't turn.

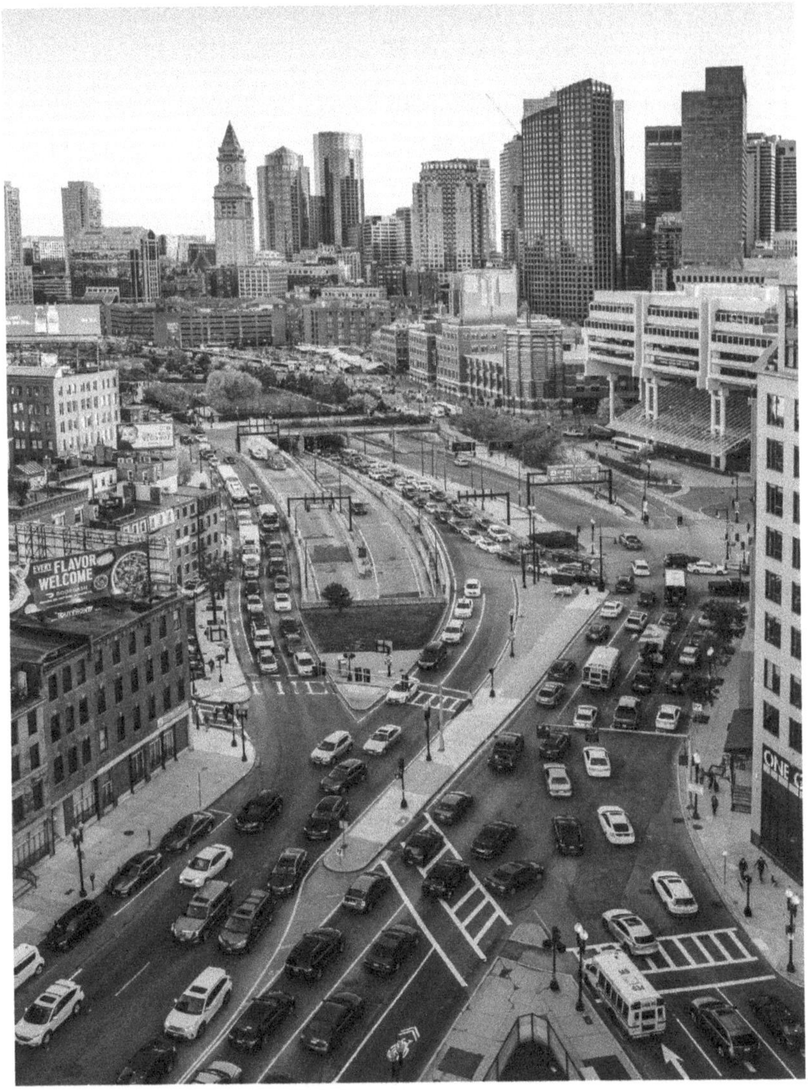

FIGURE 0.1. Forever altering the physical form of the city, the construction of Interstate 93—Boston's constantly congested Central Artery—sliced a wide swath of elevated highway through the downtown core only to be demolished and replaced two generations later with a tunnel, surface access roads, and a 1.5-mile contemporary linear park. Image courtesy of Michael Prince.

FORGING STRONGER LINKS: MOBILITY, RESILIENCY, AND LEADERSHIP

The Commonwealth of Massachusetts has 351 individual towns and cities.[7] While Boston is recognized as the commercial and cultural hub of the region, the surrounding suburban cities and towns have jealously guarded their status as independent communities. Our parochial governance structure provides each municipality with some level of autonomy and control, but it stymies our capacity to do big things. Many of our most difficult challenges need to be addressed through a regional lens. Whether it is advancing a well-networked (and sufficiently capitalized) public transportation system or addressing the dire impacts of climate change and sea level rise, a regionalist ethic that transcends municipal boundaries and political jurisdictions is necessary.

In "Transportation: Metrics and Movement," Alice Brown and Michelle Danila build on the need for a more comprehensive transportation network that diminishes our reliance on the automobile. The authors describe how we've designed our streets in the past, the means by which we create them today, and how we can evaluate their performance in the future. If the primary goal of transportation engineers (until now) has been to move vehicles as efficiently as possible, then we are looking to solve the wrong problem. Investing in new metrics that place equal emphasis on alternate modes of transport will simultaneously reduce car dependence and enhance livability. We need to reframe issues of access and mobility and overcome the pervasive mindset that prioritizes the car over other means of travel. Brown and Danila argue the need for more effective tools and techniques that preference other modes of transport, and while adding bike- or bus-only lanes and removing on-street parking is arduous in a historic city like Boston, contemporary technologies are forging new opportunities. How does the Boston region introduce other measures to improve transportation as the urban population increases and the transit system, in its current configuration, offers little opportunities for adding capacity?

In a coastal region such as Boston, planning for resilience is of paramount concern. Like all waterfront cities where the effects of climate change are amplified, the city is seeking to comprehend, measure, and address their sobering impacts. Large-scale infrastructure solutions are being prototyped at a variety of scales that take into account increasing temperatures, rising sea levels, and more intense and frequent storm events. Yet for now, individual development projects address resiliency largely on a site-by-site basis.

As capital-intensive engineering proposals dominate the sustainability discourse, and where ecological solutions have yet to mature, Antonio Raciti, Rosalyn Negrón, and Rebecca Herst argue that we may be missing the point; the focus on "design" is limited. In "Social Resilience in the Face of the Unexpected," the authors offer a guide to understanding resilience that is more social than infrastructural or ecological. Using the East Boston neighborhood as a test case, they discuss possibilities for enhanced collaboration between institutional and noninstitutional agencies to work on planning strategies that cope with the reality of the unpredictable. Their chapter develops a theoretical framework that expands the definition of resilience and showcases the richness of Boston's cultural and ethnic diversity. In so doing, they shed light on local communities that are largely left out of essential decision-making processes and are disproportionally low-income and communities of color. How is planning for resilience conceptualized and implemented in the Boston metro area, and who stands to gain or lose from local projects that increasingly face global environmental challenges?

Anne-Marie Lubenau is the former director of the Rudy Bruner Award for Urban Excellence, a national design award that "recognizes transformative urban places distinguished by their economic, environmental, and social contributions to the vitality of American cities." In this role, she has a unique perspective on an impressive inventory of transformative projects from around the United States. In "Leading with Design: Cultivating Urban Excellence," Lubenau notes that despite the tremendous growth and development that is taking place throughout the city there remains a lingering air of conservatism that suppresses design innovation in our buildings and public spaces. Granted, Boston is blessed with a multitude of nationally recognized design firms, yet much of the design acumen gets exported away. Simply put, the city is not always associated with progressive design. Lubenau draws from examples around the county and provides six recommendations about how Boston can cultivate a civic culture that aspires to urban excellence. As cities and regions compete for talent, how can Boston cultivate a civic design culture that is as innovative, entrepreneurial, and world-renown as its education, health care, and technology sectors?

LEVERAGING OUR DIVERSITY: EQUITY, ECONOMY, AND EXPRESSION

No American city is a model of equity and fairness, and in the Greater Boston region, the gap is widening. According to the Brookings Institution, Boston has one of the most pronounced income inequalities of any American city.[8] If economic gains are to be broadly shared by all, the city and state need to make that happen with the right ground rules, the right enforcement mechanisms, and the right strategies for building consensus.

Unfortunately, as urban redevelopment occurs, it often happens against a backdrop of neglected areas. There are contested spaces of poverty that intermingle with concentrations of affluence; growth and stagnation coexist in close proximity. Dozens of luxury condominium towers and vast biotechnology labs are filling in around the core, but their presence is fueling animosity between those that have financial resources and those that service them. Boston is a city of firsts in many categories, but unfortunately, it is also near the top of the list of American cities in terms of income inequality. As referenced by Richard Florida in *The New Urban Crisis,* our cities and metro areas are "ironically—and troublingly— . . . both more diverse and more segregated at the same time," with patchworks of racially concentrated poverty and racially concentrated affluence.[9]

These inequities have become even more pronounced due to the deleterious impacts of the COVID-19 global pandemic, increased racial strife, political bifurcation, and amplified social and economic discrimination. Such systemic challenges simply cannot be addressed in isolation. In "Power, the Economy, and Interdependence," Imari K. Paris Jefferies and Marie-Frances Rivera connect with Maria Elena Letona and James Jennings to discuss these issues, and how the pandemic has exacerbated the region's economic inequalities. Yes, the downtown area is growing in population, but is progress really fair if only a small percentage of the population can actually take advantage of the increased quality of life that comes with a robust economy?

In "Social Justice and Urban Environmental Policy," Ted Landsmark builds on this conversation and proposes a shift in Boston's race relations with new public policy and financing mechanisms to incentivize equitable outcomes. He acknowledges the city's legacy of discrimination, and contends that Boston continues to be "*aggressively tribal and insular,*" maintaining a conflicted sense of identity when it comes to race relations. Conversation alone is not enough. How can Boston find a way forward that confronts racism directly and takes steps forward to build bridges to people different from ourselves?

Kate Gilbert's chapter, "Embracing Artists at Every Turn," argues that compelling art in public spaces is the ultimate manifestation of civic engagement, allowing participants to create new strategies, processes, and collaborations to support and sustain. She advocates for a greater role for activism in temporary artwork that lowers barriers for emerging artists and celebrates the increasing diversity of the city. Engaging artwork also generates economic activity, which adds to the reasons to live, work, and play in the city. Boston's Museum of Fine Arts has diversified its collection to include more non-Western art, and in the last decade the Institute of Contemporary Art opened its seasonal East Boston Watershed across the harbor, but a more robust and well-financed public art program will not only reflect the city's increasing diversity but also *express* it. How can Boston advance new forms of democracy that leverage the power of the temporary to celebrate our diversity and showcase our uniqueness?

FIGURE 0.2. A performer calls out to the crowd at BAMS Fest, featuring nineteen Afro-centric and Black artists on two stages with live mural arts, in Franklin Park, Boston, on June 11, 2022. Produced by Boston Art and Music Soul (BAMS) Fest Inc. Image © KBarber Photography.

ENHANCING THE OVERALL NETWORK: PUBLIC HEALTH AND OPEN SPACE

Public health was barely on the general public's radar in early 2020. And yet, by the time of this writing in summer 2022, COVID-19 continues apace, with over 6,350,000 worldwide deaths and 1,000,000 in the United States as a result of the pandemic. A disproportionate number of these deaths are minorities and individuals of color.[10] As the severity of the health crisis plays out across our landscape, we are realizing with increased fidelity the interconnected nature of what it means to live a healthy lifestyle and how it relates to other aspects of our life. Indeed, public health is intertwined, in one way or another, with every other theme in this collection. One's health is affected by one's race, employment, neighborhood, housing, access to open space, transportation options—everything!

In the Greater Boston region, communities such as Chinatown and Chelsea have healthcare disparities that are especially pronounced. In these dense areas of the city, access to quality open space is restricted, and air quality is compromised as a result of surrounding transportation infrastructure. In a roundtable conversation that brought together representatives of not-for-profits and academia, Doug Brugge, Lydia Lowe, Maria Pilar Botana Martinez, Martha Ondras, Jeanette Pantoja, and I discuss the impacts of the pandemic on public health *as it is playing out.* The conversation examines the region through a health lens, and the intersectional frameworks that are essential for addressing gaps in the system. How do we measure, represent, and communicate the stresses on public health for our most urbanized and vulnerable populations when their geographies are constrained by industry and infrastructure?

Finally, Boston's explosive growth in the eighteen, nineteenth, and early twentieth centuries was a result of its deep harbor and extensive transportation network. As more and more industry gets displaced farther afield, Marie Law Adams and Dan Adams assert that traditional industry and contemporary notions of urbanism need not be in a constant state of conflict. We need to recognize that local decisions with regard to industrial production and distribution have regional, national, and even international consequences. Simply moving places of production further afield from consumption and shifting industry to peripheral sites has negative consequences for the system as a whole. In "Productive Tensions," the authors argue that, as a culture, we simply don't understand where things are made or how they get distributed and delivered. One needs to reconsider the relationship of the city to active industrial uses, and that the relationship *can be designed.* As Fredrick Law Olmsted did 150 years ago, Boston can "reintroduce nature into the heart of the harsh, unhealthy metropolis."[11] The city's land use decisions need to guard against sanitizing sites that render industry increasingly difficult to function efficiently. As rail lines, truck routes, shipping piers, and stockpiles get systematically replaced by high-end housing and urban parks, what does this mean for the existing infrastructures that enable those very economies to thrive?

At our country's founding, the city of Boston's landmass was approximately 30 percent smaller than it is today. Sometime between now and perhaps one hundred years from now, the core's coastline will shrink back to its original configuration as the sea level rises to approximately eight feet higher than it is today.[12] Few geographies have land use tensions as pronounced as waterfronts. Boston is a city where active industries that rely (or once relied) on water and rail access are increasingly threatened by high-end residential, office, lab, and entertainment enclaves. One need only go to the South Boston

FIGURE 0.3. Integrating both active industry and public access to the waterfront, the PORT (Publicly Organized Recreation Territory) converts a thirteen-million-gallon oil tank farm into a shared-use waterfront road salt terminal, public recreation, and wildlife habitat landscape. Image courtesy of Landing Studio.

Seaport to witness the transformation of what was once a raw, industrial rail and transportation nexus into an urban entertainment and residential retreat.

In the twenty-first century Boston is becoming more diverse, not less. As mentioned in Renée Loth's foreword and described in Marilynn Johnson's "The New Bostonians," "Although greater Boston has long enjoyed a reputation as an immigrant-friendly destination, global forces and national and state policies since the 1990's have resulted in a chillier welcome."[13] This is a very different state than when *Surging Cities* was published in 1948, proclaiming that "foreign immigration is no longer an important factor in population growth in the United States."[14] A textbook for civic high school students, the book provides a glimpse into the thinking of the Greater Boston region as it emerged from the shadows of World War II and suffered from congestion, obsolescence, and unguided development. Written three-quarters of a century ago, it documents another time of immense change in the city and region. Its tone underscores the autocentric ambitions of the day and urban planning strategies that sought "drastic remedies" and "swift action" for an overcrowded downtown that was beginning to lose population and a nation on the cusp of suburbanization and sprawl.

Surging Cities signaled that more radical changes (and turbulence) were to come as the region transitioned away from an economic base of manufacturing and industrialization and into health care, high tech, and biotechnology. Massive urban renewal and highway construction projects in the 1950s and 1960s would forever alter the physical form of the Boston area and accelerate the out-migration into the periphery which spurred the growth of America's "Technology Highway" (Route 128). However, such top-down initiatives also "birthed a radical grassroots political agenda intolerant of government-led efforts to reorder urban space through exclusionary, abusive and antidemocratic means" as chronicled in Karilyn Crockett's *People before Highways*.[15] Residents were able to stop highway construction in some of the city's most vulnerable neighborhoods and cultivate a community-based advocacy agenda that endures to this day.

There is a future orientation to these chapters. Many books about urban planning, development, and design are grounded in specific cities and motivated largely by the histories that shaped those cities—that is, how the projects, plans, people, and cultures of the past affected the way the place looks and functions today. The chapters in *Idea City* ground their perspectives in Boston's history but are interested primarily in what must be reexamined to ensure a successful *future*. The authors write from a shared vantage point that recognizes our past and is firmly grounded in the present but looks ahead. They seek to develop new and as-of-yet unimagined practices. How must our city and region adapt and change in order to prosper for everyone, and what conventions, theories, and practices are inhibiting our ability to do this?

What form will this city take when Boston celebrates its quadricentennial in 2030, and who will truly feel included in its expression? If we continue along our current course, the city will be not a model of an equitable, well-connected city but rather a shining example of haves and have-nots with amplified social and economic disparities. At this pivotal moment, we have a unique opportunity to harness the talent and intelligence of the region and create a right-sized, strong core with resilient edges and a regional network of partners. We must leverage the relationships we have across disciplines and forge new ones. For all its challenges, the Greater Boston region has immense potential. Our seemingly intractable issues of unaffordability, transportation gridlock, climate change, racial inequities, and health care disparities (together with the other themes outlined in this collection) are not, as Donald Schön wrote in his 1983 *Reflective Practitioner*, "problems to be solved, but (rather) problematic situations characterized by uncertainty, disorder and indeterminacy."[16] Interdisciplinary thinking is urgently needed to formulate new solutions to these vexing problems.

Founded in 1630, Boston is one of the oldest American settlements. However, it is rapidly evolving, and the incremental manner in which development happens, on a parcel-by-parcel basis, belies the fact that the character of entire swaths of the city become almost indistinguishable from one generation to the next. It is the sharp relief of historic buildings directly adjacent to contemporary design that has emerged as one of our defining characteristics; Boston has historically embraced both tradition and change. Examples of such juxtaposition abound in the urban design of our city, like the sweeping Christian Science Center aligned with South End brownstones, Boston's modernist City Hall looming over historic Faneuil Hall, or the iconic reflection of the Richardsonian Romanesque Trinity Church on the glass curtain wall of 200 Clarendon Street (formerly known as the John Hancock Tower).

As the city continues to grow and change, tensions between new and old are becoming increasingly amplified. These chapters reveal the potential of the American sensibility to constantly build a new can operate within a historic setting. With all of our innovative companies, engaged citizenry, academic institutions, and strong philanthropic sectors, we are poised to make Boston live up to its greatest aspirations.

NOTES

1. Colin Woodward, *American Nations: A History of the Eleven Rival Regional Cultures of North America* (New York: Penguin, 2011), 5.
2. U.S. Census Bureau, 1940-2020 Decennial Censuses; Boston Mayor's Office of Housing Analysis of Boston Inspectional Services Department Building Permit Data, January 2019 to September 2022.
3. Chapter 40B is the state's Affordable Housing Law. In light of the fact that Massachusetts is such an expensive place to live, an Affordable Housing Law was enacted with the goal of making at least 10 percent of every community's housing affordable. The law allows developers to build affordable housing by streamlining the permit process and allows for more flexible zoning rules. The process is available to developments that devote at least 20 to 25 percent of their units to low and moderate income families. Unfortunately, many communities have not met the 10 percent threshold and residents frequently strive to stop such projects from advancing. CHAPA, *Chapter 40B Affordable Housing: Frequently Asked Questions* (Citizens' Housing and Planning Association, 2018).
4. A micro-unit is a very small apartment typically no larger than a one-car garage and ranging in size from 250 to400 square feet.
5. I am indebted to David Luberoff at Harvard's Joint Center for Housing Studies for this keen insight.
6. The Massachusetts Bay Transportation Authority is the public agency responsible for operating most public transit in the region and includes light rail, commuter rail, subway, bus, and ferry lines. The agency is seeking to increase the amount of affordable housing near transit through its 2022 MBTA Communities legislation.
7. There are fourteen counties, with thirty-nine cities and 312 towns.
8. Boston ranks sixth nationally in terms of household income inequality, slightly ahead of New York City and behind Atlanta; Washington, D.C.; Providence; New Orleans; Miami; and San Francisco. More information can be found at Brookings, https://www.brookings.edu/research/city-and-metropolitan-income-inequality-data-reveal-ups-and-downs-through-2016/.
9. Richard Florida, *The New Urban Crisis: How Our Cities Are Increasing Inequality, Deepening Segregation, and Failing the Middle Class—and What We Can Do about It* (New York: Hachette Book Group, 2017), 116.
10. Latoya Hill and Samantha Artiga, "COVID-19 Cases and Deaths by Race/Ethnicity: Current Data and Changes Over Time," *Kaiser Family Foundation*, February 22, 2022, https://www.kff.org/coronavirus-covid-19/issue-brief/covid-19-cases-and-deaths-by-race-ethnicity-current-data-and-changes-over-time/.
11. Alex Krieger, *City on the Hill: Urban Idealism in American from the Puritans to the Present* (Cambridge, MA: Belknap Press, 2019), 151.
12. I am indebted to Julie Wormser, senior policy advisor at the Mystic River Watershed Association, for this insight.
13. Marilyn S. Johnson, *The New Bostonians: How Immigrants Have Transformed the Metro Region since the 1960s* (Boston: University of Massachusetts Press, 2015), 8.
14. Theodore T. McCrosky, Charles A. Blessing, and J. Ross McKeever, *Surging Cities: A Secondary School Textbook in Two Parts* (Boston: Greater Boston Development Corporation, 1948), 177.
15. Karilyn Crockett, *People before Highways: Boston Activists, Urban Planners, and a New Movement for City Making* (Amherst: University of Massachusetts Press, 2018), 15.
16. Donald A. Schön, The Reflective Practitioner: How Professionals Think in Action (New York: Basic Books, 1983), 16.

AFFORDABILITY

CHAPTER ONE

LIVING COMPACT

TAMARA ROY

As the fifty-year trend toward suburbanization reverses itself in the United States, downtowns have been experiencing growth among all demographics. Household sizes are shrinking—currently 68 percent of Boston households consist of one or two people,[1] while the housing stock of predominantly three, four, and five-plus bedroom units built in the early 1900s is not well matched to the demand.[2] At the same time, the costs of education, health care, and food are going up faster than incomes, leaving large segments of the population—workforce and entrepreneurial singles and couples, single parents, divorcees, minorities, and the elderly—priced out of the housing market. This chapter focuses on two things: first, the challenges that currently limit the production of units that would meet the demand of smaller households, and second, solutions that could positively affect compact, affordable, and middle-income housing production.

But first, some context. Boston has had one of the longest economic booms of any U.S. city in the past fifty years. It continues to outpace much of the country and attracts knowledge companies with high wage earners, even during the Great Recession, and except for a short pause, it has rebounded during and after the pandemic. Before the pandemic, the *Greater Boston Housing Report Card* of 2019 was blunt:

> To some extent Greater Boston has become . . . the victim of its own success. Having failed to produce an adequate supply of housing for decades, the region is not prepared to accommodate the population

> growth that is being propelled by the current economic boom. Strong job growth has attracted more people into the region and pulled more residents into the job market—both of which serve to increase the number of new households being formed and correspondingly, the demand for additional housing. For a region with a track record of sluggish housing production, this has predictably resulted in demand outstripping supply, sending both rents and home prices soaring.[3]

By 2021, with a focus on housing inequity for low-wage workers, immigrants, and the Black and Latinx population, the *Greater Boston Housing Report Card* stated that the "lack of housing affordability was already an untenable crisis. Stagnant wages in low-paying jobs and increasingly high rents have created a chronic housing affordability crisis in Greater Boston and the state."[4]

In this climate of Boston's overall economic success alongside a high wealth gap, it is vital to figure out how we can best deliver economical housing to those who need it most. There are two poles to the demographic spectrum of demand: the many low- and middle-income single and two-person households who cannot find housing that fits their needs (and who, by necessity, must cohabitate in larger units), and the low-wage, often multigenerational families who cannot afford larger "family units." Certainly, the two issues are intertwined, and efforts to solve the former could benefit the latter.

As the "Mother of the Micro Unit," my team and I have dedicated ourselves to designing high quality compact living environments,[5] prototyping them, and changing people's attitudes through a market testing process. We have worked with the city of Boston on policy changes that streamline design and permitting. In the past ten years we have seen the adoption of micro-studios and micro-one-bedroom units in luxury projects across the city, which has had an impact on supply but not on affordability. The production of efficient, economical small-unit housing at scale, either deed-restricted or simply offered at a cost low- and middle-income people can afford, has lagged behind.

There is overwhelming agreement from the public, press, governmental agencies, nonprofits, and social advocates—even from developers themselves—that an enormous unmet demand exists for less expensive, low- to mid-rise housing, often called, "the missing middle."[6] Yet the market economy has not been able to deliver it. Why?

Simply put, we cannot easily build our way out of the crisis we are in, certainly not in the way Boston did in the early 1900s, when there was an abundance of empty land, merchant builders, immigrant labor, and inexpensive materials. New buildings today are extremely expensive to construct, land prices are prohibitively high, infill sites can be contaminated, and neighborhoods ardently resist density. But we need to find ways to improve our current situation, and an in-depth look at factors the city can control will produce solutions that we can implement, while bold ideas can lead to "outside the box" solutions that could change the dynamic cost disparities in today's housing industry.

MY MICRO-HOUSING STORY

When I was a twenty-six-year-old graduate student at the Berlage Institute in Amsterdam (where my degree cost $15,000 rather than ten times that at a private American university), my husband and I were lucky enough to get a three-hundred-square-foot one-bedroom apartment in the city center. Our flat had two rooms: a combination kitchen/living room with a small refrigerator, tiny sink, two-burner stove, and futon sofa for guests, and a bedroom with a small bathroom. Each room was only eight feet wide by fifteen feet long and had a good-sized window.

Our days were spent studying at the institute, often late into the evening, and there was a communal kitchen with a table that sat sixteen. Loving to cook, I quickly became one of the people who collected money from the others, went to the grocery store, and enjoyed an inexpensive meal with individuals from over twenty countries. When my husband and I returned to our apartment to sleep, we never once thought, "Wow, this apartment is too small"—at that time in our lives it was exactly what we needed.

I didn't know then that my experience would become a model that would guide my future architecture practice designing multifamily residential projects and would develop into my passionate advocacy for policies to encourage lower-cost compact unit rental and condominium developments with shared social amenities. It wasn't until I my husband and I designed the MassArt Tree House—home for nearly five hundred students, with shared commons and no parking on a state college budget—that I became convinced that micro-housing was an economical answer to our city's housing conundrum.

FIGURE 1.1. The MassArt "Tree House" Residence Hall, designed by Add Inc., now Stantec, epitomizes compact living principles of reduced personal space, more communal space, zero parking, and highly sustainable construction (LEED Gold). Image courtesy of Chuck Choi.

WHO NEEDS MICRO-HOUSING?

Compact living is not a new idea. During the late nineteenth and early twentieth centuries, residential hotels, SROs (single-room occupancies), lodging houses, and boarding houses were built in downtowns across the country primarily for singles who came to the city for work.[7] Boston, by one count, had over thirty-six thousand short-term rental residential apartments in the early 1970s. While some were unhealthy tenements, many of the dormitory-style buildings run by churches, the YMCA, women's universities, and so on provided the first apartment to those seeking a job in cities, and inexpensive places to live for singles and the elderly. Today their number is approximately three thousand. They were zoned out in the 1970s campaign to eliminate the seedy associations that plagued some of them.

In the article "Boardinghouses: Where the City Was Born," Ruth Graham makes a strong case for bringing back this efficient and economical means of housing the working class. She says, "For a population accustomed to living with extended family, boardinghouses represented a first step toward the radical autonomy that we now take for granted in modern urban life."[8]

The mismatch between current household sizes and housing stock in Boston is staggeringly lopsided. We are becoming a majority city of singles and couples (and single parents) who desire walkable urban environments over suburbs yet cannot find appropriately sized and priced housing. Widows, widowers, and divorcees with limited incomes would benefit from units smaller than two or three bedrooms. As seniors age, they want to downsize, but there are no small units in their communities for them to move to. Our service economy workforce, as well as students and college graduates, many with starting salaries below $40,000 or in debt, desire inexpensive housing as an alternative to living with their families or roommates. The lack of studios and one-bedroom units often push adults to cohabitate, and with each person's monthly budget being at or below $1,000, their combined rent payment of $3,000 is driving up average asking rents for family units, pushing families out.

CHALLENGES TO BUILDING HOUSING TO MEET THE DEMAND

The production of housing is a complex endeavor, involving inputs that each need to be taken separately to drive out cost savings, many of which I will cover here. This complex web of interrelated forces and conventions that drive costs up for all projects built in the Greater Boston region each play a role. For compact units, there are additional barriers within affordable and workforce projects. The next section is devoted to exposing some of the most common challenges that need to be addressed to recalibrate housing production toward addressing the need.

OUTDATED ZONING LEADS TO HIGH LAND COSTS

With limited land area and a lack of as-of-right zoning (see chapter 2 in this volume) to support reasonable housing density, Boston and many communities in Massachusetts suffer from an intrinsic tension between balancing the need for new housing with the preservation of existing community "character." Property owners who want to maximize their selling price and real estate brokers who benefit from escalating land costs create bidding wars where the land value is determined by speculation and developers propose luxury high-density developments to offset what they spent to purchase the land. Developers are at serious risk as they bet on getting a larger scale project approved than the neighborhood might accept.

If reasonable density could become the zoning norm, and the city could hold to that zoning rather than allow developers to exceed zoning through various legal mechanisms, much of the speculation would diminish. A developer would buy property knowing exactly how much height and density could be built there, and owners and brokers could not push up the value in the "hope" that more units could be permitted. This would give communities predictability as to where and what size development is allowed.

While the *Imagine Boston 2030* city engagement process and *Housing a Changing City: Boston 2030* did an excellent job of highlighting individual neighborhood needs, neither resulted in location-specific master plans that were codified into zoning regulations.[9] While several neighborhoods, such as Jamaica Plain and Dot Avenue in South Boston, have gone through master planning processes, the rezoning process has been slow. Each year more neighborhoods should be prioritized, community engagement and education strategies should be developed, areas should be found for efficient housing production, and funding subsidies should follow. Without clear as-of-right zoning, land speculation will continue unabated.

ARDUOUS COMMUNITY REVIEW

In Boston, because the as-of-right zoning allows for only a one- or two-story building, developers need variances for height, volume, floor-area ratio (FAR), setbacks, and parking, and they are at the mercy of neighbors to pass through multiple public meetings before any zoning variances are granted. In an open-ended process, communities review projects for density, uses, design, traffic, construction, and shadow impacts, wielding great power in framing the resulting development. Abutters, citizen groups, and area business leaders can prolong permits if agreement cannot be reached. The lack of contemporary, neighborhood-specific plans creates a community backlash against density that further lengthens the design review process.

For projects over fifty thousand square feet in Boston, the timeline to complete the permitting process can range from six months to two years or more (for smaller projects, Boston has succeeded in reducing permitting to less than two months on average—this is a great success). The long timeline creates a system where only the largest developers can afford permitting, squeezing out mid-sized developers and contractors with lower costs and overhead. Along the way, impact studies result in often costly mitigation measures that developers must agree to before their projects will be approved.

Through the impact advisory group process (a committee of appointed members tasked with determining the impact of a project on its location and extracting mitigation from the developer), the city of Boston effectively outsources the cost of neighborhood improvements onto the balance sheets of private developers. The thinking goes that if a project adds, for example, two hundred residents and one hundred cars to a neighborhood, it has a detrimental effect on the area and the developer should pay for that impact. For affordable housing developers to keep rents low, they need to limit the scope of improvements to within their site boundaries.

In practice, civic groups use the Article 80 Large Project Review process to fund improvements to streets, sidewalks, crosswalks, lighting, and add green spaces, bus and subway stations, and climate resilience measures that should be paid for by the city. While this may make sense for very large developments that have considerable impact on existing infrastructure, it is an unfair burden to a single project and a huge cost added to housing projects that are trying to be economical.

CHANGING COMMUNITY PERCEPTION OF COMPACT LIVING

Regarding the need to build more efficient units, the current system of community review can be challenging. There is a misperception that smaller units translate to transient lodging, noisy students, taxing of infrastructure, and more traffic. Most neighbors do not understand (or believe) that small units can help their community. They aren't aware that:

- studios and one-bedrooms respond to a demographic need in their community;
- compact living buildings can house more people in less space;
- micro-unit buildings can result in smaller buildings overall; and that
- based on new car-sharing trends and higher use of transit, small households have less need for parking.

When I was the president of the Boston Society of Architects in 2016, I led an initiative with the mayor's Housing Innovation Lab to increase

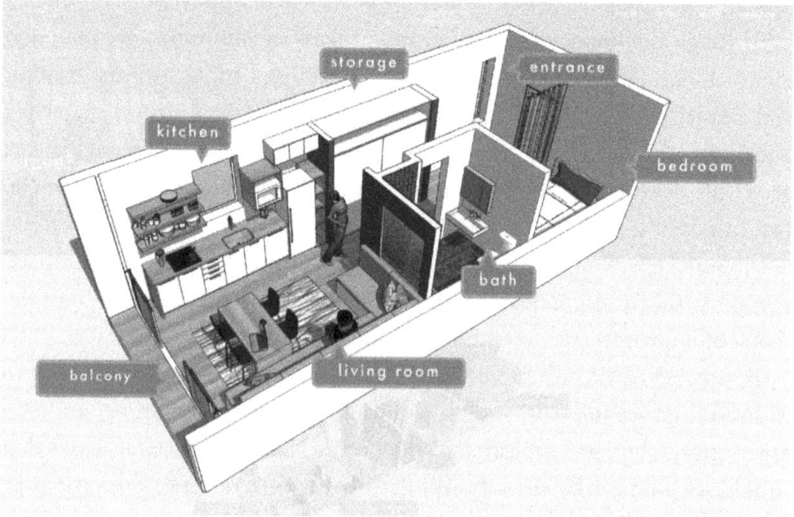

FIGURE 1.2. One tangible solution to educating the public about the small-unit shortage was the "uhu," a 385-square-foot prefabricated "urban housing unit." Built in partnership with the mayor's Housing Innovation Lab and the Boston Society of Architects, the modular apartment on wheels traveled to eight Boston neighborhoods during the summer of 2016, spreading the news that small units are critical to addressing our housing shortage, livable, and nothing to be afraid of. Able to be stacked up to four stories high, the uhu is an innovative and affordable prototype for multifamily residential projects. Image courtesy of Add Inc.

awareness of the need for small-unit housing and set the groundwork for creating the Compact Living Pilot. The "uhu" (urban housing unit, pronounced "yoo-hoo") was built in three weeks at a factory in Pennsylvania and traveled to eight neighborhoods in Boston to gather community input. The model showed that it was possible to quickly produce a 385-square-foot well-designed studio for half the cost of traditional construction. Two uhus side by side, which result in a 770-square-foot three-bedroom unit, would also provide a compact family unit that is easily prefabricated.

FIGURE 1.3. The "uhu" has a large entrance foyer, queen bed alcove, extra-large closet and storage cubbies, walk-in shower, full kitchen, two pull-out sofas for guests, and dining for up to six. Image courtesy of Add Inc.

The uhu was a living lab, gathering feedback from over three thousand city residents. The positive reception gave then mayor Marty Walsh the public engagement response he needed to change unit-size minimums and codify the Compact Living Pilot.[10]

Many people said some version of the following:

- "There's more than enough space; it's just what I need."
- "I'd really like to see a project with units like this come to my neighborhood; when will that happen?"
- "This is bigger than what I live in with my spouse, and better designed."
- "If students are looking to get out on their own, this is a perfect apartment for them."

FIGURE 1.4. Two "uhus" can be combined to create a 770 square-foot family unit with a large living room, kitchen, dining area, three bedrooms, and one bath. Image courtesy of Add Inc.

- "The bathroom is spacious—easy to get in and out of the shower."
- "Having the bedroom separate from the living area is brilliant."
- "I'm a senior, and my house is dark, cluttered, and too large for me. I wish I could move into the 'uhu'!"
- "I love the large windows, and the small outdoor deck is an added plus."

The focus of my research and professional work has been to identify user needs, design prototypes and pilots, and test compact units in the marketplace. Depending on who the end user is and the rents they can afford to pay, there are many creative ways to reduce space (and costs) that have remained unexplored in Boston.

We asked our focus groups these questions:

- How small can a kitchen get and still be workable?
- Can we devote less floor space to bedrooms that get used only while sleeping?
- What do you think about beds, tables, and sofas that fold up into the wall when not in use to save space?
- How much storage do you need in the unit itself?
- What types of program spaces outside of your unit would benefit you?

Answers varied based on age, gender, income level, and location, and we gained insight into the ways that today's lifestyles are shifting away from a one-size-fits-all approach. Flexibility and adaptability are critical components of good small-unit design. Most important is the final rent that the user can afford to pay; many participants have told us that with $1,000 as their budget, they would share everything except a bathroom. Imagine if developers could respond to that demand.

If we want to retain lower-paid single workers, who provide the backbone for the service economy, we need to allow for communal living options such as the old single-room occupancy model that save money by reducing the amount of private kitchens and baths. In our new sharing economy, there should be much more choice by price level than currently exists.

PARKING REQUIREMENTS

Current parking requirements that require a simple ratio of parking spaces per unit are clearly a disincentive to building compact units. They are a blunt instrument that mandates the same amount of parking spaces per unit regardless of the size of the unit or number of occupants. For example, if a developer has a site where they can build ten thousand square feet, they could choose to build thirty micro 330-square-foot units or ten three-bedroom one-thousand-square-foot units. With a static parking ratio of .5 applied, in the first case they would need to provide fifteen parking spaces, whereas in the second case, only five. With site area at a premium, developers choose to build fewer units with less parking.

The city of Boston has now become a leader in parking policy across the country, by encouraging a zero policy for all compact units as part of the Compact Living Pilot.[11] By scrapping higher parking ratios, the city has succeeded in two goals: first, eliminating a costly amenity that drives up the average unit cost, and second, reducing overall parking in the city to meet the latest sustainability and climate change goals.

A study released by the Metropolitan Area Planning Council surveyed "nearly 200 apartment buildings inside Route 128 and found that about 30 percent of their parking spaces go unused, even in the wee hours of the morning, when most residents are likely home."[12] In Boston, according to the American Community Survey, over 35 percent of city residents do not even own a car.[13] With one of the most comprehensive public transit systems in the nation, it makes sense for Boston to look at reducing or eliminating parking as a way to reduce housing costs.

Another win for reducing costly parking premiums was the city council vote in 2021 to relax parking rules for affordable housing. "We know that every unit lost due to delay or the cost of unnecessary, mandated parking is a lost housing opportunity for someone who badly needs it," said councilor Kenzie Bok, who cosponsored the bill with councilor Matt O'Malley. "It's time to make sure we are putting homes for people first and doing away with parking minimums that don't reflect our current needs."[14]

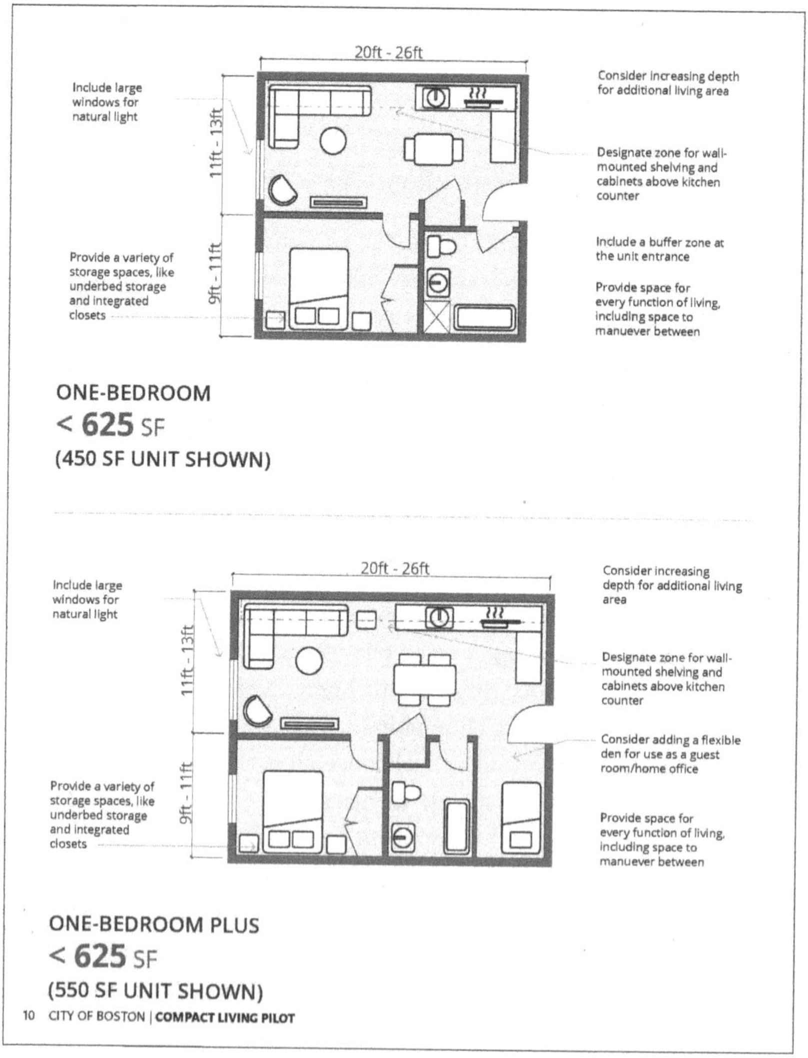
20ft - 26ft
Include large windows for natural light
11ft - 13ft
9ft - 11ft
Provide a variety of storage spaces, like underbed storage and integrated closets
Consider increasing depth for additional living area
Designate zone for wall-mounted shelving and cabinets above kitchen counter
Include a buffer zone at the unit entrance
Provide space for every function of living, including space to manuever between
ONE-BEDROOM
< 625 SF
(450 SF UNIT SHOWN)
20ft - 26ft
Include large windows for natural light
11ft - 13ft
9ft - 11ft
Provide a variety of storage spaces, like underbed storage and integrated closets
Consider increasing depth for additional living area
Designate zone for wall-mounted shelving and cabinets above kitchen counter
Consider adding a flexible den for use as a guest room/home office
Provide space for every function of living, including space to manuever between
ONE-BEDROOM PLUS
< 625 SF
(550 SF UNIT SHOWN)
10 CITY OF BOSTON | COMPACT LIVING PILOT

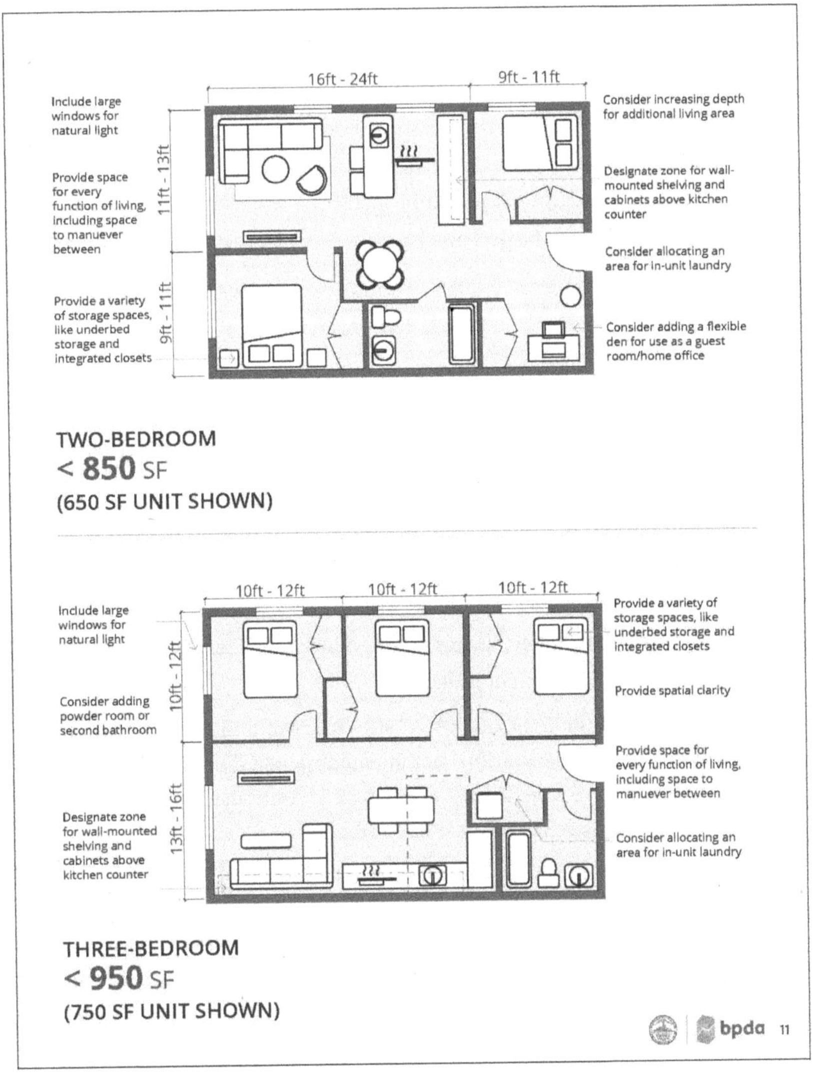
16ft - 24ft
9ft - 11ft
Include large windows for natural light
Provide space for every function of living, including space to manuever between
Provide a variety of storage spaces, like underbed storage and integrated closets
11ft - 13ft
9ft - 11ft
Consider increasing depth for additional living area
Designate zone for wall-mounted shelving and cabinets above kitchen counter
Consider allocating an area for in-unit laundry
Consider adding a flexible den for use as a guest room/home office
TWO-BEDROOM
< 850 SF
(650 SF UNIT SHOWN)
10ft - 12ft
10ft - 12ft
10ft - 12ft
Include large windows for natural light
Consider adding powder room or second bathroom
Designate zone for wall-mounted shelving and cabinets above kitchen counter
10ft - 12ft
13ft - 16ft
Provide a variety of storage spaces, like underbed storage and integrated closets
Provide spatial clarity
Provide space for every function of living, including space to manuever between
Consider allocating an area for in-unit laundry
THREE-BEDROOM
< 950 SF
(750 SF UNIT SHOWN)
bpda 11

FIGURES 1.5 and 1.6. "Compact Living Guidelines," Boston Planning and Development Agency.

HIGH CONSTRUCTION COSTS

In 2015, the Dukakis Center for Urban and Regional Policy concluded from studies of over two hundred projects in the Boston area that hard costs for land and construction are such a high percentage of overall costs that moderate rent proformas are untenable.[15] Construction costs have continued to escalate as our region experiences job growth and a general building boom.

Factory prefabrication of various building components has been increasing, and a few modular projects have been constructed.

In addition, union construction is a hot-button issue in Boston, as open shop projects in the surrounding region come in at up to 30 percent less than Boston projects. Unions considered a lower "wood-frame residential rate" for low- and middle-income projects, but it remains to be seen whether the reduction is large enough to be seen in the final pro forma.

OVERLAPPING CODES RELATED TO UNIT SIZE

There are many codes related to unit size and clearances that, while well intentioned, make designing compact units tricky and potentially risky for the developers who build them. These include but are not limited to:

- Minimum unit size, city of Boston Zoning. After a period of experimentation in the Innovation District, where 20 percent of units were encouraged to be below the city minimums, the Boston Compact Living Pilot became a much clearer set of policy guidelines for developers who hope to build efficient units.
- Massachusetts Building Code 780 CMR 5304, Minimum Room Areas has several references to room size guidelines, including that "every dwelling unit shall have at least one habitable room that shall not have less than 150 square feet of gross floor area."[16]
- The Fair Housing Act and Massachusetts Architectural Access Board describe minimum clearances for compliant kitchens, baths, doorways, closets, foyers, bedrooms, and living rooms, and these dimensional requirements must be followed for 95 percent of the units in new construction. The FHA limits many creative small-space solutions that are seen in other countries, such as sleeping lofts, half baths, etc.
- The Americans with Disabilities Act rules result in larger clearances for wheelchairs. Since this is required for only 5 percent of all units, the requirements are reasonable related to the proportion of units and the needs of a population with physical disabilities. There are many examples of elderly housing around the country that follow ADA rules and result in compact units. Those examples are constructed as part of a larger facility with common lounges, cafeterias, etc., and the occupant is not expected to cook or entertain large groups in their ADA unit. One could argue that this is the prototypical small household arrangement.

While it is possible to create a beautiful and functional three-hundred-square-foot studio or one-bedroom according to all applicable codes, these codes can limit creativity. It is critical to hire an architect who has experience with compact units to reduce the risk of making costly mistakes during design and construction.

MARKET REALITY

Chipping away at each of these challenges can help to reduce costs and bring more nonprofits, small contractors, and local, mid-sized developers with lower overhead and profit into the middle-income housing market, increasing the pool of producers, and spurring innovation at various scales. While we reduce unnecessary costs for construction, permitting, codes, and parking requirements as much as possible, we also need to acknowledge that lower rents will not be the inevitable result. In a market economy such as ours, with extremely low vacancy rates, to hope that a lucrative system of market-rate development will internally subject itself to price controls is wishful thinking.

The past decade has shown that saying that the market will solve the problem through additional supply is a fallacy. If we continue in the direction we are heading, nearly all new construction will be high-priced units that serve a small percentage of the demand. More neighborhoods will be gentrified to the point that residents have to move out of Boston to afford a place to live. Cities need to aggressively disrupt the trend toward new luxury construction if they hope to have any effect on the production of economical housing.

MOVING FORWARD IN SMALL STEPS

It behooves politicians, citizens, corporations, and universities to diversify the typology of units typical in Boston neighborhoods and embrace compact living buildings. Small-unit developments can contribute to vibrant, authentic, and diverse neighborhoods and can house the majority of our population who do not have traditional family households.

First and foremost, there are strategies that are already working that should be supported by incentive programs, increased public funding, and/or policy improvements. These are what I refer to as small steps, working within and improving the existing housing production system. They include:

THINGS THE CITY OF BOSTON COULD DO:

- Up-zone. Neighborhood-based master planning efforts outside of Boston have produced more realistic as-of-right zoning that respects neighborhood character while raising density. Providing clear caps on density and adding incentives that support affordable housing will help reduce land price escalation and give communities more trust in the public process.
- Expedite permitting and reduce costly mitigation requirements for projects with a higher percentage of affordability. Ideally, a clear policy that tells developers "If you provide xx percent affordability, you get xx relief" would be a welcome step forward. The mayor's Housing Innovation Lab has proposed expedited permitting for pilot projects that are near transit and include compact units, higher affordability, and less parking. At a small scale, these experiments can prove what is possible with alternative approaches.
- Change parking regulations based on number of bedrooms rather than number of units. In today's market, where roommate situations are common, parking should be based on data collected on recent projects and not be punitive toward smaller units.
- Increase the percentage of income-restricted units required with new construction permits. Boston's Inclusionary Development Policy, created in 2000, has set this at 13 percent. This program has produced over four thousand units of rent capped housing units in twenty years. Somerville's city council notably raised their percentage of inclusionary zoning to 20 percent of all new units produced. This is a result of citizens speaking out loudly to fight gentrification while still allowing new development to take shape in Somerville, and it is likely that Boston will follow their lead.
- Continue to push for more student housing on or near Boston colleges. There are over 150,000 students in Boston alone, with universities providing only 40,000 student beds on or near campus. At most institutions, housing is not guaranteed after freshman year. In the past, the city has been exerting pressure on universities to include housing in their institutional master plans, effectively linking the desire for new academic buildings to the production of housing. This is an excellent policy that relieves market pressure and gentrification in Boston's neighborhoods by consolidating student housing near universities, while also prioritizing compact unit housing, since nearly all student housing is by definition micro-housing, i.e., singles, doubles, or triples with shared baths, kitchens, and common space, with zero parking.

THINGS THAT NONPROFIT AND PRIVATE DEVELOPERS CAN DO:

- Build more wood-frame projects, ideally four to five stories or less (with more than five stories, an expensive concrete or steel podium is required by code, ameliorating the savings). One of the best solutions to reducing construction costs is to build more wood-frame buildings rather than mid- and high-rise concrete or steel towers. Wood and cross-laminated timber projects have lower embodied carbon and are easier and cheaper to build with a less expensive labor force. Certain common dimensions of wood construction, such as twelve-to-fourteen-foot spans and thirty-foot-deep units also support studios under four hundred square feet efficiently.
- Renovate existing public housing to preserve affordable units and increase the number of small units. Many Boston Housing Authority (BHA) apartments are taken out of commission every year due to health and safety violations that the authority does not have the money to fix. Several large BHA projects that could have replaced thousands of decrepit affordable units in kind through clever partnerships with market-rate and nonprofit developers have been stalled due to lengthy community review in Charlestown, Jamaica Plain, and elsewhere. These projects and others must find the money and political will to go forward; to have even one existing unit sit empty when there is such a long waiting list is deplorable.
- Shift toward providing more units for one- and two-person households. In private development, the shift is slowly occurring, as the market for two- and three-bedroom units becomes oversaturated and tenants become less likely to want to live with roommates. For nonprofits, some agencies are recognizing the shortage of housing for singles and seniors and are funding projects that provide more studio and one-bedroom units. One such project is 117 Union Street in New Bedford (see figure 1.7).
- Prioritize affordable senior living building construction and financing. Many seniors live in houses and apartments that no longer serve their needs, isolate them, and are difficult to maintain. Freeing up those homes for families is an important side benefit. This demographic is perfectly served with what micro-housing offers—a private, well-maintained place to sit, sleep, and bathe. Communal kitchens save precious dollars and create a sense of community. Friends meet at the cafeteria, game room, lounge, and front porch. Sounds a lot like the boardinghouse model, doesn't it? There are some excellent current examples, one of which is O'Connor Way Senior Housing in South Boston.[17]

THINGS THAT THE SURROUNDING TOWNS AND CITIES IN MASSACHUSETTS CAN DO:

- Support 40B developments in surrounding suburbs of Boston. Compared to many other towns, Boston actually has a larger share of affordable, deed-restricted housing than most Massachusetts municipalities, though it may not feel that way as housing prices continue to escalate. 20.6 percent of Boston's housing inventory is subsidized, one of the highest percentages in the state, second only to Aquinnah.[18] Upping the percentage of affordable units outside the city creates more parity for the entire region, and placing them near public transit connects residents to jobs.

FIGURE 1.7. With over half of the units being under five hundred square feet, 117 Union Street in New Bedford creates affordable housing where the New Bedford Housing Authority had the most demand: in single-person households. The percentage of ADA units is higher than required, in the expectation of a high percentage of elderly with mobility issues. Image courtesy of Add Inc.

BOLD THINKING IS NEEDED

1. Set aspirational goals.

In 2016, mayor Bill de Blasio of New York City made the creation and preservation of 200,000 affordable housing units his target; as of 2020, over 215,000 units had been built or renovated. During the same time period, Boston Mayor Walsh's housing goal was 69,000 total units, but he did not specify how many of those would be affordable, operating under the misguided assumption that simply increasing the overall supply of housing will lower rents. The result, the creation of only approximately 1,000 affordable units per year, was the disappointing result.

Mayor Wu has not made that mistake. During her mayoral campaign, she and her staff outlined clear goals around affordability. Her focus is on housing justice, prioritizing housing for low-income individuals and those experiencing homelessness, and housing stability.[19] As her first priority in office, her budget includes investing $106 million in affordable home ownership.[20] These are exactly the aspirational goals needed.

2. Include a high percentage of affordable small units in all new city master plans.

There are quite a few areas of Boston that await master plans and rezoning for new density from the city's Imagine Boston planning efforts that should include reasonably priced home ownership and rental housing. Some ideas for how this could be implemented:

- Limit height in certain areas to three to five stories to encourage affordable wood-frame construction and keep costs and land speculation down.
- Give incentives for minority- and mission-driven developer participation.
- Demand that percentages of housing units address shortages and needs of seniors, the disabled, young people, the formerly homeless, etc.
- Provide city housing grants and subsidies specifically connected to each master plan.
- Suggest that market-rate developers set aside a significant percentage of residential units as affordable and mid-priced.

3. Add to the subsidized housing funding pipeline by taxing real estate transactions above $1 million.

In 1985, the Martha's Vineyard Land Bank Commission was created and funded by a 2 percent tax on most real estate sales. Since then, 7 percent of island land has been preserved as conservation land, a terrific success.[21] Now towns across the island have voted in favor of establishing a similar bank for affordable housing. As explained by the *Vineyard Gazette*, "The housing bank would establish a new regional government entity funded by a two per cent transfer fee on most real estate transactions over $1 million.

The money would be used to expand and develop more affordable housing on the Vineyard through grants and loans from the housing bank."[22]

Imagine how much revenue could be produced for affordable housing if the city received $20,000 for every $1 million dollar unit sold, and $200,000 for every unit that sold for $10 million? Developing a stable funding stream for affordable housing that is tied to escalating real estate costs at the higher margins is an idea that most citizens, even the wealthiest, could see the logic behind.

4. Increase private donor funding for affordable projects.

New funding streams are needed to support affordable housing of all types, from homeless and elderly supportive housing to other forms of purpose-built underserved populations. The Pine Street Inn's new building in Jamaica Plain, partially funded by the Yawkey Foundation, is a great example.[23] After the death of George Floyd, many wealthy companies pledged that they would do more to correct systemic racism in this country; helping to provide more affordable housing is one way to do exactly that. If a mayor put out a clarion call to wealthy donors at every fundraising event, one wonders if and how they might respond. Certainly, donors put their names on health centers and university buildings. Why not housing?

5. Redirect the use of public land toward affordable and middle-income housing.

One important tool the city and state should wield is to stop leasing or selling their land to the highest bidder and instead devote underused and industrial properties to mission-driven affordable housing developers, community development corporations, and others willing to build deed-restricted units. One good example of redirecting public sites to affordable housing has been the scattered site development that Boston's Department of Neighborhood Development has been doing in Boston's Nubian Square. On six city-owned sites that have been designated, over five hundred affordable units have been planned, and several have been built or are in construction.[23]

If the Boston Planning and Development Agency, Massport, and MassDOT were to release their larger sites for moderately priced housing projects, a much higher quantity of low-cost housing could be put into the pipeline. This would take a significant shift in the priorities of leadership to accomplish, but given the shortage of available large parcels of land, it could drive affordable housing production at a scale not seen in Boston in years.

6. Encourage modular construction.

Prefabricated structure, walls, floors, and roofs have become standard methods for reducing the time it takes to build on-site construction (often in bad weather conditions). Factory-built kitchens and bathrooms are becoming more economical. Truly modular construction of the entire unit in a factory is still rare, but it shows promise in improving quality and eventually leading to a less expensive project. A thorough review of off-site housing manufacturing possibilities can be found in Jack S. Goulding's *Offsite Production and Manufacturing for Innovative Construction*.[24] Together with redirecting the use of larger tracts of public land toward housing (see number 5 above), an entire neighborhood could be produced economically through prefabrication and shipped to the site. The same could be true if larger industrial sites were rezoned for four- to five-story housing construction. With smart design and repetition, and deep subsidies for brownfield reparations, we could see more affordable housing at the scale that we need to meet the demand.

7. Require large companies to provide employee housing or in lieu payments.

One neglected chapter in the history of micro-housing has been the construction of "factory towns" during the industrial era, when companies built inexpensive apartments for their employees. Where those living quarters were sparse and dormitory-like, we designers of today could imagine small independent bedrooms augmented with lively game rooms, collective kitchens, and sun-filled lounges, similar to the transformations that have happened to the millennial workplaces of many high-profile, high-tech employers.

After the story of a Google employee who slept in her car in the office parking lot went viral, one would think that tech companies should realize they can't attract and retain their best and brightest in places where housing is expensive and limited. Large high-tech companies that profit from Boston's knowledge economy are significantly benefiting from being located in the city at the same time that their highly paid workers' salaries are part of the cause of the housing price escalation. The mayor's staff should look to create a housing requirement and/or generate a funding vehicle to offset the gentrification occurring from the influx of highly paid workers.

8. Transform existing housing into city-owned affordable housing buildings.

One way to drastically change the housing economy of a city is to remove a high percentage of units from the private sector, in effect stabilizing the housing stock and insulating it from the large pricing swings of the general market. Cities such as Washington, D.C., have a right of first refusal to pay market rate for properties that they can add to their affordable housing portfolio. San Francisco, Dallas, Minneapolis, and Portland, Oregon, are trying similar strategies. In an article from *Fast Company* titled "The Radical Ways Cities Are Taking Control of the Housing Market," the former head of the Cambridge Housing Authority outlined ways that his city is buying properties to grow their affordable housing portfolio.[25]

CONCLUSION

With more than one-third of Boston households spending over 50 percent of their income keeping a roof over their heads, the need for solutions is at a crisis level. It is important to crowd-source all possible ideas from every perspective and quickly condense them into a clear plan that will have measurable outcomes. It is the right time to support what is working, fix what is broken, and take bold steps to build and maintain our affordable housing stock now and for the next generation of Bostonians.

Since the production of inexpensive housing relies on the convergence of so many diverse factors, city leaders must pull every lever they have, in all areas mentioned above, to make a significant difference in the upward trajectory of housing costs, while nonprofit and market developers must be given incentives and financial support to provide reasonably priced rentals and home ownership.

Ongoing support for the mayor's Housing Innovation Lab—and other creative pilot programs—is critical. These experiments to spur affordable and moderate-income housing production are concrete rather than theoretical. Following the rapid prototype process of product designers, they propose building initial ideas, testing them in the communities they serve, improving them as they go, rewriting city codes as needed, and then providing developers with incentives to implement them at scale. In every case, community feedback has played a strong role in shaping how these ideas are carried out in the future.

I believe that if politicians, architects, planners, mission-driven developers, contractors, funders, communities, and our associated partners work together, we can lead our city toward a less polarized and more equitable housing future.

NOTES

1. "Boston at a Glance—2021," BPDA report, accessed August 27, 2022, https://www.bostonplans.org/getattachment/989b6bac-c7bb-484d-aae5-62aca094788d.
2. "Boston in Context: Neighborhoods, 2015–2019 American Community Survey," Boston Planning and Development website, 8. 68.2 percent of all units are two-, three-, and four-plus bedrooms.
3. *Greater Boston Housing Report Card 2019,* Boston Planning and Development website, 6.
4. *Greater Boston Housing Report Card 2021,* Boston Foundation, Boston Planning and Development website, 12. For prepandemic patterns, pandemic impacts, and economic inequality with regard to race and ethnicity, see the entire annual report for 2021.
5. Credit Add Inc./Stantec.
6. Daniel G. Parolek, *The Missing Middle: Thinking Big and Building Small to Respond to Today's Housing Crisis* (Washington D.C.: Island Press, 2020).
7. Wendy Gamber, *The Boardinghouse in Nineteenth-Century America* (Baltimore, MD: The Johns Hopkins University Press, 2007).
8. Ruth Graham, "Boardinghouses: Where the City Was Born—How a Vanished Way of Living Shaped America—and What It Might Offer Us Today," *Boston Globe,* January 13, 2013.
9. *Imagine Boston 2030,* City of Boston, accessed August 27, 2022, https://www.boston.gov/civic-engagement/imagine-boston-2030; "Housing a Changing City: Boston 2030," City of Boston, accessed August 27, 2022, https://www.boston.gov/finance/housing-changing-city-boston-2030.
10. "Compact Living Guidelines," City of Boston, accessed August 27, 2022, https://www.boston.gov/departments/new-urban-mechanics/compact-living-pilot.
11. "Compact Living Guidelines."
12. Tim Logan, "Study Finds 30 Percent of Parking Spaces in New Apartment Buildings Are Going Unused," *Boston Globe,* updated July 24, 2019.
13. For means of commuting, see "Boston in Context: Neighborhoods, 2015–2019," 15—.
14. Tim Logan, "Boston City Council Votes to Relax Parking Rules for Affordable Housing," *Boston Globe,* updated October 20, 2021.
15. "Dukakis Center Housing Cost Analysis," Boston Foundation, 2015, https://www.tbf.org/tbf/51/~/media/ACFE028AAA5647188A3B23184C21DAFB.pdf.
16. "780 CMR: State Board of Building Regulations and Standards / Building Planning for Single- and Two-Family Dwellings," Mass.gov, https://www.mass.gov/doc/780-cmr-state-board-of-building-regulations-and-standards-building-planning-for-single-and-0/download.
17. "Grand Opening of O'Connor Way Senior Housing Development Celebrated in South Boston," City of Boston website, accessed August 27, 2022, https://www.boston.gov/news/grand-opening-oconnor-way-senior-housing-development-celebrated-south-boston.
18. Chapter 40B is a state statute, which enables housing developers to bypass local zoning for affordable housing developments under flexible rules if at least 20 to 25 percent of the units have long-term affordability restrictions. "Department of Housing and Community Development Chapter 40B Subsidized Housing Inventory (SHI) as of December 21, 2020," City of Boston, accessed August 27, 2022, https://www.mass.gov/doc/subsidized-housing-inventory/download.

19. "Michelle for Mayor" website, accessed November 2, 2022, https://www.michellefor-boston.com/issues/housing.
20. Marta Hill, "Here's How Mayor Wu Is Planning to Turn Renters into Homebuyers," Boston.com, April 26, 2022, https://www.boston.com/news/local-news/2022/04/26/heres-how-mayor-wu-is-planning-to-turn-renters-into-homebuyers/#:~:text=The%20proposed%20%24106%20million%20investment,three%20years%2C%20totalling%20%2410.2%20million.
21. Martha's Vineyard Land Bank Commission, accessed August 27, 2022, https://www.mvlandbank.com/.
22. Julia Wells, "After Key Win at Town Meetings, Housing Bank Coalition Turns to Elections," *Vineyard Gazette*, April 12, 2022, https://vineyardgazette.com/news/2022/04/12/west-tisbury-kicks-busy-night-town-meetings-overflow-crowd.
23. Hill, "Mayor Wu."
24. Lyndia Downie and Ray Hammond, "Boston Has What It Takes to End Homelessness," *Boston Globe*, February 22, 2022, https://www.bostonglobe.com/2022/02/22/opinion/boston-has-what-it-takes-end-homelessnness/.
25. Nate Berg, "The Radical Way Cities Are Tackling Affordable Housing," *Fast Company*, April 27, 2021, https://www.fastcompany.com/90618596/the-radical-way-cities-are-tackling-affordable-housing.

ZONING

CHAPTER TWO

ZONING 3.0

Guiding Land Use in the Contemporary City

MATTHEW J. KIEFER

Suddenly, zoning is notorious.

For most of its life, zoning as a general topic interested only land use professionals. But zoning is suddenly the focus of intense debate as U.S. cities grapple with housing access, climate resilience, and other existential challenges—most recently the effects of the COVID-19 pandemic. Cities are indispensable engines of opportunity, innovation, and culture. Some form of land use regulation is indispensable to make them work for everyone. Yet the current focus on zoning as a tool to manage urban change is largely misdirected because it accepts the current rule-based zoning paradigm and merely seeks to adjust the rules.

Zoning arose in the early decades of the twentieth century to protect homeowners from the impacts of urbanization. But from its beginnings, zoning has been problematic in ways that are increasingly evident today, and we have learned enough from a century of experience to radically improve it. Zoning works by dividing a city into districts and setting uniform rules within each district regarding uses and structures. Zoning has evolved in countless ways to encompass new urban land use imperatives, but cities change at an accelerated pace, and zoning rules are often behind the curve—a patchwork quilt that's too rigid in some ways and not comprehensive enough in others. Zoning's requirement for uniformity also discourages adaptability and design innovation. With its primary goal of protecting homeowners, zoning often serves as an instrument of exclusion—a way for incumbents to resist outsiders, and in the process, restrict housing supply and raise housing prices.

The age of urban reinvention has its challenges—infill development virtually always affects others. But growth addresses human needs for housing, workplaces, commerce, culture, and entertainment. Restricting it creates bigger problems than the restrictions intend to solve. Zoning's goal should be to minimize the impacts and maximize the benefits of growth in order to produce a positive growth balance sheet. Zoning needs to be fundamentally rethought to meet this challenge.

Rethinking zoning starts from the premise that its organizing principle—imposing a set of uniform land use rules and forcing landowners to justify departures under an onerous hardship standard that unduly empowers self-interested abutters—is fatally flawed, and that the now-highly evolved practice of development impact review provides a vastly superior alternative. In addition to making zoning relief obsolete, development impact review also presents the opportunity to rationalize development exactions and incentives and to subsume overlapping and often conflicting land use regulations. This shift in approach will empower local governments to better address current social and environmental imperatives in an era of rapid urban change.

This chapter traces the evolution of zoning, using the city of Boston—long a zoning innovator—as a case study. It will then address this question: how would you manage urban land use if you were starting from scratch? It will conclude with specific suggestions for how such a program might work. We begin with some stories that, while partial fabrications, are based on actual Boston zoning disputes and illustrate the inherent flaws of zoning.

Sarah, an architect, owns a house in one of Boston's historic rowhouse neighborhoods with a rental unit on the ground floor. She lives on the upper floors with her family. When her next-door neighbor, Ian, wanted to build a roof-deck, Sarah offered support at the neighborhood meeting and gave Ian informal design advice. Ian got the needed zoning variance (the neighborhood has very strict zoning controls on rooftop additions) and built his new deck and a stairway headhouse to access it. Sarah, observing how nicely it turned out, decided to pursue one herself. By the time she got a home equity loan and came up with a design she liked, Ian sold his house to Jake, a hedge fund investor.

When Sarah contacted her neighbors about her plan, Jake didn't respond. She got support and some helpful suggestions at the neighborhood meeting *and then applied to the zoning board for approval. To her surprise, Jake sent an attorney to the hearing to oppose it. The board voted to grant the variance anyway, and encouraged Sarah to meet with Jake to try to address his concerns. When she did, Jake informed her that her roof-deck and headhouse would diminish his enjoyment of his own roof-deck. He calculated that her roof-deck would add about $50,000 to the value of her house and would diminish the value of his house by at least half that amount. He offered to withdraw his opposition if she paid him $25,000. Otherwise, he would have no choice but to challenge her variance in court. Unable to afford the extra $25,000 or the cost of defending a lawsuit, and advised that she would likely lose the lawsuit anyway, Sarah abandoned the project.*

* * * * * * *

Housing First, a leading nonprofit housing developer, decided to partner with an experienced social service provider to develop supportive housing for people experiencing chronic homelessness. They focused on a large warehouse site located along a commercial corridor in an emerging neighborhood, well served by transit and targeted by the city in a recent planning study for medium-density mixed-use development. They drew up a proposal for two hundred housing units with common facilities for residents, ground floor retail use, and a limited amount of off-street parking.

They studied every aspect of this proposal during a two-year-long development impact review process that involved over forty meetings with neighbors, public officials, advocacy groups, and others. They demonstrated project need, overcame many early objections, changed the project to address other objections, and garnered approval from the city's planning board. In the meanwhile, they sought financial support from government and private sources, which required evidence of zoning compliance. Although the project was designed to meet the city's new district planning guidelines, the neighborhood's thirty-year-old zoning had not been updated, so the project required several zoning variances, including one for reduced off-street parking—an important cost-saving feature, which Housing First had carefully made the case for during impact review based on the very low vehicle ownership of their target population.

At the zoning board, many spoke in support of the project, but some spoke against it. None of the objectors said they were opposed to the project's principal use; all found other aspects of the project to object to, including Simon, an abutting business owner who objected to the inadequate parking. The board granted the requested variances anyway and directed Housing First to try to address the objectors' concerns. Predictably, this proved fruitless, given that parking and other topics had been the subject of many previous meetings, studies, and project changes.

Simon filed suit to challenge the variances, citing in particular the lack of adequate off-street parking. The pending litigation caused the state housing finance agency to withdraw its preliminary funding commitment and allocate it to another shovel-ready project. Housing First and other affordable housing advocates submitted a petition to eliminate the minimum parking requirement for affordable housing from the zoning code, which eventually passed, reducing Simon's leverage and inducing him to withdraw the lawsuit in exchange for a financial settlement to compensate him for the alleged loss of value of his property.

In the meanwhile, Housing First sought approval from the conservation commission, a nonzoning body, for construction in an area of the site potentially subject to flooding given projected sea level rise. Because climate resilience had been a component of development impact review, Housing First had already designed the project to put all habitable space and building systems above anticipated future flood levels, and the conservation commission readily approved this design. But a different group of abutting homeowners filed a lawsuit to challenge this approval on grounds that the project could increase future flooding risk on their property.

As of this writing, the zoning and wetlands challenges have delayed the project by two years and imposed meaningful additional cost, and the fate of Housing First's project is uncertain.

* * * * * * *

Public control over the use and improvement of land is as old as cities. Land use regulation balances the interests of landowners with those of others, including the broader public, and evolves to reflect changing needs and circumstances. There is no more conventional and time-tested form of land use regulation than zoning. By providing predictable rules, zoning aims to reward private investment while also protecting others from its impacts.

ZONING 1.0: SEPARATION

Zoning arose in the reformist Progressive Era—an era when foundries, slaughterhouses, and glue factories coexisted with housing—to rationalize land use and thereby minimize land use conflicts instead of relying on courts to redress them after the fact.[1] Zoning began to spread outside New

York City after the U.S. Department of Commerce published a popular zoning primer and a standard state zoning enabling act in the 1920s and the U.S. Supreme Court upheld this approach.[2]

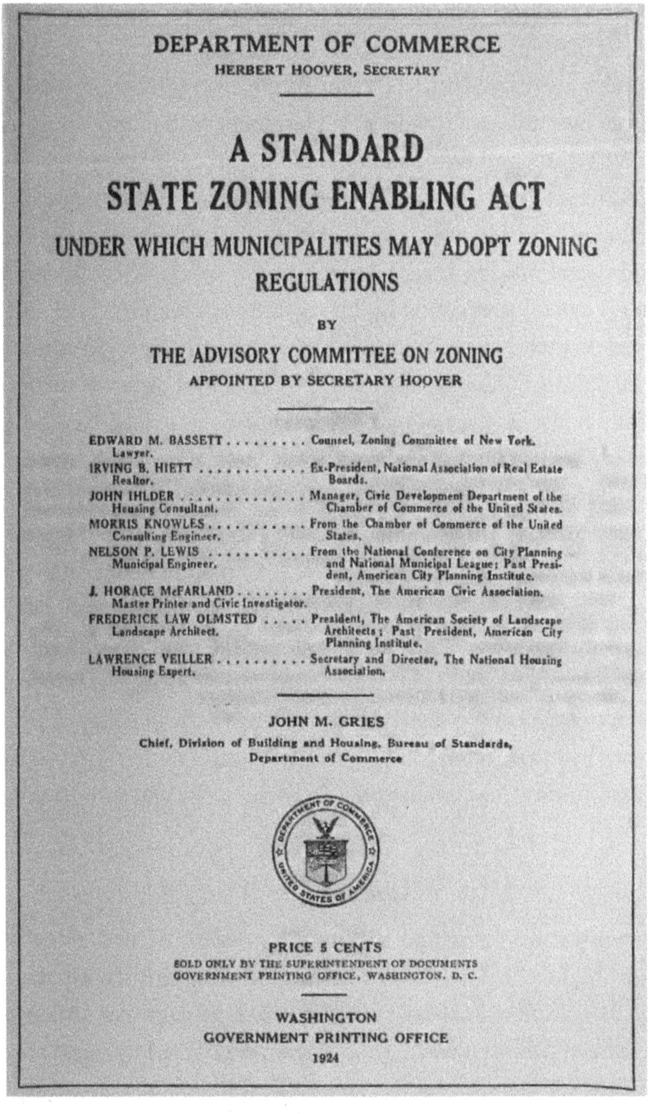

DEPARTMENT OF COMMERCE

HERBERT HOOVER, SECRETARY

A STANDARD
STATE ZONING ENABLING ACT

UNDER WHICH MUNICIPALITIES MAY ADOPT ZONING REGULATIONS

BY

THE ADVISORY COMMITTEE ON ZONING

APPOINTED BY SECRETARY HOOVER

EDWARD M. BASSETT . . . . Lawyer.	Counsel, Zoning Committee of New York.
IRVING B. HIETT . . . . Realtor.	Ex-President, National Association of Real Estate Boards.
JOHN IHLDER . . . . Housing Consultant.	Manager, Civic Development Department of the Chamber of Commerce of the United States.
MORRIS KNOWLES . . . . Consulting Engineer.	From the Chamber of Commerce of the United States.
NELSON P. LEWIS . . . . Municipal Engineer.	From the National Conference on City Planning and National Municipal League; Past President, American City Planning Institute.
J. HORACE McFARLAND . . . . Master Printer and Civic Investigator.	President, The American Civic Association.
FREDERICK LAW OLMSTED . . . . . Landscape Architect.	President, The American Society of Landscape Architects; Past President, American City Planning Institute.
LAWRENCE VEILLER . . . . Housing Expert.	Secretary and Director, The National Housing Association.

JOHN M. GRIES

Chief, Division of Building and Housing, Bureau of Standards, Department of Commerce

DEPARTMENT OF COMMERCE · UNITED STATES OF AMERICA

PRICE 5 CENTS

SOLD ONLY BY THE SUPERINTENDENT OF DOCUMENTS
GOVERNMENT PRINTING OFFICE, WASHINGTON, D. C.

WASHINGTON
GOVERNMENT PRINTING OFFICE
1924

FIGURE 2.1. Local zoning was promoted by the U.S. Commerce Department under its secretary (and future U.S. president) Herbert Hoover. Hoover appointed an advisory committee that included attorney Edward M. Bassett, who led the adoption of New York City's 1916 zoning ordinance, and landscape architect Frederick Law Olmsted Jr. The Advisory Committee on Zoning, *A Standard State Zoning Enabling Act Under Which Municipalities May Adopt Zoning Regulations* (Washington, DC: Government Printing Office, 1924).

Zoning was conceived as a tool to harmonize two conflicting goals: allowing business and industry to expand, and promoting homeownership in the burgeoning auto-age metropolis, where uses could migrate freely—homeowners being then (as now) the primary constituency for zoning.[3]

Euclidean zoning (so-called because of the Supreme Court case that upheld it and not, as planning students often surmise, because it uses geometric formulas) divides a city into districts, each with its own uniform use restrictions and controls over the size, shape, and placement of buildings on their lots. Proposed structures and uses that conform can proceed "as-of-right." Departures are subject to discretionary review by a citizen board, generally based on a showing of hardship justifying the grant of a variance for unique features of the land parcel making it very difficult to use productively in compliance with zoning. Lawful preexisting buildings and uses are protected, but limits are imposed on their expansion and continuation after a period of non-use.

Such Euclidean zoning was, in a sense, all about separation. It put the single-family house at the top of a pyramid of uses. It separated businesses from housing and separated industry from virtually everything else. After a hiatus during the Great Depression and World War II, modern Euclidean zoning took off during the sustained postwar economic boom. Massachusetts adopted a new statewide zoning act in 1954; a separate new enabling act for Boston was approved in 1956.[4] By 1964, a new comprehensive zoning code was in place in Boston. Today, all fifty states have zoning enabling acts, mostly patterned on the Standard State Zoning Enabling Act, delegating zoning power to local governments.[5] Zoning eased the expansion of early twentieth-century cities and promoted their suburbanization after World War II. It proved remarkably successful—or at least influential—in shaping city and suburb alike.[6]

ZONING 2.0: ADAPTATION

Just as urbanization instigated zoning controls in the first place, several forces soon highlighted Euclidean zoning's limitations. In an attempt to overcome them, and to adapt to evolving urban imperatives, urban zoning codes have been tinkered with in the last several decades, mostly by grafting provisions for features such as design and impact review, impact fees, performance standards, overlay districts, and inclusionary housing onto a traditional zoning framework. These patches, described in the following sections, each have their virtues, but they have not addressed the inherent limitations of urban zoning, resulting in an ungainly patchwork-quilt urban zoning ordinances, and have often led to unintended consequences.

First, it has proven impossible to set workable uniform rules to guide growth in reurbanizing pre–auto age cities such as Boston, which developed their distinctive character before zoning arose, and zoning has also proven cumbersome to amend, often behind the curve of rapid urban change. This limitation is magnified by the unworkable variance standard for most departures that is easy for any abutter to challenge, thus giving those with the least objectivity the strongest voice in reshaping cities. From its beginnings, zoning had an exclusionary subtext; this flaw has allowed it to be weaponized as an instrument of exclusion in growing cities such as Boston.

Second, designed to prevent harm, zoning has since been adapted to promote ideal urban conditions through providing incentives and exactions. But this advance lacks a clear organizing framework and often involves excessive case-by-case negotiation, resulting in inequitable and sometimes suspect results. Finally, zoning's promise of comprehensiveness has proven elusive as new regulatory programs for cultural and natural resource protection have arisen outside the zoning framework, leading to conflicting mandates and unpredictable outcomes.

Land use regulation has always evolved in response to social change and technological advances.[7] The most significant recent advance in land use planning and regulation is impact review, and the increasingly sophisticated modeling and visualization tools that accompany it, which have vastly reduced the need for uniform rules and rewarded innovation by allowing impacts to be forecast in advance. Impact reviews also present opportunities to rationalize exactions and incentives and to make urban land use regulation more comprehensive. By leveraging the power of impact review, we can improve both cities and city-making, to the benefit of all of the actors in the land use arena.

Five key social forces and the zoning adaptations intended to address them are addressed below.

1. Urban Form

Zoning 1.0 was based on separating buildings and uses in the interest of reducing land use friction and promoting homeownership in the ever-expanding metropolis. Once the results expressed themselves clearly on the landscape, they were questioned by urbanists—most famously, Jane Jacobs.[8]

These critiques highlighted how prevailing planning ideals and the zoning codes that enforced them undermined the very value proposition of the city—its tendency to promote interactivity, variety and adaptability. The last half century has witnessed a tectonic shift from dispersed auto-oriented separation to concentrated walkable versatility as the organizing principle for urban form. Jane Jacobs, the empirical incrementalist, may only have fought Robert Moses, the rationalist master builder, to a draw in mid-twentieth-century New York City,[9] but her view of cities has emphatically triumphed since.

As the pace of urban change accelerates, zoning has struggled to keep up. This is only partly because it started with imperfect rules. More fundamentally, no set of rules can produce the complex, responsive, even improvised urban places we now seek or protect them where they already exist. Some antidotes to the determinism of Euclidean zoning have emerged over the last several decades.

Planned Unit Developments

Planned unit developments (PUDs) became popular in the 1970s, mostly in smaller towns and suburbs. A big-city equivalent is Boston's Planned Development Area (PDA), a special overlay district for large-scale projects, generally in more high-density districts. Once approved by the city's planning board and zoning commission for a specific project, a PDA development plan supersedes underlying zoning. The first PDA was adopted in 1968 for the expansion of John Hancock Life Insurance Company's Back Bay headquarters, which included Henry Cobb's instantly iconic—and controversial—tower.[10] Well over one hundred PDA development plans have been approved since.

Design Review

Neighborhood design overlay districts are a big-city equivalent to the town character or traditional neighborhood development zoning adopted in many smaller towns and suburbs in the 1990s. Boston's design overlay districts, adopted in several low-density residential neighborhoods not protected by historic designation, establish design guidelines and layer staff-level design review on top of underlying zoning. In 1986, Boston's zoning code was amended to establish a thirteen-member civic design commission to review projects over 100,000 square feet or of "special urban design significance." This review is only advisory but has proven influential in

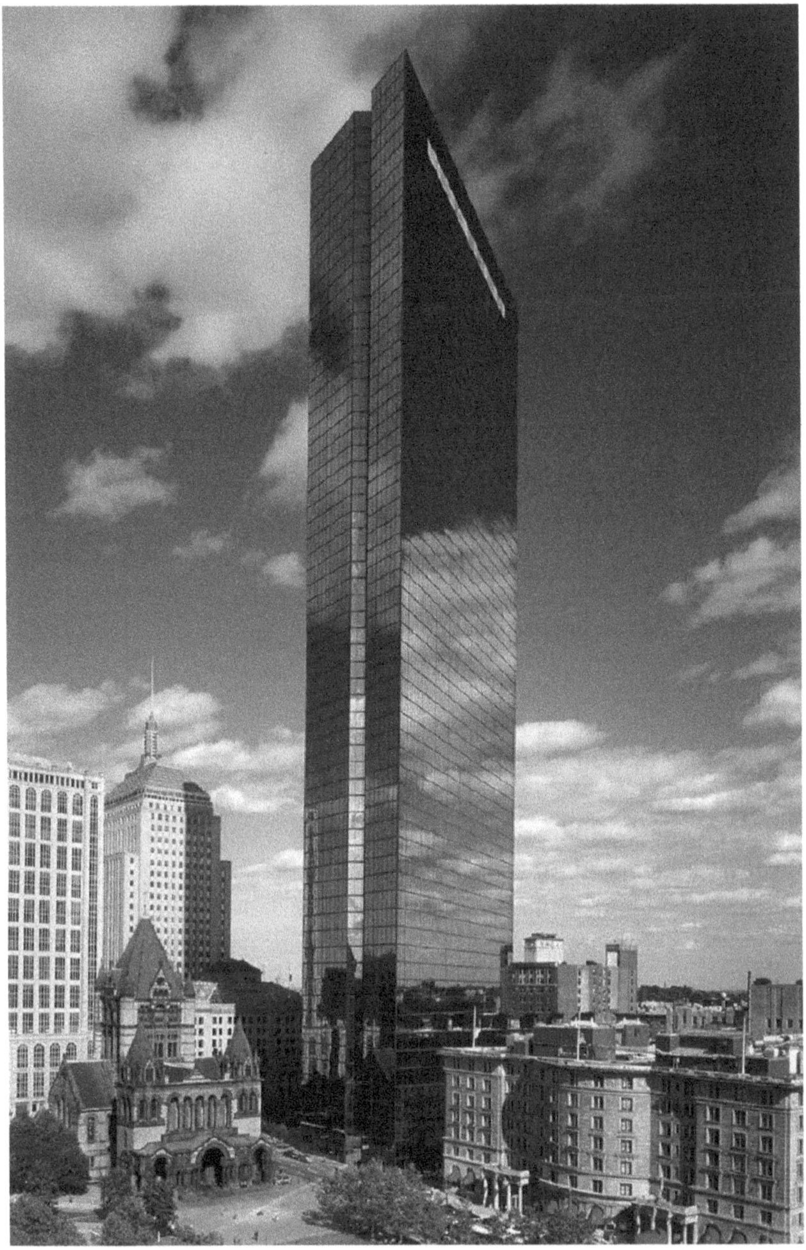

FIGURE 2.2. Projects such as the Hancock Tower along Boston's "High Spine" needed so much zoning relief that the Boston Zoning Commission adopted a special zoning mechanism to accommodate them just four years after the citywide zoning code took effect. Image © Peter Vanderwarker.

improving design quality and raising awareness of the importance of urban design.

These reviews do not take the place of zoning compliance nor eliminate the need for zoning relief.

Form-Based Codes

As an antidote to sprawl, form-based codes championed by the new urbanist movement leave uses generally unregulated, acknowledging that the departure from cities of most heavy industrial uses—whose expansion helped spark zoning in the first place—creates the opportunity to allow use flexibility in urban districts.[11] However, this flexibility as to use is matched by determinism as to dimensions. These codes aim to produce an ideal urban form based on the mixed-use walkability and legibility of pre–auto age (and thus prezoning) neighborhoods by mandating smaller lot sizes, lower parking ratios, and specific building shapes and sizes, often varied by district along a density gradient. So in fixing one problem—needless use separation—they accentuate another one—dimensional rigidity—perpetuating one of Euclidean zoning's fundamental flaws.

Historic Districts

Though the earliest historic districts predated urban renewal by two decades,[12] passage of the National Historic Preservation Act in 1966 accelerated historic district protections as another regulatory response to the thoughtless urban destruction of the postwar era of urban renewal and highway building. These have unquestionably been effective in protecting the character of urban districts, but they are generally administered outside of zoning. This leads to conflicting requirements, duplicative reviews that consume public resources and burden stakeholders, and additional risk and uncertainty for proponents. They also impose design rigidity that often impairs natural evolution.

2. Environmental Impact

By the 1970s, the side effects of dispersed urban settlement were also being questioned on environmental grounds, based on urban sprawl's tendency to consume excessive land, promote auto-dependency, destroy natural habitat, and compromise air and water quality. The resulting growth control movement reframed development not as a generator of economic benefits that should be encouraged but as an impact generator that should be carefully managed. Land use measures to address this included urban growth boundaries, growth moratoria, impact fees, and especially impact reviews.[13]

Impact Review

The now-widespread process of impact review started with the National Environmental Policy Act of 1969, the "magna carta" of environmental protection.[14] Many states passed so-called mini-NEPAs. Massachusetts passed its version in 1972,[15] applying impact review not only to public projects like roads and prisons but also to private projects that obtain state permits, funding, or land and exceed impact thresholds. Project proponents undertake an iterative environmental assessment, with each step subject to public and agency review and comment, in order to identify and incorporate "all practicable means and measures" to avoid or minimize environmental harms into a project before it can proceed.

Site plan review has long been a feature of many suburban and smaller city zoning ordinances, but this path-breaking concept of impact review—site plan review on steroids—has now been incorporated into many big city zoning codes, which require a multistep development impact review for projects above certain size thresholds. Because of its importance to this chapter's central thesis, it is described in some detail here. The city of Boston first adopted citywide development impact review in 1988 for new construction or expansion of more than 50,000 square feet and substantial rehabilitation of more than 100,000 square feet. (There are lower size thresholds in some zoning districts.) It originally required assessment of impacts in five broad areas: transportation, urban design, historic resources, utility infrastructure, and the environment, with additional focus areas in open space districts and along the waterfront. More recently, reviews have been added to address housing, handicap, broadband and language access; climate resilience and green building features; and the diversity of project teams.[16]

The proponent submits a series of increasingly detailed reports—preliminary, draft, and, if required, final—that describe the project, its likely impacts in each applicable subject area, and measures to address those impacts or to provide public benefits to offset those that cannot be eliminated. Each such report is subject to public comment, review by a project-specific citizens advisory group appointed by the mayor, and focused review by public agency staff. Based on principles of transparency and accountability, the process is rigorous. The detailed transportation, wind, shadow, noise, air quality, energy modelling, flood protection, and other required studies and questionnaires have spawned specialized consultants in each subject area. The process involves extensive neighborhood and stakeholder input and takes months or years to complete. It informs agency permit decisions and results in detailed, binding mitigation agreements in each subject area. It has become the crucible in which the design and operation of urban projects are shaped, often in fundamental ways. As addressed below, the effectiveness of impact review presents the opportunity to reform zoning.

Local Environmental Controls

Other locally administered regulatory programs have arisen outside zoning in the interest of environmental protection. In Boston, these include wetland protection and flood control, and a parking freeze program to limit air emissions, each requiring a discretionary approval by a separate nonzoning body. The need for these separate approvals is increasingly unclear as the scope of development impact review has expanded to encompass the issues they address.

3. Exactions and Incentives

The late twentieth-century rise of development exactions and incentives as instruments of public policy has also affected zoning's efficacy. Until the second half of the twentieth century, city-making roles and responsibilities were fairly clear: government set zoning rules and laid out streets, sewers, and parks, funded mostly by the property tax; private landowners, regulated by zoning, filled the spaces in between. Land use regulation generally had no affirmative objective other than to reduce land use conflicts, and private parties were not expected to create or directly fund public infrastructure.

Once the seeds of urban decline took root, cities became the objects of affirmative public policy. During the heyday of federal funding for urban renewal from the 1950s to the 1970s, local governments began deploying public incentives such as land assembly and disposition, property tax breaks, and infrastructure investments in order to stimulate private investment. By the 1980s, federal funding for urban renewal had starkly diminished, the economy was growing, and the growth control movement was questioning the benefits of growth. Local governments began to view private development as a potential generator of public benefits to offset its impacts, imposed as conditions to development approvals—often called exactions. In a pair of decisions, the U.S. Supreme Court set outer limits on such exactions, requiring that they be both targeted toward and roughly proportional to a likely project impact, thus in effect ratifying the importance of impact review as a means to justify exactions.[17]

During the current era of neoliberal city-making, exactions take varied forms, many of them zoning-based.[18] Impact fees and inclusionary development requirements (addressed in the following section) are formula-based and embedded in zoning ordinances. Many exactions, however, are the product of negotiation during the discretionary approval process. For instance, in order to gain permission to build a large apartment building, the proponent may be required to install or upgrade a nearby park, traffic signal, or sewer line or to provide on-site public realm improvements or affordable cultural space. Cities often down-zone as a means to increase opportunities to attach permit conditions as a condition of allowing additional density. (Boston's extensive down-zonings in the 1980s and 1990s are described below.)

The excessive case-by-case negotiation of exactions is on the other end of the spectrum from the rigidity of Euclidean zoning, and creates problems for all participants. Proponents must prepare for increased cost, time, and uncertainty, leading them to try to reduce risk in other areas, such as housing affordability, climate resilience, or architectural quality. Neighborhood residents believe they need to participate vigorously, in their free time and of course without compensation, in every project approval process to make sure their interests are advanced. Needless to say, "the public" rarely speaks with one voice, often adding complexity, rancor, and confusion to the process. The exaction regime forces the public agency to simultaneously regulate development and shake the benefits tree on which they have become increasingly dependent, sometimes compromising and often leading critics to question the integrity of regulatory decision making.

All actors exert pressure to keep the benefits close to the source project. Neighbors believe they are due compensation for the impacts they will suffer; the proponent wants to benefit from its own largesse by garnering the support of project neighbors and improving the setting of its project; and the public agency wants to achieve consensus that allows the project to proceed. This means that public improvements are opportunistic. They arise in the desirable districts where private development occurs, their arrival timed with development cycles, rather than where and when they are most needed.[19]

Boston's Zoning Innovations

In the 2000s, the Boston Redevelopment Authority—since renamed the Boston Planning and Development Agency—began to experiment with incentive zoning, form-based codes, and performance codes (addressed below), often in combination. In response to several uncoordinated development proposals, the agency convened four major landowners to jointly plan an area of mostly parking lots and underused historic warehouses in the emerging South Boston waterfront, known as the 100 Acres. The resulting district plan identified open spaces and circulation improvements that were ultimately embodied in a special zoning overlay district adopted in 2007.

This new zoning district gave each landowner base development rights of about two-thirds of the density they sought; they could unlock the last third only by dedicating land or paying into an infrastructure fund for the district-wide improvements identified in the plan. This clever use of incentive zoning had the significant virtues of defining exactions in advance and directing them toward preidentified district-wide improvements, thus creating greater predictability for all parties and more useful planning-based public realm improvements than site-by-site negotiated benefits.

Zoning innovation was taken one step further in the Stuart Street District, adopted in 2016 for a corridor along Boston's "High Spine."[20] The zoning followed a multiyear planning process involving major landowners and representatives from three bordering historic rowhouse neighborhoods. The new zoning article combined form-based, performance, and incentive zoning provisions. It identified parcels suitable for additional height and density to reduce pressure to demolish historic or character-defining early twentieth-century commercial buildings. This density could be earned through meeting performance standards regarding wind and shadow impacts, satisfying building design criteria intended to make the new development compatible with its existing context, and choosing from a menu of public realm, affordable housing, transportation and other public benefits, mostly established by formula, thus reducing case-by-case negotiations.[21]

This combination of features improves on Euclidean zoning in important respects—though it is still hostage to the prevailing zoning framework.

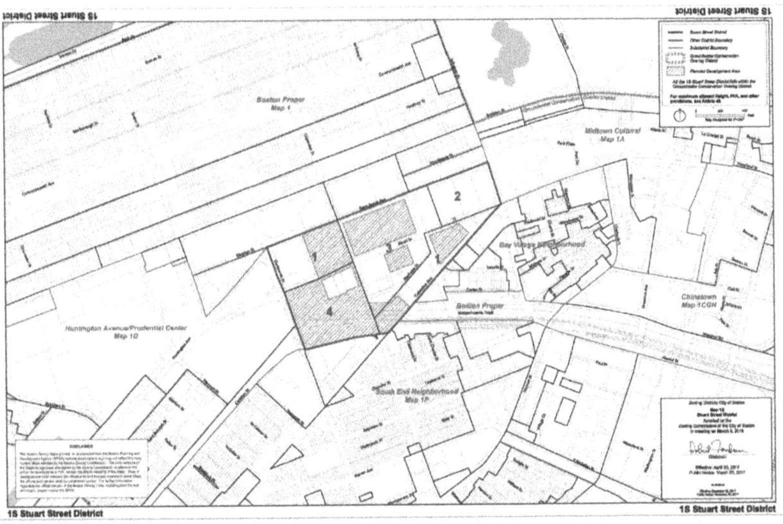

FIGURE 2.3. The Stuart Street zoning district allows additional density on carefully identified sites along a mixed-use corridor in central Boston.

4. Public Participation

Zoning's effectiveness as a land use tool has also been affected by heightened citizen participation—and its evil twin, self-interested development opposition, popularly known as NIMBYism,[22] a perhaps more pernicious form of land use friction than the conflict between homeowners and industry that gave rise to zoning in the first place. The modern era of citizen participation in planning and development decisions dates to the urban renewal era, which unmistakably demonstrated that public participation was a necessary corrective to the autocratic methods of the master builders. (We are still fixing their city-destroying mistakes by burying or dismantling elevated urban highways, remaking public housing projects, and breaking up superblocks.) Following the public interest activism of figures such as Jane Jacobs, Rachel Carson, Saul Alinksy and Ralph Nader,[23] the growth control movement, in reframing growth as an impact generator, deputized informed citizens as impact police. New environmental legislation, in addition to mandating public comment periods on impact studies, broadened standing rules to challenge governmental action.

Project proponents are of course self-interested and, left to themselves, are often oblivious to or willing to externalize the impacts of their projects, so those most affected by development must have a voice to ensure development accounts for its impacts. Conceived to address air and water pollution and habitat destruction, impact review has been adapted in urban settings to address noise from rooftop mechanical systems, light pollution from site illumination, and shadows on neighboring roof-decks as urban residents have developed steadily diminishing tolerance for perceived threats to their quality of life and their property values. It is unrealistic to expect citizen participation to be altruistic, but although often cloaked in concerns about protecting the neighborhood or the environment, it has often become intensely self-interested. This is especially true in dense urban neighborhoods, full of vigilant incumbents who strongly resist change to their immediate environment.[24]

Euclidian zoning is inherently biased against newcomers, making it easy for disgruntled abutters (like Jake and Simon in the fictionalized accounts above) to exercise the leverage it affords them to vindicate their self-interest at the expense of allowing broader urban needs to be accommodated. This disempowers local government in advancing citywide policy goals and has become a particular obstacle to improving housing access.

5. Housing Access

Conceived primarily to protect homeowners, zoning has always had a subtext of preserving racial and economic homogeneity.[25] African American migration to industrializing cities before and during World War I led to explicit racially restrictive zoning ordinances in Baltimore and other cities. When the U.S. Supreme Court struck down Louisville's version in 1917,[26] exclusionary zoning went underground, shifting to "economic zoning." Single-family zoning districts had the effect of restricting neighborhoods to those with the means to purchase a house (a much smaller cohort before federal mortgage insurance, amortizing mortgages, and other Depression-era advances) and effectively excluded most Blacks and immigrants.

This approach was sanctioned when Supreme Court justice George Sutherland noted, in the 1926 *Euclid* case mentioned above, that "very often the apartment house is a mere parasite" and that, in single-family residential districts, apartment houses "come very near to being nuisances." In suburban contexts, such economic zoning soon came to include minimum lot or house sizes and other features designed to ensure economic homogeneity. As inflation and housing shortages turned homeownership into an investment and home appreciation became a major goal of middle-class families, high-voting homeowners became property value protectors, often deploying environmentalism to promote restrictive zoning.[27] Conceived as a way to accommodate growth with less land use friction in outwardly expanding cities, zoning has become a barrier to growth in reurbanizing cities; protection from impacts has morphed into a form of protectionism.

In Boston, a decade-long rezoning campaign in the 1990s established neighborhood districts, each with their own use, dimensional, and other controls that were both more nuanced and more restrictive than the base code they replaced. These down-zonings were geared toward insulating incumbent residents from change and they significantly increased the proportion of projects requiring discretionary zoning relief. By preserving the status quo, such zoning restricts housing supply in growing cities such as Boston, where job creation far outpaces housing production. The resulting supply-demand imbalance increases housing prices and reduces housing access more broadly. High housing costs limit labor mobility and hamper economic opportunity. Restricting housing growth is also a form of generational discrimination by older homeowners against those trying to get a foothold in rising housing markets.[28]

The stakes are high for addressing housing access. In addition to the consequences to the regional economy, high housing costs are a main driver of segregation, income inequality, and wealth gaps. Transportation accounts for as much as a third of CO_2 emissions, so the jobs/housing imbalance also hampers our ability to address climate change.

Inclusionary Housing and Affirmatively Furthering Fair Housing

To address urban housing access, many cities with strong housing markets have adopted inclusionary zoning, which requires that a portion of new housing units in a project be affordable as a condition of zoning approval. Since the cost of delivering such affordable units exceeds their restricted sale price or rental value, the requirement is often accompanied by increased development density to help cross-subsidize the cost. Boston's program, first adopted in 2000 and adjusted several times since, requires any project that proposes multiple new market-rate rental or ownership housing units to create affordable housing on-site as part of the project, create affordable housing off-site in the neighborhood, or pay into a city-controlled fund for the creation or preservation of affordable housing. In recognition of market differences throughout the city, the program establishes tiered percentages for calculating the required contribution in zones of high, medium, and low housing values. The program has produced or preserved over six thousand income-restricted housing units since its inception, with no public subsidy—and no density bonus.

The importance of housing access nationally led the Obama administration in 2015 to implement an almost-forgotten provision of the 1968 Fair Housing Act that requires cities that receive federal funds to "affirmatively further" the fair housing purpose of the statute. This HUD rule requires cities that receive federal housing money to create a plan to rectify barriers to fair housing.[29] The City of Boston responded by integrating fair housing into the development impact review processes for large residential projects. Project proponents must look backward to consider whether there has been a history of exclusion in the neighborhood that the project could address, and must look forward to assess whether the project creates a future risk of displacement at and around the project site. Based on this assessment, the proponent can then choose from a menu of affirmative marketing, enhanced affordability, and other options. Adopted in 2021, the affirmative fair housing program is too new for its effects to be evaluated.

These programs are important examples of how zoning and impact review can be adapted to meet policy imperatives, but they are layered on top of base zoning, so projects that require zoning relief are vulnerable to—and, given their increased density and affordability, often targeted for—obstruction.

New District Plans

Beginning in 2015, Boston took major steps to reset development expectations in a city with significant development pressure. First, it undertook detailed studies to quantify housing needs, describe climate threats, and address transportation needs. Then it embarked on a very public citywide planning effort—the first since adoption of the 1964 base zoning code. Dubbed *Imagine Boston 2030*, the plan set aspirations for housing, open space, mobility, climate resilience, and other spatially influenced urban needs, and identified former industrial areas, low-scale transit-served commercial corridors, and other areas that could accommodate additional growth.[30]

The next step was to develop district plans in several growth zones, which, like the 100 Acre and Stuart Street rezonings described above, combined increased density and use flexibility with higher expectations for mitigation measures and public benefits. But the plans proved controversial, and the rezonings that were intended to codify them have not, as of this writing, gone forward. Thus, even projects that conform to the plans are vulnerable to zoning challenges, as illustrated in the Housing First example above.

ZONING 3.0: INTEGRATION

Any effort to reconceive zoning must start with an appraisal of its advantages and limitations as a city-making tool. Zoning is battle-tested, widely practiced, and versatile. The degree of flexibility cities have in fashioning it varies by state, but it can be shaped and amended to respond to local conditions and needs.[31]

But as noted, zoning is cumbersome to amend on a district scale—the Stuart Street zoning article described above took eight years after the planning effort before it commenced, and the rezoning for more recent district plans has still not proceeded due to local opposition—so zoning mandates are often behind the curve. Zoning is also slow-acting; by itself, it does not produce outcomes on any defined timetable—it merely regulates the voluntary actions of private landowners over time. It is therefore also inadvertently inequitable—it is more influential in growing cities and districts than in struggling or declining ones.

More fundamentally, traditional zoning is overly deterministic in some ways, based on the implicit belief that controlling the uses, dimensions, and placement of buildings and site improvements can produce desired social outcomes, and insufficiently intentional in others, generally leaving the determination of exactions and incentives to case-by-case negotiation with few clearly articulated guidelines or goals.

Rule versus Discretion

This illustrates the central tension in zoning between rule and discretion—the timeless yin/yang underlying all forms of regulation. Neither a pure rule-based system nor a purely discretionary one works well in the land use arena. A discretionary system rewards innovation and adaptation, but unbridled discretion opens the door to arbitrariness, exclusion, and unpredictability that can hamper private investment and lead to potential abuses.

Rules are consistent, predictable, and efficient—but also inflexible. In zoning's infancy, its proponents believed that newly urbanizing cities could fashion workable rules to solve straightforward early twentieth-century problems of land use friction.[32] But using uniform rules to appropriately refashion existing cities to meet twenty-first-century challenges is much more challenging; decades of experience suggest that in a pre-auto age, topographically complex and mostly unplanned city such as Boston, where the very quirkiness, walkability, and texture that are key to its vitality arose only in the absence of zoning rules, it may be a fool's errand.

Consensus on the appropriate rules is also difficult to achieve. Developers want expansive rules on use and development density to accommodate financial feasibility, which constantly changes along with interest rates, construction costs, and market rents; the neighbors want highly restrictive rules. Issue-oriented advocates want zoning to advance housing affordability, climate resilience, high quality design, and other worthy goals. Public officials must navigate this minefield to arrive at a compromise that makes everyone equally unhappy so that private investment in urban needs can proceed at the least political cost.

So, the resulting rules, no matter how well-intentioned, rarely work for all projects. Many—especially larger development projects—need zoning relief. If this zoning relief requires variances, it places a high burden of proof on the property owner. As previously noted, the hardship finding that the zoning board must make gives the challenger the advantage, and often leads abutters to oppose projects even after they have undergone rigorous impact review with vigorous community participation. Because zoning was conceived to prevent land use injuries, and those closest to a proposed project were thought to be the most likely to be injured, the standard zoning enabling act gives any single abutter legal standing to challenge the grant of zoning relief.

Nobody seeks to put glue factories or slaughterhouses next to single-family houses in the contemporary city. Yet, after a century of experience, we still have a system based on imperfect rules that gives those with the least objectivity the most leverage to challenge departures from them. In essence, it hands each abutter a club and forces project proponents to try to convince them not to use it. This is fundamentally undemocratic, allowing a single property owner or handful of property owners to hijack public agency decision making and determine development outcomes that affect everyone.

Fortunately, the extraordinary success of impact review over the last half century provides an opportunity to craft a workable alternative—a synthesis of rule and discretion. Impact review is not an exact science—it is subject to interpretation and evaluation. More importantly, there is no such thing as "zero impact" development, so some discretion is required to determine what level of impact is acceptable in light of project benefits. But the general effectiveness of impact review raises an obvious question: if the impacts of a project can be accurately forecast in advance and addressed after a public process, why require strict adherence to anticipatory rules designed to avoid impacts? Just as zoning rendered nuisance law virtually obsolete, impact review can render rule-based zoning obsolete.

Starting from Scratch

- Update citywide goals and set specific objectives by neighborhood to reflect best practices in city-making.
- Require development impact review for all projects over modest size thresholds to gather public and agency input, shape projects, and establish permit conditions.
- Set "safe harbor" rules for small projects such as home and small business improvement, but allow them to opt in to impact review to gain greater flexibility.
- Formulate clear guidelines for mitigation, exactions, and incentives.
- Make exactions planning-based and decoupled from their source projects where appropriate.
- Make the public agency's finding of consistency comprehensive (the only required discretionary approval) and accord it a presumption of validity.
- Require "no fault" postoccupancy impact evaluation.
- Regularly update goals and objectives, and refine guidelines for mitigation, exactions, and incentives based on experience.

A New Model

The wide latitude that the U.S. Supreme Court has set in fashioning land use regulation creates an opportunity to establish a new urban zoning template that fulfills the objectives of versatility and comprehensiveness that zoning's originators aspired to.[33]

The first obvious step, in the current era of urban reinvention, is to update citywide planning, design, and development goals, as Boston has done with *Imagine Boston 2030,* and then to develop district or neighborhood plans that advance these goals. Like the Boston's 100 Acre and Stuart Street rezonings described above or PLAN:East Boston, currently underway, these district plans can specify desired uses, the scale and urban design characteristics of buildings, and public benefit expectations. Some districts may favor large-scale manufacturing or other job-creating uses and discourage or even forbid residences in the interest of employment opportunity; in some low-density residential districts, nonresidential uses would be subject to more rigorous review in the interest of housing stability. But many or most districts would accommodate a mix of uses and both housing and employment growth in appropriate locations.

These district plans can be followed by district rezonings that set clear baseline zoning rules for as-of-right development for projects below development impact review thresholds so that homeowners and small businesses aren't needlessly burdened with exacting public review. These baseline rules would conform to district goals with fewer detailed use and dimensional parameters than existing neighborhood zoning and might include light design review to ensure contextual compatibility.

A key step is to require development impact review for projects over the "baseline" threshold. (Projects below the size thresholds could also opt in to achieve greater flexibility.) Crucially, this comprehensive development review would assess consistency with newly updated citywide goals and district standards and would encompass resource protection programs, such as those for wetlands and historic resources, that have arisen outside zoning. Once impacts have been studied and mitigation measures and public benefits have been identified, the administering agency would make a finding of consistency. This finding would constitute zoning compliance and no further discretionary approval would be needed from any municipal board or agency—only construction-related approvals would be required.[34]

The public agency determination of consistency and the conditions it contains will assume new importance once it becomes a final discretionary approval. As a result, a critical step is to formulate guidelines for determining mitigation and public benefits and eligibility for incentives such as property tax relief or infrastructure funding. This is an arena where, in fact, more rigor would be helpful. Impact tolerances for noise and wind impacts might be citywide; other standards might vary by district and would establish what level of project-specific mitigation is expected based on the local system's capacity to absorb impacts. These guidelines can set planning-based public benefits in place of the often heavily negotiated case-by-case on-site public benefits that result from the existing system.

In some districts—former industrial zones or disinvested neighborhoods with vacant land—growth could be encouraged with planning-based development incentives like density bonuses, expedited permitting, or a waiver of impact fees. Developing an accepted cost/benefit methodology for incentives would also be helpful, with standards for what amount of public benefits in what categories and over what period of time will justify a given level of government support.

Exactions and incentives can be more intentionally used to achieve equitable growth by spreading its benefits to the locations where they're most needed—which may or may not be in the vicinity of the source project. Proponents of large projects could also be required to submit postoccupancy evaluations of built projects that compare their actual impacts against forecasts, on a "no fault" basis, so that impact review methods can be continuously refined.

Enforceable timelines can be established for agency action, which can vary by project size, to set expectations for project proponents and for public participants and avoid lengthy and inconclusive public reviews.

A final key point: the agency's finding of consistency, as well as any required zoning relief for baseline projects, should be subject to an "abuse of discretion" standard, like most administrative actions. This would reverse the lopsided burden of proof that bedevils the existing as-of-right/variance dichotomy. Standing requirements could also be changed to require, for example, ten registered voters to mount a legal challenge.

* * * * * *

Relieved that the city transformed its approach to land use regulation, Sarah resumed her pursuit of a roof-deck. Though it was too small to require development impact review, Sarah opted in. She consulted the city's guidelines for roof-decks in historic rowhouse neighborhoods like hers. She submitted a succinct report that mapped the location of the windows and roof-decks of abutting houses and the view obstructions and shadow and noise impacts of her headhouse and other deck improvements on her neighbors, and described how she had changed the design to minimize impacts. She met with her neighbors (Jake chose not to attend) and did her best to address their concerns. In response to comments from the historic district commission (now in an advisory role), she moved her headhouse back two feet from the front parapet to make it invisible from across the street. In response to a request from the parks department, she agreed to contribute a modest impact fee (using a formula based on deck area) into a fund for public parks in neighborhoods without adequate public open space, based on parks department guidelines for optimum open space per household. When she received a certificate of consistency and applied for a building permit, Jake, advised by his attorney that the agency determination likely met applicable legal requirements, did not challenge it. Within sixty days of starting the process, she was under construction with a design that even Sarah acknowledges was improved over her original proposal.

* * * * * * *

By the time Housing First completed development impact review and redesigned their project to conform to the neighborhood plan, to provide mitigation measures on flood storage in response to advisory conservation commission review, and to earn their density bonus by providing the public benefit of

FIGURE 2.4. Roof-decks, most of them set back from the front parapet, punctuate the roofscape of the South End, Boston's largest historic rowhouse neighborhood. Image © Peter Vanderwarker.

deeply affordable housing with supportive services to address the city's acute homelessness crisis, the city planning agency had adopted a zoning amendment to make any project that completes development impact review zoning-compliant on a finding of planning consistency. This finding also encompassed and superseded wetlands review. Simon and the neighbors did not mount a legal challenge, aware that it would likely be unsuccessful.

Once Housing First received their certificate of consistency, they were off and running, garnering the public subsidies they sought and beginning construction on schedule. By the time the project was ready to be occupied, there was a waiting list for the project's two hundred supportive housing units. They and their operating partner are looking for additional sites.

CONCLUSION

Land use regulation is no longer merely about conflict avoidance. Land use regulation can be a potentially powerful set of tools that must be continually refined to address evolving urban needs. It can advance social imperatives by minimizing the impacts of growth, harnessing it to spread its benefits, and channeling it to where it is needed.

The current zoning paradigm is increasingly ill-suited to the challenges of the twenty-first-century city. Rather than trying to perfect zoning rules, we should be perfecting development impact review to reduce reliance on rules. Rather than trying to negotiate our way to the good city one project at a time, we can use planning-based impact review to produce more equitable and predictable results.

Rather than requiring strict adherence to a set of detailed rules and making any departures vulnerable to challenge, this approach would encourage innovation, eliminate the veto of self-interested abutters, increase predictability for all participants, and empower local government to achieve shared urban ambitions with less erosion of the civic fabric.

Cities, once viewed as a set of problems, are now recognized as a set of solutions. As they recover their importance as engines of economic opportunity, cultural expression, innovation, and environmental progress, it should be a high public policy priority to manage their land use more effectively.

NOTES

1. This generally falls under the legal concept of nuisance—a use of land that interferes with the legal rights of others.
2. New York City's 1916 zoning ordinance, which famously controlled building heights and setbacks by zone, is often cited as the first U.S. example. But it was a particular response to the rising office economy and advances in building technology that enabled ever-larger skyscrapers in Lower Manhattan to deprive the street and neighboring properties of light and air—essential workplace attributes in the early days of mechanical ventilation and electric lighting, when office rents depended on distance from the window line. See Jason M. Barr, *Building the Skyline: The Birth and Growth of Manhattan's Skyscrapers* (Oxford: Oxford University Press, 2016). Sarah Bradford Landau and Carl W. Condit point out that "it was not architects or planners or even those concerned with health and safety who got the law passed. It was the real estate men, the corporate owners, the syndicators, and the investors—the very financial interests that had created the skyscraper in the first place, those whose primary concern was to protect property values." Sarah Bradford Landau and Carl W. Condit, *The Rise of the New York Skyscraper, 1865–1913* (New Haven, CT: Yale University Press, 1996), 395. The City of Boston restricted building heights to 125 feet in commercial districts and to 80 to 100 feet in residential districts as far back as 1892, largely on grounds of fire safety, and other cities followed suit. The lower residential restriction withstood legal a challenge in *Welch v. Swasey*, 214 U.S. 91 (1909). In 1923, the height limit was raised to 155 feet; a 1927 zoning ordinance allowed downtown building heights to exceed 155 feet if certain setbacks to protect light and air at street level, like New York's, were observed. Robert M. Fogelson, "The Sacred Skyline: The Battle of Height Limits," *Downtown: Its Rise and Fall, 1880–1950* (New Haven, CT: Yale University Press, 2001). These protozoning efforts were overtaken by the more

comprehensive approach of the Standard State Zoning Enabling Act described below. On the U.S. Supreme Court upholding this approach, see "A Standard State Zoning Enabling Act under Which Municipalities May Adopt Zoning Regulations," Advisory Committee on Zoning, U.S. Department of Commerce (Revised 1926), *Village of Euclid, Ohio v. Amber Realty Co.*, 272 U.S. 365 (1926).

3. It is no coincidence that the first state zoning enabling act, passed in 1927, coincided with the first national highway act. See Henry Petroski, *The Road Taken: The History and Future of America's Infrastructure* (London: Bloomsbury, 2016).
4. The Massachusetts statute is at General Laws Chapter 40A (amended many times since its passage); Boston's is Chapter 665 of the Acts of 1956, amended less frequently.
5. Arden Rathkopf, Daren A. Rathkopf, and Edward H. Ziegler, Jr., *Rathkopf's The Law of Zoning and Planning*, at Section 1.9, Thompson Reuters, updated Nov. 2022.
6. According to U.S. Census data, only 45 percent of U.S. households were homeowners in 1920. Although influenced by factors in addition to zoning, the homeownership rate reached almost 70 percent prior to the 2008 financial crisis and, as of the 2020 census, stands at about 65 percent.
7. As Supreme Court Justice Sutherland observed in upholding zoning in Euclid, "While the meaning of constitutional guaranties never varies, the scope of their application must expand or contract to meet new and different conditions which are constantly coming within the field of their operation" (387).
8. Jane Jacobs' seminal critique of post–World War II city-making, *The Death and Life of Great American Cities* (New York: Alfred A. Knopf / Random House, 1961), was influenced by *The Exploding Metropolis: A Study of the Assault on Urbanism and How Our Cities Can Resist It*, edited principally by William H. Whyte; *Fortune Magazine* (1958); and Grady Clay's "Metropolis Regained," *Horizon Magazine* (1959), reproduced with an introduction by Sandy Isenstadt in *Places Journal* (November 2015).
9. See Anthony Flint, *Wrestling with Moses: How Jane Jacobs Took on New York's Master Builder and Transformed the American City* (New York: Random House, 2009).
10. The unanticipated groundwater and wind impacts of this sixty-story tower helped instigate Boston's impact review mandate addressed below.
11. We may be coming full circle with the rise of the maker economy and its "productive frictions."
12. The trend began in the South: the first was in Charleston, South Carolina (1931); followed by the Vieux Carré (French Quarter) of New Orleans (1936); San Antonio, Texas (1939); Alexandria, Virginia (1946); and Williamsburg, Virginia (1947). Boston's first historic district, Beacon Hill, was created in 1955, followed by the Back Bay in 1966.
13. Increased environmental awareness also led to the adoption of programs regulating air emissions, water discharges, and alteration of wetlands and other natural resource protections. Even when locally administered, they are generally implemented outside of zoning.
14. Codified at 42 U.S.C. §4321 et seq.
15. The Massachusetts Environmental Policy Act is codified at M.G.L. c. 30 §§61 through 62I.
16. See the Boston Planning and Development Agency website at https://www.bostonplans.org/.
17. *Nollan v. California Coastal Commission*, 483 U.S. 825 (1987); *Dolan v. City of Tigard*, 512 U.S. 374 (1994).
18. Long before the exaction era bloomed, New York City combined exactions and

incentives in a 1961 zoning ordinance that gave developers a density bonus for incorporating plazas and other public amenities into their projects according to a set of formulas. The legacy of the ordinance is decidedly mixed, highlighting the difficulty of an overly prescriptive approach to something as site-specific and nuanced as open space. See Jerold S. Kayden, *Privately Owned Public Space: The New York City Experience* (New York: John Wiley & Sons, 2000).

19. See Matthew J. Kiefer, "Public Planning and Private Initiative: The South Boston Waterfront," in *Urban Planning Today: A Harvard Design Magazine Reader* (Minneapolis: University of Minnesota Press, 2006).
20. The concept of a "spine" of tall buildings from Faneuil Hall in downtown Boston through the Back Bay, a component of the 1961 Architects' Plan for Boston, was conceived as a way to accommodate growth while protecting the historic rowhouse neighborhoods on either side. The concept is often attributed to Kevin Lynch, a consultant to the Committee on Civic Design of the Boston Society of Architects, which drew up the plan. See Robert S. Sturgis, AIA, "The Architects' Plan for Boston," *Journal of the American Institute of Architects* (January 1962).
21. This general rezoning approach has been followed in Boston zoning enactments for the Harrison-Albany Corridor and the South Huntington Avenue Corridor. Although this new zoning is too recent for its effects to be evaluated, it has allowed at least one large-scale project to proceed as-of-right—a rare occurrence in Boston—after a multiyear impact review process.
22. "Not in My Backyard" is succinctly described by Wikipedia as "a pejorative characterization of opposition by residents to a proposal for a new development because it is close to them." "NIMBY," Wikipedia, last accessed February 22, 2023, https://en.wikipedia.org/wiki/NIMBY.
23. In *Public Citizens: The Attack on Big Government and the Remaking of American Liberalism* by Paul Sabin (New York: Norton, 2021), the author observes that this public-spirited assault on government decision making has had the unintended effect of reducing government resources and effectiveness.
24. Connor Dougherty deftly captures this self-interest, and the YIMBY movement that has sprung up as a counterpoint in the San Francisco Bay Area, in *Golden Gates: Fighting for Housing in America* (New York: Penguin Press, 2020). See also Matthew J. Kiefer, "The Social Functions of NIMBYism," *Harvard Design Magazine*, Spring /Summer 2008.
25. See Richard Rothstein, "Racial Zoning," in *The Color of Law: A Forgotten History of How Our Government Segregated America* (New York: Liveright, 2017).
26. *Buchanan v Warley*, 245 U.S. 60 (1917). Racially restrictive deed covenants, widely used in housing subdivisions as a companion to single-family zoning, were not invalidated until *Shelley v Kraemer*, 334 U.S. 1 (1947).
27. William A. Fischel observes that growth control, while cloaked in public purpose, is often a cover for exclusion and protection of property values. "An Economic History of Zoning and a Cure for Its Exclusionary Effects," *Urban Studies* 41, no. 2 (February 2004).
28. Connor Dougherty, in *Golden Gates*, quotes Harvard economist Edward Glaeser as calling restrictive zoning the most important shift in the U.S. housing market since the automobile.
29. Although rescinded by the Trump administration, the rule has been reinstated by the Biden administration, which has gone further to propose a competitive grant

program to fund jurisdictions that eliminate exclusionary zoning and expand housing access to low or moderate income people. "President Biden Announces New Actions to Ease the Burden of Housing Costs," Whitehouse.gov, May 16, 2022, https://www.whitehouse.gov/briefing-room/statements-releases/2022/05/16/president-biden-announces-new-actions-to-ease-the-burden-of-housing-costs/.

30. "*Imagine Boston 2030* Implementation," Boston Planning and Development Agency, last accessed February 22, 2023, https://www.bostonplans.org/planning/imagine-boston-2030-implementation.
31. The powers of municipalities are governed by state law. In "home rule" states, cities have greater regulatory autonomy; in "Dillon's rule" states, they are subject to closer state control. Massachusetts (and thus Boston) is on the Dillon's rule end of the spectrum. Gerald E. Frug and David J. Barron, *City Bound: How States Stifle Urban Innovation* (Ithaca, NY: Cornell University Press, 2008). Cities are generally free to experiment with new zoning techniques as long as they tend to protect public health, safety, and general welfare and "encourage the most appropriate use of land." See, e.g., *Rodgers v. Village of Tarrytown*, 276 A.D. 1019 (N.Y. App. Div. 1950).
32. These contrasting approaches were debated during deliberations on the Standard State Zoning Enabling Act in the early 1920s. Planners on the committee (including Frederick Law Olmsted) favored rules, distrusting that a citizen "board of appeal" would apply guidelines competently. The committee chair, the nation's leading zoning lawyer, believed flexibility was key to the acceptance and workability of zoning. Ruth Knack, Stuart Meck, AICP, and Israel Stollman, AICP, "The Real Story behind the Standard Planning and Zoning Acts of the 1920s," *Land Use Law & Zoning Digest* 48, no. 2 (February 1996). The resulting compromise came down on the "rule" side of the debate: the SSZEA, the source code of most zoning ordinances, envisions uniform rules and a "hardship" standard to vary them. As noted, this "original sin" bedevils zoning implementation to this day.
33. Aspects of these proposed regulatory approaches can be accomplished by simple zoning code amendments; others may require amending state zoning enabling acts or specific legislative authorization, e.g., to subsume historic district, wetland protection, and other programs with independent statutory authorization into a comprehensive land use approval process.
34. A model for this is the Massachusetts Comprehensive Permit Program created under Massachusetts General Laws Chapter 40B in 1969. Intended to remove barriers to affordable housing in cities and towns with little of it, the program allows a proponent of housing meeting certainly affordability requirements to obtain a single municipal permit that overrides local zoning, supersedes local discretionary approvals, and has limited appeal rights. Though often locally resisted, it has been highly effective in producing affordable housing in suburban communities.

REGIONALISM

CHAPTER THREE

TECHNOLOGY AND THE GROWTH OF THE BOSTON METROPOLITAN REGION

ANDRES SEVTSUK

The Boston metropolitan area has witnessed remarkable growth in the last two decades. Its population grew by a tenth between 2000 and 2020, adding close to 300,000 new residents. The metro area's GDP grew by 30 percent in the past twenty years, driven largely by a strong innovation economy. Despite two serious economic crises—the 2008 credit crash and the 2020 pandemic—real estate prices remained high and construction cranes never disappeared, making unaffordability rather than growth the key planning issue.

What role has technology played, if any, in this latest growth spurt of one of America's oldest cities? As in past waves of urban expansion, technology in the twenty-first century has influenced Greater Boston's growth by determining the location of production and development, and by enabling the movement of people, goods, and information. But unlike times past, the location of economic production is no longer dictated by the availability of raw materials, the presence of industrial machinery, or the availability of cheap land. Rather, present-day job production and development activity follow workforce preferences. Where skilled labor wants to live and work, capital follows and urban development flourishes. Instead of water currents or railroad or highway connections, present-day urban growth in Greater Boston is driven by technology-oriented employment clusters that boast high density, mixed land uses, transit, and amenity-rich environments, which increase housing demand around them.

This "winners take all" urbanism, where growth is dictated by corporate high-earners,[1] has left the area vulnerable to acute gentrification and affordability challenges. To sustain its economic advantage, Boston—like other rapidly growing cities in the United States—needs strong public sector leadership (see chapters 1, 6 and 8 in this book) that will deliver equitable investment into public transit infrastructure and affordable housing along transit-oriented growth corridors. Better connecting inner-city job clusters with regional, rail-oriented town centers and their affordable housing stock would extend high-quality lifestyles to more people and enable more equitable economic growth for decades to come.

Boston was founded in 1630 on the banks of Massachusetts Bay and two rivers, the Charles and the Mystic. Access from both the Atlantic Ocean and the inland rivers facilitated the movement of people, goods, and animals on waterways—a vital technological advantage that enabled access at roughly one-fiftieth of the cost on a per-mile basis compared to movement over land by horse-drawn carriage.[2] All early European colonies in North America were established on the seaboard, access to which depended on either wind and river currents or human and animal power.

The invention of the steam engine in 1781 revolutionized freight movement along inland rivers and gave rise to a new economy of artificial canals that could connect towns, hinterlands and factories that lacked the fortune of downstream water connections to urban markets and ports.[3] Before steamboats, products could be readily floated downstream, from farms to markets, but it was far more difficult to transport them back up against the currents. Barges and riverboats accumulated at downstream ports, where it was often more economical to burn them for firewood than to pull them back up against the flow. The steam engine made it possible to sail upstream almost as fast and easily as downstream, causing an explosion in travel and shipping and radically catalyzing development in inland areas. The Middlesex Canal, completed in 1803, established a waterway between Boston and Lowell, spurring manufacturing and trade between Boston and a series of mill towns along the Merrimack River. It inspired the Erie Canal between New York City and the Great Lakes, completed in 1825, which ultimately helped New York overtake New Orleans as the most important port in the country.[4]

The steam engine technology also gave rise to railroads.[5] The first major rail corridor in Massachusetts was created in 1830 as the private Boston and Lowell Railroad. By the mid-1800s, the Boston metropolitan area grew along a number of newly established rail corridors that linked the historic city with the mill economy along New England's rivers, providing an even more rapid and cost-effective pathway for goods and products to reach ports and markets in central Boston. The towns of Lowell, Worcester, Springfield, Waltham, Lawrence, Framingham, and many others, which till this day mark key junctions on the commuter rail network (see figure 3.1), defined the loci where nineteenth-century timber, paper, and textile profits found their *spatial fix*.[6]

At the turn of the twentieth century, Boston's growth was driven by the next transportation technology—the streetcar—dedicated to the transportation of people rather than goods. Streetcar lines spanned out from job clusters in central Boston and spurred speculative housing developments on fields and meadows surrounding the congested city.[7] Whereas horse-and-carriage rides were reserved for the relatively few who could regularly afford them, streetcars provided a daily return trip from verdant suburbs to city-center jobs for a mere nickel, turning "commuting" into a middle-class phenomenon. Working-class Bostonians could commute into the city from newly built homes in Mattapan, Dorchester, or Roxbury, which until then had remained the privy of the wealthy. Streetcar connections expanded the city's footprint to a number of additional suburbs, including Newton, Stoneham, Dedham, and Somerville.

The growing city produced growing horsecar and streetcar traffic. To mitigate congestion, Boston built America's first underground passenger rail line along Tremont Street in 1897—a precursor to the present-day MBTA Green Line. This was followed in 1901 by the Main Line Elevated, which itself was a precursor to the Orange Line and, in 1904, by the East Boston tunnel, a precursor to the present Blue Line. In 1912, a tunnel was added to connect the subway network with Cambridge via Longfellow Bridge, and a Dorchester extension opened in stages from 1927 to connect grade-separated mass transit to Mattapan. Unlike London, where the first subways ran on steam engines spewing ash and soot into the dark tunnels, Boston's subways ran on electric engines invented by Frank Sprague in 1886.

Streetcars and horsecars were gradually overtaken by the automobile that opened up even greater access to undeveloped land around the metropolitan core. The first truly mass-produced car—Ford's Model T—came on the market in 1908. By the mid-1920s, automobiles had overtaken most of the horses and carriages on city streets. Not only did automobiles sell beyond anyone's expectation, they quickly shifted planners' focus from new towns, garden cities, and "city-beautiful" visions to designing cities for the automobile. "The flood of motors made the gridiron street pattern, which had formed the framework for urban real estate for over a century as obsolete as a fortified town," argued Clarence Stein.[8] Due to small city blocks of preautomobile cities, "pedestrians risked a dangerous motor street crossing 20 times a mile."[9] Major urban utopias, such as Le Corbusier's Radiant City plan (1930), Frank Lloyd Wright's Broadacre City (1932), and General Motors' Futurama exhibit of 1939, all shared a fascination with the automobile as a mechanism for revolutionizing modern life and reshaping the concepts of space and time in twentieth-century urban planning. In the Boston area, large swaths of underdeveloped land became single-family homes, facilitating white flight from downtown neighborhoods after World War II and spurring downtown department stores to give way to suburban malls on the North Shore and the South Shore, and in Natick, Burlington, Brockton, and Dedham, among others.

Popularization of the automobile wasn't achieved through market forces alone. Federal policies and subsides played a critical role in enabling its adoption. First, scenic *parkways* for automobile commuters would extend to Roxbury, Rosendale, and further suburbs, such as Weston along the Charles River. As the popularity of the automobile grew beyond the upper-middle class, the Federal Highway Acts of 1944 and 1956 established massive federal subsidies for high-speed automobile infrastructure for the masses, covering nine out of ten dollars, if cities built out highways and interchanges that linked up with a federal network. In Boston, the Department of Public Works released a master highway plan in 1948, which proposed the construction of eight radial expressways (I-90, I-93, and I-94) and state highways (East Boston, Northeast, Northern, Northwest, Western, Southwest, and Southeast Expressways and the Central Artery), including a central belt route, called I-695, which was to connect the high-speed motorway network together as a circular Inner Belt.[10]

A broad-based coalition of activities stopped major parts of these plans by 1972, advocating for greater and more equitable investment in public transport instead, though a number of segments were already built by then. Suburban growth driven by motorization was literally driving jobs out of the city center toward newly established edge-cities, most notably along the Route 128/I-95 beltway, which became Boston's own Silicon Highway.[11] Along with the rest of the country, the Boston metropolitan area witnessed a large economic boom between the 1960s and 1980s, resulting in the development of large amounts of auto-oriented office and residential space in the suburbs, now spilling further out to the second beltway around the city—Interstate 495—that opened in 1957 (see figure 3.1).

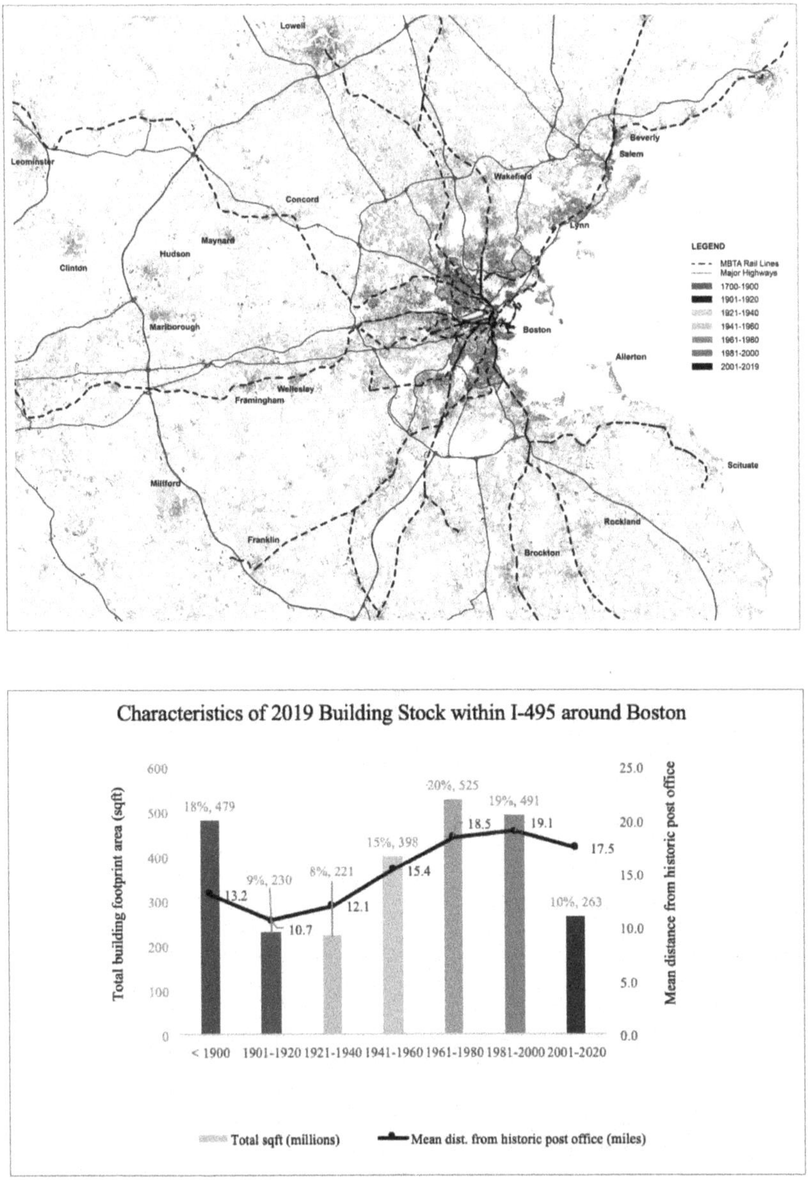

FIGURE 3.1. (*Top*) Map of current building footprints in Greater Boston by period of construction. (*Bottom*) The black curve on the secondary axis in the chart illustrates the average distance between structures constructed in each period and Post Office Square in the Financial District of Boston. It shows how the rise of streetcars, and most prominently the popularization of the automobile, drew development gradually further away from the historic core. The years between 1961 and 1980, which delivered the biggest building boom in the city's history, adding over half a billion square feet of footprints, were also located the furthest from the historic city, attesting to their car-oriented character. Images courtesy of Andres Sevtsuk.

The map in figure 3.1 illustrates Greater Boston's building stock in 2019, dated by period of construction.[12] Roughly 18 percent of buildings within the I-495 outer beltway date from before 1900. The majority of these and early twentieth-century structures are found close to the historic city center and along rail corridors fanning outward, many of them still in old mill towns. The largest amount of building footprints date from the periods 1960–80 (20 percent) and 1981–2000 (19 percent), which are mostly distributed throughout the low-density suburbs and exurbs between the first (Route 128) and second (I-495) ring roads around the city.

The past two decades of Boston's metropolitan growth have diverged from the predominantly outward expansion seen in the second half of the twentieth century. While development still continues apace in the suburbs, new construction has increasingly emerged closer to downtown, producing several newly built or substantially regenerated inner-city districts. The Union Square development, currently nearing completion in Somerville, provides a compelling example. Anchored around the new Green Line rail transit extension, Union Square development boasts high-density office, residential, and laboratory space in much taller structures than found in the otherwise

FIGURE 3.2. Union Square redevelopment proposal along the newly developed Green Line Extension in Somerville, with downtown Boston in the background. Image courtesy of US2, master developer of the Union Square Revitalization.

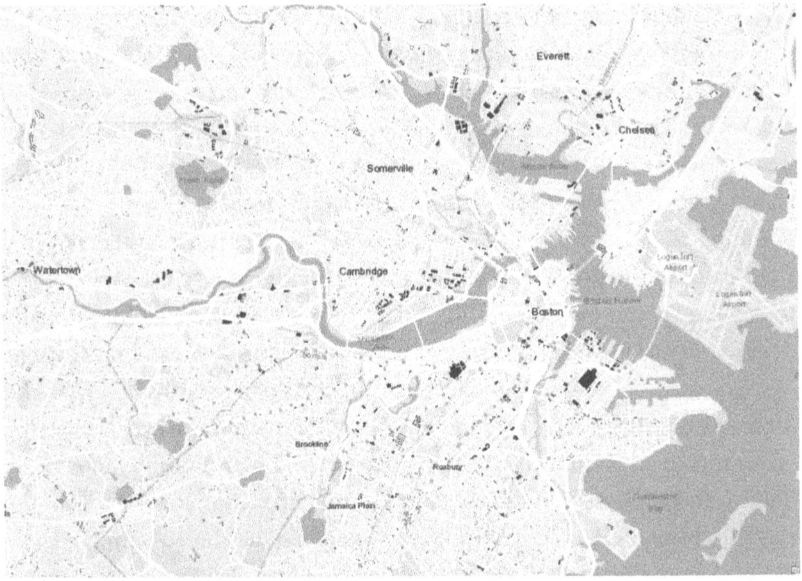

FIGURE 3.3. Building footprints built between 2001 and 2019 (*dark gray*) and transit stations (*circles*). Image courtesy of Andres Sevtsuk.

lower urban fabric around it (see figure 3.2). A broadly similar pattern characterizes the Seaport District, the East Boston waterfront, SOWA (South of Washington Street), North Point and Kendall Square in Cambridge, Assembly Row in Somerville, the upcoming Dorchester Avenue, a transformed Fenway-Kenmore area, and the North Station area (see figure 3.3).

Boston's economy is driven by technology-oriented sectors—professional, scientific, and technical services, as well as healthcare industries. Life-science innovation firms, pharmaceuticals, and research-oriented hospitals have made the Greater Boston area one of the biggest life-science employment clusters in the world. Global digital technology firms, including Amazon, Google, and Facebook, along with numerous smaller companies have established a firm footing in several of Boston's new employment clusters. Amazon, which already houses hundreds of staff at Kendall Square, is constructing additional space for two thousand workers in the Seaport District.

The technically skilled, highly paid, and increasingly international labor force that drives the innovation economy is influencing the location choice of capital investments and real estate developments with its milieu and place preferences. Unlike the nineteenth century, when development activity gravitated to sites of industrial production, or the post–World War II era, when development fostered around suburban highway corridors in the urban periphery, *new economic clusters are growing at more central sites.* Capital is attracted to environments where talent wants to work—amenity-rich, pedestrian-oriented, and transit-accessible sites. A common denominator among the newly emerging districts is a denser, mixed-use and walkable character at transit-served locations that the tech-economy labor force is willing to pay for. In lieu of the suburban office park along the I-93, the I-90, the I-95, or Route 128, Boston's new employments clusters are closer to downtown and public transit options. They are denser and boast a more diverse mix of land uses, typically including office, housing, and retail space.

While getting to these new clusters from far-flung suburbs is slower and more frustrating by car, they compensate for this inconvenience by enabling occupants to reach lunch on foot, bike or walk to surrounding multifamily homes, and stick around for retail, food, and entertainment services in the evening. New residential developments are being developed within a short distance from these urban knowledge-worker hubs, enabling workers to get to jobs by public and active transportation. But despite working in transit-rich locations, the city's upper-middle class still keeps vehicles at hand, contributing to "transit gentrification," whereby households living next to transit do not actually use transit.[13] They are instead drawn to the amenities and convenient locations that transit-oriented developments offer.

This recent reurbanization trend in American cities has been described by journalist Alan Ehrenhalt (2012) as the *great inversion.*[14] Inner-city districts that lost middle-class residents along with purchasing power and property taxes as part of white flight in the second half of the twentieth century are witnessing a return of more affluent residents. Downtowns and former industrial zones around them, as well as formerly working-class districts nearby, are increasingly occupied by middle- and upper-middle-class households who used to stay in the suburbs. Predictably, a large influx of wealthy residents triggers new residential construction and sets off a contentious gentrification struggle for these areas' longer-term residents. Lower income households are pushed out to the suburbs, flipping the twentieth-century urban dynamic between decaying urban cores and prospering suburbs on its head. In 2019, there were almost three times as many families below the poverty line in suburban towns within the I-495 ring road around Boston as there were within the city of Boston itself.[15]

The concentration of development capital around high-income and predominantly white technology clusters has significantly contributed to spatial inequality and housing unaffordability in Greater Boston. Large wage differences between incoming residents on the one hand, and existing residents and businesses on the other, is pressuring long-standing neighborhood inhabitants and businesses to make way for higher bidders.

The Berkeley-based economist Enrico Moretti has argued that each innovation and technology sector job (e.g., a Facebook job) produces around five other jobs through economic ripple effects—service sector jobs, construction jobs, education jobs, and so on.[16] Though good for the economy as a whole, innovation-based jobs exert pressure on housing locally, whereby limited housing supply near good job locations is outbid by the high-earners. The five out of six workers that support the innovation clusters have no other option than to move further out. Boston and its neighboring inner-city municipalities that harbor lucrative innovation-driven employment clusters and accommodate much of the wealthy workforce within a few miles around them face an acute affordable housing shortage. Even median-income residents now struggle to find suitable homes that can accommodate a family within the city's core. While luxury housing production has advanced rapidly in a number of emerging districts, affordable housing production has lagged far behind. Very few net public housing units have been added since the 1980s.

Faced with minimal housing options in the city, a large share of the workforce is once again driven out of Boston to more affordable homes in far-flung suburbs. Quincy has become the new Chinatown. Brazilians in Somerville are increasingly driven to the more distant suburbs of Framingham and Everett. As mentioned in Renée Loth's foreword, East Boston's Latin American diaspora is being pressured by luxury condos on the waterfront. This is contributing to spatial inequality, forcing the middle- and working-class population, especially minority ethnic groups, to devote a disproportionately large share of their income to transportation between service sectors jobs in the city and increasingly remote homes in the suburbs. Gentrification is also affecting access to public goods such as schools, parks, public transport, amenity-rich main streets, and civic institutions that tend to follow municipal taxes, and now concentrate in denser inner-city locations where the tax base is growing. Despite a temporary decline during the COVID-19 pandemic, bumper-to-bumper traffic on major highways during morning and evening commuting hours has been increasing each year as a result of the "great inversion."

In order to counter this market-driven, unequal urbanization pattern, Greater Boston needs stronger and higher-quality government intervention.

It needs bold investments into rail and bus transportation that would provide a dignified, car-free commuting experience for many more beneficiaries and open up large amounts of new affordable building stock along commuter rail corridors outside of the historic center. And it needs more aggressive affordable—and indeed public—housing development in the inner city and close to public transit.

In January 2020, the Massachusetts Bay Transit Authority (MBTA) advisory board endorsed a bold plan to revitalize the commuter rail network that surrounds the metropolis.[17] The planned improvements promise to deliver fifteen-minute service headways system-wide, and more frequent "subway-like" service in denser core areas, generally within Route 128 around Boston. They also suggest system-wide station upgrades, a collective fare system, other transit services, and partial electrification, which could help reduce the state's greenhouse gas emissions, transportation energy consumption and noise levels near tracks. These improvements have yet to secure financing, and the COVID-19 pandemic created a cloud of uncertainty around them. Yet it would be wise, and indeed essential, for the metropolitan area's future to find the funding and follow through.

Around 1.8 million people live and 1.5 million people work within a one-and-a-half-mile radius of a commuter rail station in Greater Boston[18]—close to 40 percent of the metropolitan area population.[19] In 2018, the commuter rail system served approximately thirty-two million trips per year. But due to a number of factors, ridership has been declining, down from about forty million trips in 2002. The decline is two-pronged: first is the increasing wealth in the region, which has led to more car sales, and second is the poor service quality and relatively high commuter rail fares. Furthermore, while Boston and its surrounding towns have gone through a significant economic and real estate boom in the last decade, relatively little of that growth has occurred near commuter rail stations outside of the city center. New office development has centered around subway stations in the inner city but largely avoided outlying towns along commuter rail corridors. Unlike the regenerated city center, exurban and suburban developments have largely remained car-centric and have shifted potential riders away, rather than toward, commuter rail stations.

Public transport, especially rail transport, remains unrivalled in its capacity to foster dense and mixed-use development. The efficiency of different transport technologies is often compared by the number of passengers a system can transport through a typical ten-foot way per hour per direction (figure 3.4). Private cars typically achieve up to one thousand passengers per hour per direction on a road lane. If a lot of these vehicles carry multiple passengers, the number can go up to around fifteen hundred. If the same ten-foot way is given to pedestrians, it can funnel through up to five thousand pedestrians per hour without causing uncomfortable congestion. With bicycles, the upper limit is about the same as pedestrians. But public transport is in a different league. Buses can move up to around eight thousand people per hour per direction, and if those buses are given an exclusive bus rapid transit right-of-way, capacity can go up to around fifteen thousand.[20] This is on par with a light rail system. With heavy rail underground or over-ground tracks—that is, Boston's Commuter Rail network—capacity can reach as high as twenty-five to fifty thousand passengers per hour. The upper range of this requires longer trains and highly efficient signaling that reduces headways between trains to only about a minute or two during peak travel periods. What this means from an urban design and planning perspective is that both bus and rail public transportation can move far more people using a limited amount of space. Instead of wasting valuable urban land on asphalt, Greater Boston's Commuter Rail system can serve as a veritable movement artery that ties the metropolitan area's growth from the innovation job centers clustered around downtown to further-out transit-oriented towns on rail connections, thereby opening access to large amounts of additional affordable housing outside the inner core and enabling transit- and pedestrian-oriented lifestyles to many more Bostonians.

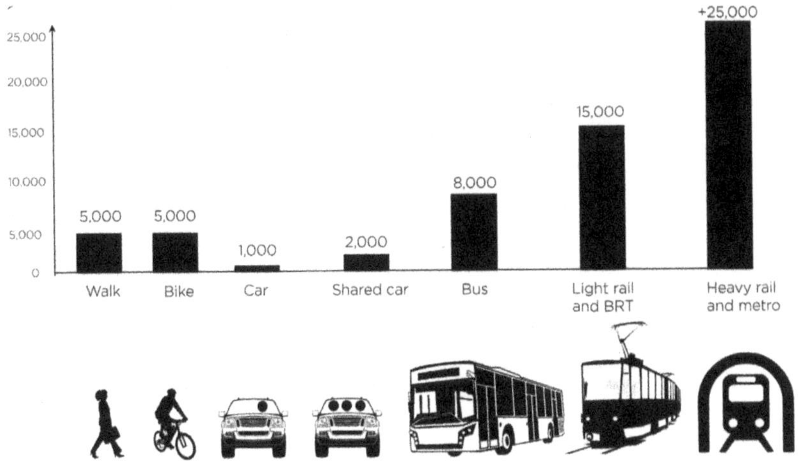

FIGURE 3.4. Maximum throughput capacity of a typical ten-foot lane per hour per direction on different transportation modes. Image courtesy of Andres Sevtsuk.

There are 141 stations in the current commuter rail network, connecting historic towns and subcenters to Boston's and its neighboring towns' employment opportunities. Vacant land, underutilized buildings, and parcels within walking range of stations offer an ideal setting for transit-oriented development. If enhanced rail service and building regulations near stations, coupled with street improvements to ameliorate walking and biking to stations, could attract future development into transit-connected suburbs and gateway cities, commuter rail improvements could generate more inclusive and economically productive growth and open up housing supply well beyond Boston and its inner suburbs (figure 3.5). It is also vital to provide reliable and convenient bus connections from the stations to surrounding homes and jobs, extending the rail catchment beyond the immediate walksheds around the stations. Similar regional rail investments

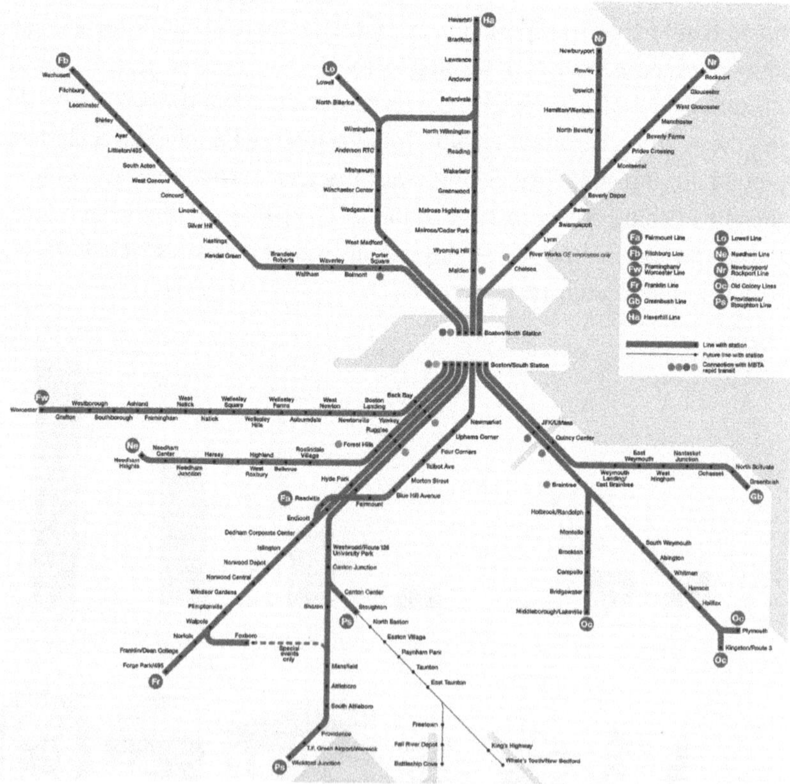

FIGURE 3.5. Present-day MBTA commuter rail network. Source: Wikimedia Commons. Original map by the Port of Authority. Updates by Pi.1415926535. CC BY-SA 3.0, https://creativecommons.org/licenses/by-sa/3.0/deed.en.

were put in place by a number of European and Asian cities decades ago, turning Copenhagen, Stockholm, Paris, London, Tokyo, Seoul, and Taipei into truly transit-oriented metropolises. With the rail corridors and rights-of-way already in place, Boston shares this opportunity to pivot its future growth toward rail corridors and embark on a sustainable and equitable expansion trajectory for the twenty-first century.

In addition to improving regional transit connections to the city, Greater Boston also needs to significantly increase new affordable housing production, while protecting existing affordable homes (see chapter 1). It should reestablish a new public housing development program. The current affordable housing requirements, which mandate developers of market rate housing to ensure that 15 to 20 percent of the units be made available at affordable rates, have worked too slowly to deliver sufficient supply. The lack of clear as-of-right development regulations has led numerous luxury housing projects to circumvent the requirements (see chapter 2). Affordable housing requirements differ across municipal boundaries, creating an uneven playing field in the metro area as a whole. Even in the best cases, where inclusionary housing programs do ensure that one-fifth of newly built homes are affordable, the share of jobs with below-area-median incomes (currently $79,350 in Boston for a one-person) at inner-city locations tends to be far greater than the corresponding supply of housing units. When new housing units in inner-city neighborhoods gradually replace older units, the process can turn majority affordable neighborhoods into minority affordable neighborhoods (e.g., one-fifth), tipping the balance in favor of luxury housing and contributing to displacement and inequality.

Other cities around the world have learned that affordable housing at scale can be achieved with publicly housing interventions. European capitals such as Vienna, Amsterdam, London, Paris, and Berlin each manage a large portfolio of public housing units that help city governments address housing unaffordability head-on. Economies of scale involved with centralized housing production help keep development costs under control. Coupling of housing policy and transport policy ensures that land value increases caused by new rail transit investment can be put to work in the public interest. Land around stations is acquired by municipalities or taxed with value capture instruments, allowing new public housing projects to be sited close to convenient transit stations. The international cities above have demonstrated that the quality of publicly developed housing projects can be as good as private sector housing, providing a valuable opportunity to young developers and designers, and enabling them to work with communities directly to cater to people's evolving needs. Singapore, Hong Kong, and other Asian cities, too, have endorsed a strong public housing model to combat the otherwise toxic spatial inequality that laissez faire housing markets tend to produce.

Though inequalities are innate to urban economic markets, the public sector has a critical role to play in determining how the inequalities play out. Do middle-class families need to drive to city-center jobs along congested highways from increasingly distant suburbs where the tax base is bound to shrink, dragging schools and public services downward over time? Or could they walk from an affordable, high-quality home, along a multimodal street (see chapter 4), to a modern train station that takes them to a city-center job, shopping district, or museum on a weekend? In the long run, concentrating new growth along rail corridors, along with ample affordable and public housing provisions, would concentrate scarce tax dollars, enabling smaller municipalities to pay for better schools, nicer parks, and community-oriented main streets. Such a future would require visionary planning, long-term transit investment, and a newly revamped public housing program at scale. Perhaps this could form a pillar of Greater Boston's response to the Green New Deal for which newly elected Mayor Wu has announced her support.[21]

NOTES

1. Robert Frank and Philip Cook, *The Winner-Take-All Society: Why the Few at the Top Get So Much More Than the Rest of Us*, repr. ed. (London: Penguin Books, 1996)
2. John Paul Rodrigue, "Transportation in the Pre-Industrial Era (pre-1800s)," in *The Geography of Transport Systems* (London: Routledge, 2020), https://doi.org/10.4324/9780429346323.
3. James Watts is credited for the first steam engine with rotary power that that could drive rotational mills, propellers, or wheels.
4. Until the steam engine's arrival, New Orleans had enjoyed the advantage of being downstream of the Mississippi River—a considerably larger system of hinterlands than on the Hudson—receiving produce and materials from the vast lands upstream. These canals' success prompted thousands of more man-made waterways to be developed across the country in the 1830s.
5. There were horse-drawn railroads prior to the steam engine, but these were quickly overtaken.
6. D. Harvey, *The Limits to Capital* (Chicago, IL: University of Chicago Press, 1982).
7. S. B. Warner, *Streetcar Suburbs: The Process of Growth in Boston, 1870–1900*. (Cambridge, MA: Harvard University Press and the MIT Press, 1962).

8. Clarence Stein, "Radburn, New Jersey," in *Toward New Towns for America* (1950; repr., Cambridge, MA: MIT Press, 1989).
9. C. Stein, "Radburn, New Jersey."
10. K. Crockett, *People before Highways: Boston Activists, Urban Planners, and a New Movement for City Making* (Amherst: University of Massachusetts Press, 2018).
11. J. Garreau, *Edge City: Life on the New Frontier* (New York: Anchor, 1992), 576.
12. The summary chart in figure 3.1 accounts only for building footprint sizes from each period. It therefore underreports actual built floor areas for periods that witnessed proportionately more multistory structures. Given that building activity from the last twenty years has occurred notably closer to downtown Boston—10 percent closer than in the previous two decades on average—where taller structures are more prevalent, the total building footprint area of 263 million square feet between 2001 and 2020 is a notable underestimate. What the Boston areas' newer urban form lacks in ground coverage and expanse is likely compensated for in height.
13. R. Basu and J. Ferreira, "Planning Car-Lite Neighborhoods: Examining Long-Term Impacts of Accessibility Boosts on Vehicle Ownership," *Transportation Research Part D: Transport and Environment* 86 (September 2020), https://doi.org/10.1016/j.trd.2020.102394.
14. Alan Ehrenhalt, *The Great Inversion and the Future of the American City*, 1st ed. (New York: Alfred A. Knopf, 2012).
15. American Community Survey U.S. Census Bureau, 2019 estimates and author's calculation. Number of families in poverty in Boston: 18,246. Number of families in poverty in census tracts between Boston and I-495: 50,488.
16. Enrico Moretti, *The New Geography of Jobs* (Boston: Mariner Books, 2013), 304.
17. M. Stout, "MBTA Board Commits to Ambitious Transformation of the Commuter Rail," *Boston Globe*, November 4, 2019, https://www.bostonglobe.com/metro/2019/11/04/oversight-board-vote-potential-commuter-rail-overhaul/TlX-KmleQBBalUYv3vOQpFK/story.html.
18. A. Sevtsuk, R. Morgan, and S. Fayad, *Transit Access: Improving walking and biking to commuter rail stations in Greater Boston*, Massachusetts Institute of Technology Department of Urban Studies and Planning, 2020, https://boston.transit-access.com/.
19. See https://boston.transit-access.com for reference.
20. In Curitiba's highly efficient Bus Rapid Transit system, with long buses and level platforms, throughput can be as high as twenty-five thousand per hour per direction.
21. A. Ocasio-Cortez, "H.Res.109–116th Congress (2019–2020): Recognizing the Duty of the Federal Government to Create a Green New Deal" (PDF), February 12, 2019, https://ocasio-cortez.house.gov/sites/ocasio-cortez.house.gov/files/Resolution%20on%20a%20Green%20New%20Deal.pdf.

MOBILITY

CHAPTER FOUR

TRANSPORTATION: METRICS AND MOVEMENT

Measuring Mobility and How We Measure Roadway Performance

ALICE BROWN AND MICHELLE DANILA

What a good street looks like depends on who is being asked. A good street looks different to someone behind a steering wheel than it does to someone looking for a bus stop, pushing a stroller, or riding a bike. These days, an outdoor dining spot to one person might look like a lost parking space to someone else; an "open street" event where people take over the street to walk, bike, shop, and eat might look like delays to a driver; and a red-painted bus lane might look like an empty travel lane to a driver waiting in a queue of passenger vehicles. What a good transportation system looks like is an even broader question. A well-connected network might contain highway overpasses, intersecting rail lines, a continuous protected bike lane, or a sidewalk with a ramp to a crosswalk and a walk signal that doesn't need to be pushed.

For more than a century, the success of transportation infrastructure design has been quantified by many engineers and planners using metrics that focus on the movement of cars while ignoring holistic or qualitative assessments of how people might move around in cities and towns. It's not entirely counterintuitive. Many people in positions of power and others who make such decisions use cars to get around, and anyone who has been in a car has experienced the frustrations of being stuck in traffic. It also seems obvious to people driving exactly where the problem lies—the point at which they must slow down or stop.

It can be challenging to consider the design of a road that is trying to accommodate people walking, bicycling, driving, or riding the bus when the metrics of the automotive era focus on ensuring vehicular efficiency as the primary measure of success. Using the computational models that evaluate vehicle delay, intersections are designed so that drivers don't have to slow dramatically to turn, wait too long at traffic signals, or look too long for parking along the curb. Even new development of land is measured by its potential impact on traffic on adjacent streets. The mathematical outputs of these studies infrequently anticipate or support a change in the existing street or intersection design that might remove capacity for motor vehicles throughout the corridor or the larger system. *Even where new streets are being planned, the potential needs of cars and their drivers continue to dominate both the equations and the conversation.*

In the first two decades of the twenty-first century, a broad coalition of advocates and designers who live in cities have radically shifted their thinking about the way roadways should be built and used across the United States. Though the pace of change has felt slow to many advocates, a century of city building focused primarily on accommodating automobiles cannot change overnight. It's often easier to rebuild roads to match previous designs than to reimagine the first few pieces of a comprehensive bike or bus network when they begin as fragments. Looking to European cities such as Paris, Copenhagen, and Amsterdam as well as other cities in the Americas, such as Mexico City and Medellin, has allowed municipal leaders and transportation staff to rethink the design of streets in the U.S. cities that are willing to embrace change. The Complete Streets roadway design standards, touted by the National Association of City Transportation Officials (NACTO) and modified to meet local context in different cities, illustrate how to design urban roadways.[1] The various local iterations include design guidance for protected bicycle facilities, exclusive bus lanes, narrower crossing distances for pedestrians, and an increase in sidewalk amenities, from street trees to benches. These guidelines aim to show how to create space for all modes of travel to establish best practices for roadway dimensions and other measurable attributes of safe accommodations.

At the local, state, and national level, change has been the most meaningful in places where elected officials, engineers, and engaged residents are the ones who regularly ride bikes and buses and get around on foot. Planning processes have also been most successful when public participation efforts have focused on reaching populations who don't drive and finding transportation solutions that work for them. In the same way that Tamara Roy writes in chapter 1 about all the people who would benefit from micro-housing with no parking, a large and underconsidered population in Greater Boston needs more safe and affordable ways to get around without a car.

Prioritizing roadway design for car mobility is not aligned with our present urban needs, and the metrics of success need to be reframed. In Boston, changes to travel behavior and roadway design are officially enshrined in *Boston's Complete Streets Guidelines* (2013), the *Boston Bike Network Plan* (2013), and the *Go Boston 2030 Vision and Action Plan* (2017) as well as *Boston's Climate Action Plan* (2014, updated 2019).[2] Yet as long as transportation systems in Boston and across the United States continue to focus overwhelmingly on the needs of people traveling in cars, and as long as the decision makers and the most vocal voters are reliant on private vehicles, the changemakers are fighting an uphill battle against the status quo. It may seem all but impossible to imagine a world where narrower travel lanes, reductions in vehicular parking, new standards for turning radii, and a completed network of protected bike facilities could be possible. Elected officials, transportation engineers, and the residents who testify in opposition to change at public meetings would need to put bus passengers, bike riders, and people walking ahead of drivers.

Transportation systems and streets have been based on measuring the wrong things. This chapter looks beyond design and points to metrics that can be used to evaluate transportation systems in order to build more equitable, climate-responsive, and economically vibrant cities and towns. In order to support a shift in travel modes, provide a diverse array of affordable options for people to get around, and allow denser development patterns, engineers and planners need to establish new ways to evaluate the quality of mobility—how streets, sidewalks, and intersections function for everyone using them. The majority of the data available today effectively "proves" that there is minimal roadway space available for designated uses other than automobiles. The people responsible for making change must either make a leap of faith that constructing a street for all transportation modes will attract people to those alternatives and effectively shift travel patterns across the system or have the political will to prioritize people using more equitable and sustainable travel modes over car drivers.

ROADS AND DATA DESIGNED FOR CARS

Personal vehicles were viewed as the primary solution for mobility for most of the twentieth century—the most effective way to provide people with choice and speed for getting everywhere they wanted to go. Our present built environment was designed around this assumption. As described by Andres Sevtsuk in chapter 3, developing Boston's transportation network was a gradual process, focusing first on water and then on rail. Walking around an older city like Boston, one can find streets of many different dimensions illustrating how the city was built first for pedestrians, then horses, then carriages, then streetcars, and finally for many lanes of car travel connected to a broader interstate system complete with elevated or underground highways.

Images of an ideal transportation future focused almost exclusively on smooth and seamless travel by private car, often with a driver and no passengers, with no congestion and few stops other than the desired destination. The chaos of historic downtowns was seen as outdated, and efficient engineering promised solutions in both the design of safe and comfortable vehicles and the design of a roadway system with soaring overpasses, curving exit ramps, ample parking supply, and well-timed signals that could keep cars moving through several signals at a time.

As the United States built out the interstate highway system and as arterial city streets were converted into one-way pairs to improve travel flow, first residents and then jobs moved out of city centers and into the suburbs. However, the roadway systems, as well as fixed-route transit systems, continued to serve downtown hubs and extend radially toward suburban areas.[3] Travel options designed to get people directly into downtown for jobs now required people to go through the urban core to reach jobs in other areas, putting continued pressure on the center of the system and causing congestion on major roadways. Since the problems become particularly acute during peak commuting hours, between 8:00 and 9:00 in the morning and 5:00 and 6:00 at night, many transportation solutions focus on addressing these peaks. To ensure that vehicular traffic can always move smoothly, roads have been widened, existing buildings have been demolished to clear the way, and new development has been prevented because it could cause more traffic. These changes have failed to make the promised impact because wherever new lanes have been added in response to severe congestion, they inevitably fill up more rapidly than anticipated, induced by the latent demand of people who had previously adjusted their commute times, driven less frequently, or been carpooling when it was congested.[4]

Intersections are measured with letter grades known as level of service (LOS) that compare current roadway conditions to anticipated roadway changes. As shown in figure 4.2, this measurement calculates the average amount of delay per vehicle measured in seconds at an intersection. For

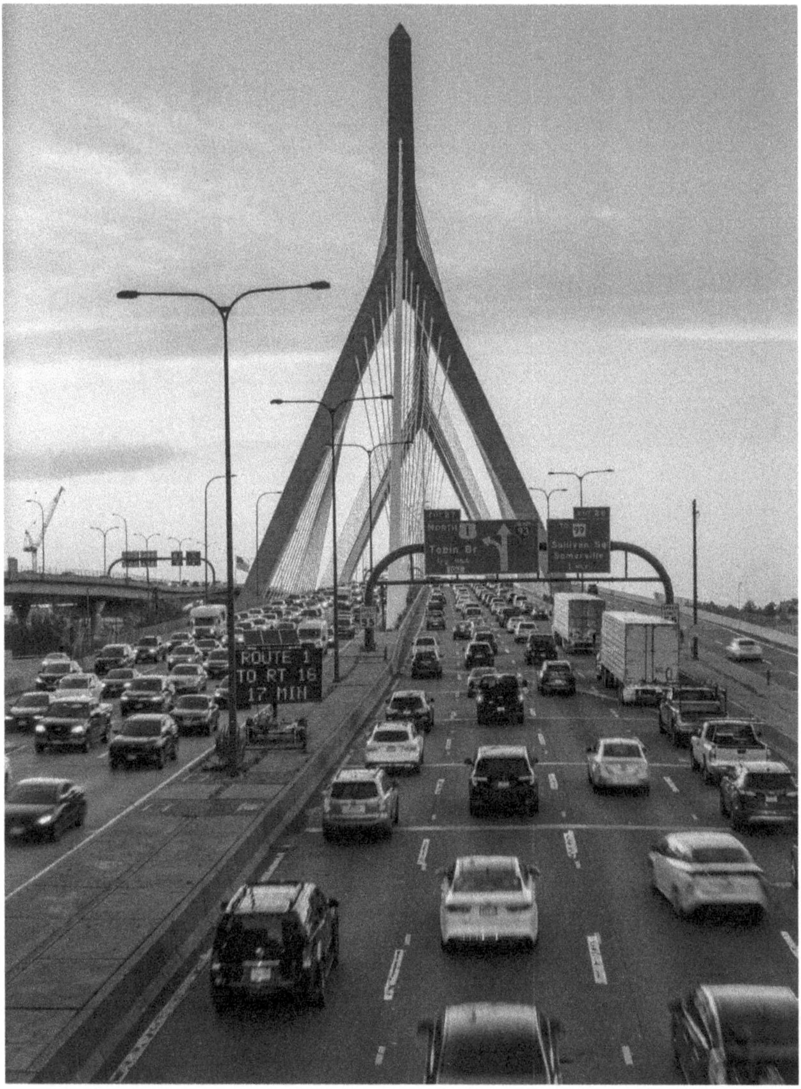

FIGURE 4.1. Vehicle congestion seen on the Zakim Bridge in downtown Boston. Image courtesy of Michael Prince.

each letter grade, there is also a description of how a driver might experience the roadway. These gradations determine when congestion has reached "unmanageable" levels with a seemingly simple scale. The Transportation Research Board's *Highway Capacity Manual* and the American Association of State Highway Transportation Officials' *Geometric Design of Highways and Streets* are national publications that enumerate the quality of traffic movement ranging from "free flow" (A) to "forced flow" (F).[5]

Traffic Signal Level of Service		
A	• Highly stable, free-flow condition with little or no congestion • No vehicle waits longer than one signal indication • Delay: < 10 seconds/vehicle	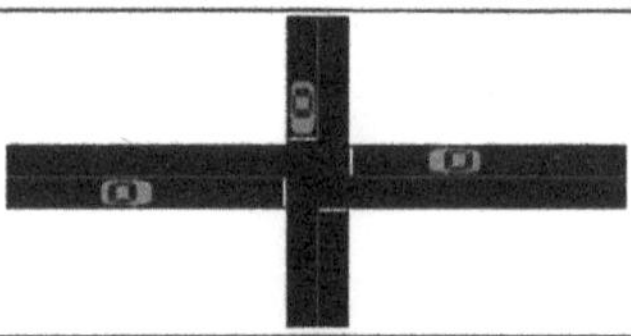
B	• Stable, free-flow condition with little congestion • On rare occasions vehicles wait through more than one signal indication • Delay: 10 to 20 seconds/vehicle	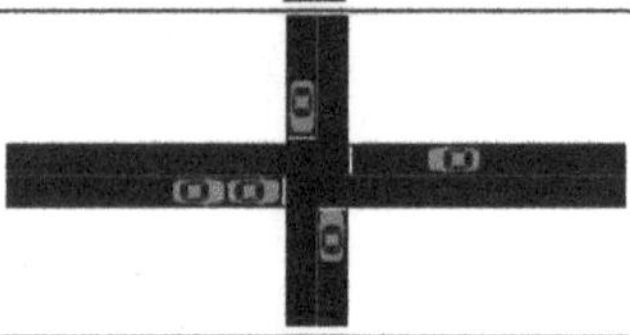
C	• Free-flow conditions with moderate congestion • Intermittently vehicles wait through more than one indication and occasional backups may develop • Delay: 20 to 35 seconds/vehicle	
D	• Approaching unstable condition with increasing congestion but without excessive backups • Level of service D has historically been regarded as desirable design in urban areas • Delay: 30 to 55 seconds/vehicle	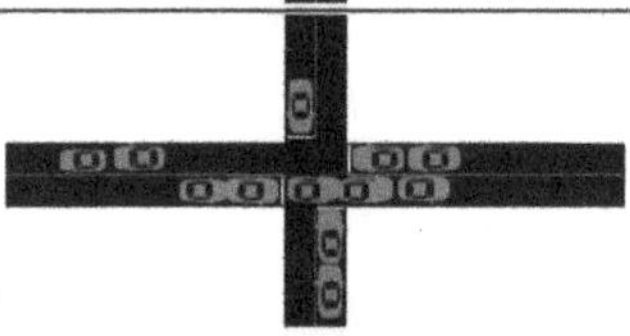
E	• Unstable, congested condition • Very long queues may create lengthy delays • Delay: 55 to 80 seconds/vehicle	
F	• Stop and go • Backups from locations downstream restrict or prevent movement of vehicles out of approach creating "gridlock" condition • Delay: >80 seconds/vehicle	

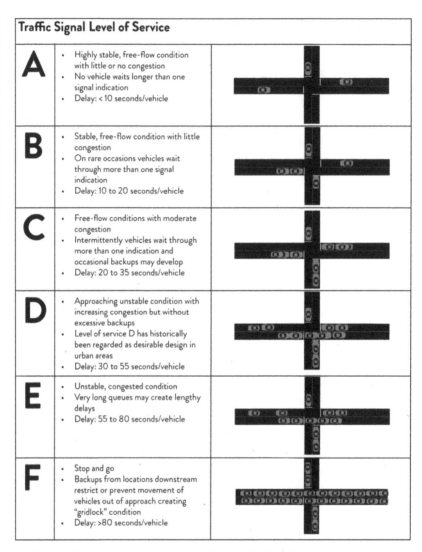

FIGURE 4.2. Illustration of the level of service letter grades for traffic signals. Image courtesy of Alice Brown and Michelle Danila.

Like letter grades at school, an A is better than an F. Unlike in school, where an A indicates significantly better performance than a C, any LOS ranging from A to C is generally accepted as a good performance for a roadway. In fact, LOS C is typically considered the gold standard for an urban setting—enough cars to indicate that it's a dense and interesting place to be, but with traffic still moving most of the time. A score of LOS D is acceptable, though it is "approaching an unstable flow" and has a "tolerable delay," while a LOS E has an "unstable flow" and "intolerable delay." The difference between these scores can be as little as a few seconds of delay for a vehicle and its passengers—not something most people in cars would notice, especially over the course of a trip.

Though scores of D or E are often acceptable when modeled for a new roadway design or development project, engineers avoid LOS F if at all possible since it is correlated with traffic jams or slow, tenuous, and unsafe driving conditions on a highway. On an urban arterial, a multilane street in a city that typically crosses through multiple districts, an F refers to "operations with extremely low speeds caused by intersection congestion, high delay, and adverse signal progression [when drivers encounter one red traffic signal after another]."[6] Though frustrating for drivers and a serious problem for bus operations, these low speeds may actually be safe and appropriate in a dense urban environment where vehicles are surrounded by people walking or biking as shown in figure 4.3. Though LOS F usually exists for only a small segment of the day, its mere potential can derail an entire project despite its possible economic and safety benefits. Drivers who are unable to speed down a street can see more of their surroundings, because they have increased peripheral vision at lower speeds. Seeing more restaurants and shops, as well as people crossing the street and biking, can lead to support for local businesses and increase both statistical and perceived safety.

The letter grades themselves are modeled using a traffic analysis software product developed from the *Highway Capacity Manual* concepts and used by traffic engineers to compare the existing traffic conditions measured in

Level of Service Criteria for Arterials

Arterial Class	I	II	III
Range of Free-Flow Speeds (mph)	45 to 30 mph	35 to 30 mph	35 to 25 mph
Typical Free-Flow Speed (mph)	40 mph	35 mph	27 mph
Level of Service	Average Travel Speeds		
A	> 35	> 30	> 25
B	> 28	> 24	> 19
C	> 22	> 18	> 13
D	> 17	> 14	> 9
E	> 13	> 10	> 7
F	< 13	< 10	< 7

Adapted from Transportation Research Board. Highway Capacity Manual, Special Report 209

FIGURE 4.3. Alternative level of service for arterial that factors in vehicular travel speeds. Image courtesy of Alice Brown and Michelle Danila.

the field to potential future traffic condition changes. The success of the project hinges on the letter grade for vehicular traffic during the peak commuting times. Even if a roadway is redesigned to better accommodate people walking, biking, or riding the bus, a model that shows a potential to delay vehicles based on LOS letter grades often leads to projects being rejected. The improvements for people walking and biking are not part of the calculation. There is not a way to measure the positive impacts of an intersection providing more time for pedestrians to cross the street or shorter crossing distances for people walking or to allow space for an exclusive bike facility. Similarly, if signal timing changes for bus priority or space for a bus lane are proposed, there is no way to consider the significantly larger number of people on a single bus than in a single automobile. This historic lack of metrics has created a problem for the planners, designers, engineers, and advocates striving to make multimodal changes to the system.

REFRAMING PLANNING OBJECTIVES AND DESIGN TOOLS

The Death and Life of Great American Cities, Jane Jacobs's famous 1961 critique of urban planning, laid out the observed benefits of multimodal streets along with a mix of land uses and a robust public transit system.[7] Donald Appleyard's less-well-known 1981 book *Livable Streets* provided a roadmap for deemphasizing traffic in cities, particularly in dense residential areas.[8] The last twenty years have provided the opportunity locally and nationally to develop new definitions for roadway success. New values and standards for quality cities and quality streets have been established by a collection of transportation planners, engineers, and advocates.

In Boston, there have been two waves of change. In the 1970s, Governor Francis Sargent announced a moratorium on highway construction in and around the city and created the plans for supporting alternatives. In the same decade, city officials pedestrianized parts of the city that were dense and well served by transit, such as Downtown Crossing, as well as tourist areas, such as Faneuil Hall and Quincy Market. Nonetheless, the final decades of the twentieth century were still highway focused. The "Big Dig," which included burying an elevated section of highway and building a park at the surface, seemed (at least in theory) to take cars off the street. However, the results included even more travel lanes and a complex parallel street network that is inextricably linked to the congestion on this underground highway. In an effort to keep vehicles moving, the design of the highway off- and on-ramps makes parts of the park difficult to navigate by bike and on foot.

Another wave of local change took place in the last decade. In 2012, under Governor Deval Patrick, the Massachusetts Department of Transportation (MassDOT) announced that there were no plans to build new highways in the Commonwealth and that the agency was working to triple the proportion of trips taken by walking, biking, and transit by reducing the proportion of trips taken by people driving alone.[9] Although LOS standards are still used, the policy charged MassDOT and many municipalities to consider changes to signals and travel lanes as part of the overall roadway design solution.[10]

Good planning has taken place. Design guidance enshrined in *Boston's Complete Streets* in 2013 redefined the characteristics of a high-quality street by requiring newly designed or redesigned streets to be "multimodal, green, and smart."[11] Within the guidelines, specific new standards attempted to focus first and foremost on the street users who didn't use cars and to carve out space from streets for other modes. In the guidelines, there are intersections that prioritize pedestrians with raised crosswalks, pedestrian signals that say "WALK" before traffic signals turn green, and reclaimed space for everything from cafés to bike parking to plantings to public art. There are similarly ambitious suggestions for the design of bicycle and bus facilities.

The *Boston Bike Network Plan,* also published in 2013, went further in developing the parameters for existing and proposed types of bicycle facilities and when to use them.[12] It also set a goal of adding 75 miles of bike infrastructure to the existing 120 miles by 2018. The city of Cambridge's bicycle plan, first published in 2015 and updated in 2021, published a bike plan with even more ambitious targets, including making all streets bicycle friendly and getting 20 percent of all trips in Cambridge to be made by bicycle by 2030.[13] In addition, the city council in Cambridge passed the Cycling Safety Ordinance, which requires the installation of approximately twenty-five miles of separated bike lanes within the next five to seven years.[14] A 2019 *Massachusetts Bicycle Transportation Plan* provided guidance for municipalities and state agencies to support the goal of making bicycling "a safe, comfortable, and convenient option for everyday travel."[15]

These bike plans and the Complete Streets guidelines reflected an evolving perspective on national standards for urban roadway design that was codified in the design guidelines of NACTO, which drew heavily on the prototyping and testing of new street designs by the New York City Department of Transportation under the leadership of commissioner Janette

Sadik-Khan.[16] State and federal regulations have followed suit, and accepted standards for street design have shifted toward slowing vehicular speeds for safety, accommodating designated lanes for bicycles and buses, and ensuring that the people walking feel like they are part of a continuous network with more crossing opportunities and shorter wait times at traffic signals, something that's particularly beneficial to people accessing bus stops on the other side of the street.[17]

The 2013 Boston mayoral election led to a surge in citywide planning across municipal departments in 2014. The 2017 mobility plan, *Go Boston 2030 Vision and Action Plan*, laid out three guiding principles: equity, climate responsiveness, and economic opportunity.[18] By reframing the core issues of mobility in this way, a city where everyone drives alone would be unable to both flourish and meet these objectives. A set of mode-shift goals reinforced the objectives. More equitable mobility and a reduction in carbon emissions can be achieved by prioritizing buses with exclusive lanes and signal phases as well as improving safety for people walking and bicycling.

Boston's 2014 *Climate Action Plan* established the goal of reducing greenhouse gas emissions from transportation by 5.5 percent of 2005 levels by 2020.[19] The 2019 update to the plan included the additional goal of making Boston a carbon-neutral city by 2050 along with a set of goals for improving and expanding active transportation infrastructure. Travel options with lower per capita emissions must be used for a greater share of trips in order to reduce the city's contribution to climate change, and with limited street space available, a conversion to electric vehicles alone is not feasible.

Many employers and business owners continue to believe that ample vehicle parking is necessary to attract their workforce and customers. However, dense concentrations of jobs cannot accommodate an on-street parking space for every employee and simultaneously maintain the spillover benefits of proximity, clustering, and networking found in areas supported by transit and other driving alternatives. Additionally, the retail streets across the nation with the highest rents per square foot are on congested streets where traffic moves slowly—where large numbers of people walk and shop while vehicles, forced to travel at lower speeds, have more time to notice the shops lining the street than they otherwise would at higher speeds. Studies in New York City and Toronto have demonstrated that where entire corridors are improved for transit and bicycling, total profits increase for local businesses.[20] Providing more ways to get to jobs and retail as well as to education and health services is encapsulated in the economic opportunity section of the *Go Boston 2030* vision.

FIGURE 4.4. Street designed to better accommodate many people using different modes of transportation. Image courtesy of Michelle Danila.

The online publication of these design tools and future plans empower more advocates and residents to join the dialogue and play a more meaningful role in redesigning cities. Using the standards, activists that support walking, bicycling, and transit have been able to develop conceptual designs that demonstrate the capacity for other modes on major roadways. Digital civic engagement tools such as Streetmix allow people to create new cross-sections for multimodal streets and test configurations that balance different uses.[21] Planners and engineers have used paper versions of this cross-section concept and other tools that look at the street from above to foster dialogue in planning meetings for districts and corridors. Private developers can also begin their projects with multimodal designs for roadways within and adjacent to their properties.

Two of the primary targets in the *Go Boston 2030* plan aim to provide high-quality transit, car sharing, bike sharing, and access to a protected bike network to every Boston resident. These targets redefine access, but they do not always have an impact on localized design review for roadways or development projects. To achieve these targets requires changing the dimensions and designs of streets, sidewalks, and intersections. What is limiting the implementation of these plans and the reallocation of street space? The uncertainty of predicting how these new streets will work stands as a major barrier to the carefully calculated level of service analysis and transportation modeling that has driven the final engineering decisions for decades.

CHALLENGES TO THE AVAILABLE DESIGN TOOLS

At every scale, from regional and citywide to neighborhood and district-wide to roadways and intersections, the primary units of measurement remain vehicles, vehicle trips, and vehicle delay. *While design standards are increasingly multimodal, nearly every standardized metric for roadway movement ignores or heavily undervalues other modes of transportation.* The *Highway Capacity Manual* that standardized level of service added a "multi-modal level of service" only in the 2010 edition, and this measurement tool is infrequently used because it is cumbersome.

Regional travel models tend to overcount potential vehicle trips in mixed-use areas where people are more likely to walk than drive within the district and to undercount the potential for shifting mode preferences when bikes or buses are better accommodated. Citywide data relies on the U.S. Census and the American Community Survey, which provides data based solely on the most frequently used commuting mode and not for all trips. The once-per-decade census is too infrequent to study mode changes, while the survey data is too thinly distributed to study mode changes at the neighborhood level.

If none of these metrics is framed in a way that considers the many ways people may choose to travel and the merits of those choices, LOS continues to pose similar problems and also provides the technical underpinnings for many concerns associated with NIMBYism.[22] Drivers who feel that wait times for traffic signals are too long or that they have to stop too often on a roadway corridor tend to focus on specific delays that inconvenience them. Their concerns can be supported by quantifiable data on a case-by-case basis even if a design change might improve travel times over the full length of the road. Philosophically and psychologically, preserving space and mobility for cars also means that adding a bike or bus lane is viewed as "the loss of a lane" rather than the allocation of the lane for others because the people who move in this new lane are not counted. Similarly, each of these countable cars must be accommodated not only when moving but when parked as well, which allows engineers to reject designs that consolidate or eliminate parking spaces.

ALTERNATIVE METRICS

Metrics for safety, access, and reliability, along with mode-shift goals, are politically powerful and palatable, but they face challenges on a case-by-case basis. In order to balance mobility for multiple modes on city streets, new tools for measuring performance must be implemented. Some apply to the streets themselves, while others apply to the urban conditions surrounding them. Streets can be evaluated on how well they normally function for all of their users, how safe they are for people not in vehicles, and how much value they generate. Measurements linked to land use can also support street design changes when new development projects are held accountable for how people access the site. Yet, regardless of the measurement, the adage that what is counted is what matters is applicable at every scale.

Here then, are six recommendations for Boston and other cities to consider when designing streets that do more than just move cars.

> New Metrics and Strategies for Regional and Citywide Change
> 1. Align budgets for capital improvements with mode-shift goals.
> 2. Adopt a Vision Zero policy to evaluate roadway designs based on their reduction of traffic fatalities and serious crashes.

Municipalities can demonstrate the value of multimodal streets by budgeting for them and allocating capital dollars to improvements that support a range of travel choices. In San Luis Obispo, California, planners created a modal hierarchy for streets that determined which streets should focus their priority on which mode of transportation. This was done in conjunction with the establishment of very progressive mode-shift goals, and in order to build the infrastructure that would support this mode shift, the city established a policy of budgeting for their desired goals. This means that while they work to achieve a 20 percent modal split for bicycling, 20 percent of their transportation spending is directed toward bike facilities. Boston has yet to adopt this practice, though significantly more funding has gone to "active transportation" since the release of the *Go Boston 2030* plan.

Another way that cities have sought to de-emphasize design for automobile speeds has been the adoption of Vision Zero policies, which focus on reducing the number of fatal traffic crashes to zero. San Francisco was one of the first cities in the nation to do so and established a goal of eliminating traffic fatalities by 2024. Boston, along with Cambridge and Somerville, have also adopted Vision Zero policies and focused renewed attention on making streets and sidewalks safer. Incidents that were once considered "accidents" are being seen as preventable collisions. Most cities that have adopted these policies are paying special attention to eliminating crashes that result in severe injuries as well, and they are working to make residential streets and school zones places where vulnerable roadway users are protected by designs that make them more visible and less susceptible to being hit by drivers, in addition to reducing vehicle speeds.

Though Vision Zero work is data driven, data collection and reporting are inconsistent, which makes the identification of the worst intersections and corridors less precise. State and local police data and corresponding Emergency Medical Services reports, if they exist, do not have the same format and are not all part of the same system. Where there is good data for a roadway corridor or intersection, there have been substantive redesigns, but it takes time to collect data on the absence of crashes, and pressure from drivers who are forced to travel slower by design can make change temporary. In the meantime, Boston has created a crowd-sourced safety concerns map where individuals can self-report intersections and streets that they find problematic.[23] Where pedestrians feel unsafe crossing a neighborhood street because people speed through intersections, raised crosswalks or intersections slow cars and make even potential collisions less severe, trading increased safety for reduced speeds.

New Metrics and Strategies for Neighborhood and District-Wide Change

3. Support a mix of land use to improve walkability and bikeability with infill incentives, vehicle miles traveled, and walk score.
4. Create exceptions to parking minimums and LOS with transportation demand management and other criteria.

Residents who are resistant to infill housing often point to concerns about increasing traffic congestion and declines in level of service at nearby intersections when voicing their opposition. Statewide legislation in California provides a model for overcoming these arguments. California Senate Bill 743, signed in 2013, was designed to "balance the need for level of service standards for traffic with the need to build infill housing and mixed-use commercial developments within walking distance of mass transit facilities, downtowns, and town centers and to provide greater flexibility to local governments to balance these sometimes competing needs."[24] The result is that level of service will no longer apply to roadways within an "infill opportunity zone." Municipalities are working to develop new standards that will work well for their particular geographic, social, and political needs. Caltrans published the First Edition of two guidance documents in September

2020 for the analysis of transportation impacts using vehicle miles traveled (VMT): *Transportation Analysis Framework* (TAF) and *Transportation Analysis under CEQA* (TAC).[25]

Some California cities are leveraging VMT to evaluate projects. Vehicle miles traveled can be measured on a per capita basis for residential development, per employee for commercial development, and as a net total for retail and service industries. In this framework, a proposed housing project that moves people away from a congested area but leads to longer drives to reach jobs and amenities is penalized relative to a project close to the downtown core, near a neighborhood main street, within a mixed-use district, or along a transit corridor. By allowing and encouraging denser development and eliminating the study of a single intersection, future residents, workers, and shoppers can take advantage of more modes of travel.

Mixed-use developments and neighborhoods support increased walkability and bikeability. The Walk Score data used by real estate professionals makes proximity to amenities a part of the value of a property, and there are now similar versions for biking and transit access.[26] This tool shows that there is an economic benefit to proximity, but it lacks a way to evaluate the quality of the experience on foot or provide an incentive to improve the street design and make the walking experience more pleasant. A design-centered metric for walkability would include an evaluation of the infrastructure with points for access to trails, protected bike lanes, quality sidewalks, good curb ramps, and marked crosswalks as well as reliable transit access.

New development would also benefit from clear guidance to support fewer people driving. Areas with high walking, transit, or biking scores could allow for lower parking minimums. The cost of constructing parking or the additional revenue from building uses other than parking could be used as mitigation for other improvements to nearby roadways such as bike and bus lanes or better pedestrian amenities. Funding could also be for transportation demand management, which could support tenants by providing alternatives to driving from transit passes to bike share to shuttles. And, as noted by Roy in chapter 1, housing built without required parking is more affordable to future tenants.

New Metrics and Strategies for Corridor and Intersection Changes

5. Study person-throughput and delay on roadways.
6. Leverage digital tools to count all intersection and roadway users, then reallocate space accordingly.

Recognizing that the historic segmentation of pedestrian, bicycle, and transit measures into separate chapters and tools made them easier to marginalize, the *National Cooperative Highway Research Program Report 616* incorporates all of these modes into corridor and intersection measurements.[27] The revised computational tools consider the width of the sidewalk and ramp conditions that acknowledge pedestrian congestion. They also consider the experiences of a person walking; the experience of people accessing, waiting for, and riding a bus or light rail system; and how long people bicycling wait for a signal and are delayed in the space between two signalized intersections. By considering how people walking, biking, riding the bus, and driving are experiencing the current conditions and will experience future improvements for an intersection or corridor or roadway, the dialogue about a street's purpose in moving people also changes.

Currently, when bus or bicycle facilities are installed that remove a travel lane or restrict turning movements, the report on whether the intersection is operating properly focuses on LOS for vehicles only. The change in design is framed as a loss for drivers. A variety of alternative tools have been proposed as strategies to measure multimodal level of service. The first one was created in Florida, and others have been developed since then by private firms, academics, and municipalities.

Person throughput is the simplest of these tools and considers who is using a corridor or intersection in different modes and how much space is allocated to their mobility needs. Person throughput counts all of the individuals who are able to travel down a street or through an intersection, unlike vehicular throughput, which counts buses and cars equally and ignores the number of people on the bus and people walking and biking. The creation of a peak-hour bus lane on Washington Street in Boston's Roslindale neighborhood came about from a study that determined that 60 percent of people on the roadway at peak hours were on buses, so the parking lane was reallocated to buses only. Though the lane looks empty some of the time, the utilization of this space on a per capita basis is far greater than it was.

The North Washington Street Bridge leading to the Charlestown neighborhood is being rebuilt and will include designated lanes for buses and for bikes based on data captured prior to its construction. Bike lanes can sometimes be hard to justify with this tool, because riders are less likely to get stuck in traffic, and it's challenging to forecast how much bike ridership will increase with the installation of a new bike facility. In general, though, the idea of "person throughput" as the number of people who move through an intersection during a period of time is fairly easy for people to grasp even if the predictive models have not yet been fully developed. A longer pedestrian phase that increases delays for cars can add value by allowing hundreds of people to move across an intersection.

Although ample technology has been created to count vehicles, evaluating a multimodal roadway is limited by costly and cumbersome data collection for other modes. Fortunately, affordable multimodal counting methods are becoming more common. Digital bike counters have improved, and some feature daily or weekly counts to publicize the use of a new bike lane. Some companies provide data based on scraping images from video recordings that can count pedestrians and bikes as well as cars, or can study sidewalk congestion and desire lines, the routes people chose to walk that deviate from the official path. In 2015, the city of Boston began purchasing Waze data to determine if multimodal projects were having a significant impact on overall travel times in affected corridors. Initial studies showed that drivers are not delayed as much as anticipated.

THE FUTURE

A street with space for people walking, bicycling, riding the bus, driving, and lingering can be the new design consensus. A city or district should be walkable, transit-oriented, and bike-friendly. Some or all of these features appear in some of the most attractive neighborhoods in the country and support vibrant downtowns. Accommodating many modes of travel addresses many of the problems faced by contemporary cities by improving local air quality and reducing greenhouse gas emissions, providing more equitable mobility options that connect people of all ages and incomes with employment and educational opportunities, and supporting and growing a robust local economy that cannot be well-served exclusively by driving and parking single-occupancy automobiles.

People traveling without a car remain harder to count in the field, more challenging to create projected travel models for, and challenging to prioritize in designs that favor the predictability of car travel and the calculable LOS measures. Continued work is required to augment multimodal design tools with the measurement tools that will support the implementation of the less car-centric streets that form the backbone of our most livable communities. When the public sector is making a major infrastructure investment, they definitively want to know what the results will be, and the complexity of multimodal streets have made the older models and tools defunct. Such uncertainty makes changes risky and requires strong political support (and senior staff with the confidence to try it).

Advocates and community organizers, as well as real estate developers and property owners, need to learn more about and push for new tools and metrics for transportation projects that support mixed use and infill development, foster community, support density, and de-emphasize automobile dependence. As described in chapter 10, the public health sector is pushing communities to support walking, along with transit riding and biking, in order to improve air quality, reduce chronic asthma cases, lower rates of obesity, promote higher levels of fitness, and support mental health by naturally incorporating walking into residents' daily routines. With clear standards for measuring and tracking street uses and performance at the intersection, roadway, and network scale, cities can shift their goals, reallocate street uses, and better leverage mitigation measures from new development where applicable.

In the coming decade, autonomous vehicles will also affect how we measure roadway performance. Autonomous vehicles, particularly if shared, can further reduce the need for storage space and move in ways that make travel lanes more efficient. Their benefits remain murky when viewed through the lens of other transit modes. Autonomous vehicles may be able to communicate with signals or gather huge amounts of data on how people travel, but intersections still need to support travel modes that are not digitally connected. Even as technology enables cities to digitally connect with vehicles and gather data with new tools, the needs of and space for *all* roadway users will continue to be paramount for effective multimodal urban transportation design. If the new metrics continue to focus on or emphasize these cars over the needs of people walking, bicycling, and taking transit, the greatest efficiencies will never be realized.

The early months of the COVID-19 pandemic demonstrated problems and opportunities within our roadway systems. The decline in traffic volume during peak travel times when teachers and office workers were working from home showed that travel could potentially be spread out throughout the day. The emptier streets allowed cities to install new bike lanes, shared streets, and bus lanes, and even to replace curbside parking with outdoor cafés. The permanence of these changes has yet to be proven, but the pilot testing has been done. As of summer 2022, traffic volumes have returned, though people seem to be traveling in vehicles more continuously throughout the day. New bus lanes result in faster and more reliable bus service and have increased ridership along those routes. Increasingly, people working from home are requesting safe and connected facilities to walk and bike even if it is for trips that aren't commutes. We need not wait. How the good street of the future will be defined is being decided now.

NOTES

1. National Association of City Transportation Officials, *Urban Street Design Guide*, 2013, https://nacto.org/publication/urban-street-design-guide/; National Association of City Transportation Officials, *Urban Bikeway Design Guide*, 2014, https://nacto.org/publication/urban-bikeway-design-guide/.
2. City of Boston, *Boston's Complete Streets Guidelines*, 2013, https://www.boston.gov/sites/default/files/file/2019/12/BCS_Guidelines.pdf; City of Boston, *Boston Bike Network Plan*, 2013, https://www.cityofboston.gov/images_documents/Boston%20Bike%20Network%20Plan%2C%20Fall%202013_FINAL_tcm3-40525.pdf; City of Boston, *Go Boston 2030 Vision and Action Plan*, 2017, https://www.boston.gov/sites/default/files/file/document_files/2019/06/go_boston_2030_-_full_report.pdf; City of Boston, *Boston's Climate Action Plan*, 2014 (updated 2019), https://www.boston.gov/sites/default/files/embed/file/2019-10/city_of_boston_2019_climate_action_plan_update_4.pdf.
3. Fixed-route transit systems include train lines, monorails, funiculars, cable cars, and even buses that run on catenary wires or in physically separated lanes. Fixed-route transit is often seen as more dependable and durable than bus or shuttle routes that have less physical infrastructure and can get stuck in traffic or be permanently rerouted or canceled.
4. Congestion typically serves as a deterrent. Waiting too long or too often in traffic causes individuals to defer trips, to change their commute patterns in order to travel outside the peak hour, and to carpool, or to avoid the road by taking transit if that is an available option. Adding capacity to a roadway attracts drivers who would otherwise have avoided driving on that road at that time or allows them to drive alone at peak times and encourages them to make more trips by car.
5. Transportation Research Board, *Highway Capacity Manual: A Guide for Multimodal Mobility Analysis*, 6th ed. (Washington, D.C.: Transportation Research Board, 2016), https://www.trb.org/Main/Blurbs/175169.aspx. The American Association of State Highway Transportation Officials is the official body for setting standards for highway design and construction in the United States and is best known for "The Green Book" that specifically addresses the geometry of roadways and intersections. *A Policy on Geometric Design of Highways and Streets*, 7th ed. (Washington, D.C.: American Association of State Highway and Transportation Officials, 2018), https://store.transportation.org/item/collectiondetail/180.
6. Transportation Research Board, *Highway Capacity Manual.*
7. Jane Jacobs, *The Death and Life of Great American Cities* (New York: Random House, 1961).
8. Donald Appleyard, *Livable Streets* (Berkeley: University of California Press, 1981).
9. MassDOT oversees the state-owned roadways, transit and rail operations, aeronautics, and the Registry of Motor Vehicles in the Commonwealth.

10. MassDOT published the *Separated Bike Lane Planning and Design Guide* in 2015. A more recent engineering directive lays out guidance for selecting bicycle facility types based on roadway context and has improved the design of complimentary infrastructure. The *Massachusetts Bicycle Transportation Plan* was published in 2019 and can be found at https://www.mass.gov/service-details/bicycle-plan.
11. City of Boston Transportation Department, *Boston Complete Streets Design Guidelines 2013*, Boston.gov, https://www.boston.gov/sites/default/files/file/2019/12/BCS_Guidelines.pdf.
12. City of Boston Transportation Department, *Boston Bike Network Plan*, Boston.gov, 2013, https://www.cityofboston.gov/images_documents/Boston%20Bike%20Network%20Plan%2C%20Fall%202013_FINAL_tcm3-40525.pdf.
13. City of Cambridge Community Development Department, *Cambridge Bicycle Plan: Toward a Bikeable Future*, 2015, https://www.cambridgema.gov/CDD/Transportation/gettingaroundcambridge/bikesincambridge/bicyclenetworkplan.
14. The requirements and timelines of the City of Cambridge's Cycling Safety Ordinance can be found at https://www.cambridgema.gov/streetsandtransportation/policiesordinancesandplans/cyclingsafetyordinance/requirementsandtimelines.
15. Massachusetts Department of Transportation, *Massachusetts Bicycle Transportation Plan*, 2019, https://massdot.maps.arcgis.com/apps/MapJournal/index.html?appid=c80930586c474a3486d391a850007694.
16. NACTO has published the *Urban Street Design Guide* (2013), the *Urban Bikeway Design Guide* (2014), and the *Transit Street Design Guide* (2016). AASHTO's fourth edition of their *Guide for the Development of Bicycle Facilities* (2012) also moved toward designs that were more context sensitive in urban environments than they had been.
17. Federal Highway Administration, *Guidebook for Developing Pedestrian and Bicycle Performance Measures*, 2016, https://www.fhwa.dot.gov/environment/bicycle_pedestrian/publications/performance_measures_guidebook/pm_guidebook.pdf.
18. City of Boston Transportation Department, *Go Boston 2030 Vision and Action Plan*, 2017, https://www.boston.gov/departments/transportation/go-boston-2030.
19. City of Boston Environment Department, "Greenovate Boston 2014 Climate Action Plan Update," 2014, https://www.cityofboston.gov/eeos/pdfs/Greenovate%20Boston%202014%20CAP%20Update_Full.pdf.
20. The New York City DOT published their findings in a report titled "The Economic Benefits of Sustainable Streets," which can be found at https://www.nyc.gov/html/dot/downloads/pdf/dot-economic-benefits-of-sustainable-streets.pdf. The Toronto study results can be found at https://www.tcat.ca/resources/bloor-street-economic-impact-studies. The granular tax receipt data that is used to measure this is not available in Massachusetts.
21. Streetmix.net was developed by Code for America in 2013 to allow planners and the public to compare roadway lane configurations based on a given street width and context. Users can adjust the widths and sequence of sidewalks and travel lanes to compare different roadway uses between two buildings. Learn more at https://streetmix.net.
22. NIMBY is an acronym for "Not in My Backyard" and is used to describe advocacy that protects and preserves the status quo whether in zoning, housing, or transportation.

23. The map can be found at https://www.boston.gov/transportation/vision-zero. It is worth noting that feeling safe on a street can go well beyond the movement of cars and the behavior of drivers.
24. California Senate, *Senate Bill No. 743, Chapter 386*, 2013–2014 Legislative Session, 2013, https://leginfo.legislature.ca.gov/faces/billTextClient.xhtml?bill_id=201320140SB743.
25. California Department of Transportation, *Transportation Analysis Framework*, 2020, https://dot.ca.gov/-/media/dot-media/programs/transportation-planning/documents/sb-743/2020-09-10-1st-edition-taf-fnl-a11y.pdf; California Department of Transportation, *Transportation Analysis under CEQA*, 2020, https://dot.ca.gov/-/media/dot-media/programs/transportation-planning/documents/sb-743/2020-09-10-1st-edition-tac-fnl-a11y.pdf.
26. Walk Score was founded in 2007 as a way to measure the walkability in order to promote walkable neighborhoods. The tool is now targeted toward housing searches. Learn more at www.walkscore.com.
27. Transportation Research Board, *National Cooperative Highway Research Program Report 616: Multimodal Level of Service Analysis for Urban Streets*, 2008, https://www.trb.org/Publications/Blurbs/160228.aspx.

RESILIENCE

CHAPTER FIVE

SOCIAL RESILIENCE IN THE FACE OF THE UNEXPECTED

ANTONIO RACITI, ROSALYN NEGRÓN, AND REBECCA HERST

In the Boston metropolitan region, which is experiencing significant economic growth pressures, and where the free market tends to drive the policy agenda, decision making for resilience has become a contested terrain. Mainstream climate adaptation strategies search for the most innovative solutions to protect urban areas and their assets from the short- and long-term effects of climate change. This focus tends to prioritize ends over processes, and, as such, questions about how people understand problems and interact, learn, organize, and respond to achieve resilience are examined in relation to ends (e.g., how will communities respond to a proposed solution?).

On the one hand, solutions, impacts, or ends-focused approaches to resilience—important as they are—tend to frame resilience primarily as an outcome to be achieved. Indeed, the assumptions that underpin the notion of resilience as an end are embedded in most standard definitions of resilience, which is to say the ability of individuals or systems to return to a prior state after a disturbance. On the other hand, process-focused approaches to resilience orient toward ongoing systems change and transformation rather than a return to (or preservation of) a stable state as an end. Yet human action, intention, and anticipation drive continuous systems' change. Rather than thinking of resilience solely as an end to be achieved, we discuss social resilience as capacity building rooted in social relationships.

This contribution is one of the outcomes of a larger "Metro Boston Climate Adaptation Stakeholder Mapping Project" carried out by faculty and graduate students at the Sustainable Solutions Lab (SSL) at UMass Boston. The Sustainable Solutions Lab is a cross-disciplinary collaborative research and action institute whose core members have affiliations in six schools and four institutes across UMass Boston. The center's primary mission focuses on ensuring that historically excluded communities can be safe and healthy in the face of the climate crisis. We explore the concept of social resilience by analyzing collaborative relationships in metropolitan Boston's climate adaptation field. Rather than look at the entirety of the socio-ecological system that is the city of Boston and its surroundings to assess the system's resilience, we zero in on the climate adaptation field itself, which exists to build a metropolitan Boston more resilient to climate change. As we will show, an analysis of the climate adaptation field—its stakeholders, their roles, and the collaborative relationships among them—demonstrate not only how resilience, as an end, drives social action but also how collaborative interactions in themselves build resilience to unexpected shocks.

First, we map the network of climate adaptation stakeholders in metropolitan Boston. Granted, these networks are a static snapshot of dynamic social action and interaction. But an analysis of the structure and composition of the stakeholder network reveals continuous and purposeful moves to connect and cooperate around shared goals. It is these concrete capacity-building actions, we argue, through which preparedness to major shocks emerges. In fact, after mapping out the metropolitan Boston climate adaptation stakeholder network, we then look more closely at the social connections within the climate adaptation field that were activated locally in response to the COVID-19 pandemic crisis. Our stakeholder network analysis shows that the existing climate adaptation field of actors forms a social infrastructure that made COVID-19 collaboration possible. The Boston metropolitan area has a highly active climate adaptation field that includes stakeholders from multiple sectors, spanning public, private, and community organizational realms, as well as physical, environmental, and social resilience goals. As we will show, the COVID-19 crisis activated collaborative responses across sectors and resilience fields. This bodes well for metropolitan Boston's capacity to mobilize broad climate adaptation resources to build social resilience in the face of climate and nonclimate disasters.

RESILIENCE AND CLIMATE ADAPTATION

Given that cities and urbanized areas face increasingly frequent global-scale effects resulting from climate change, in the last twenty years the climate adaptation field has been searching for numerous strategies at the interface between physical and social planning. In this context, the concept of resilience has become the main label under which adaptation strategies have been proposed. Although various definitions of resilience were initially formulated in the field of ecology and later translated into multiple disciplinary settings, the link between original definitions and their use in practice hasn't always been clear.

An attempt to link existing definitions of resilience to their practical use was identified by scholars using the original conceptualizations of *engineering, ecological,* and *evolutionary* resilience as coined by Crawford S. Holling to establish reference frameworks for action.[1] Simin Davoudi and colleagues note that institutional strategies have been typically inspired by the *engineering resilience* and *ecological resilience* paradigms.[2] While the former has been used to search for the most innovative technical solutions protecting urban areas and enable them to return to their "normal" state after natural catastrophes, the latter has been trying to generate naturally oriented strategies that would restore former ecological conditions to accommodate the effects of those changes and create a new "normal" condition. In climate adaptation strategies, planners and policymakers have mainly used engineering and ecological resilience paradigms to physically organize or envision cities to face unexpected events linked to climate change.

Challenging the idea in early definitions of resilience as returning to a "normal" state, evolutionary resilience is based on the understanding that social-ecological systems are complex, nonlinear, and need to be flexible, adaptive, and critically transformative.[3] One of the most critical issues highlighted by the concept of evolutionary resilience is that human agency and intention can affect the capacity to cope with nonlinear and nonpredictable systems. This idea of evolutionary resilience urges us to think holistically about climate adaptation as a process in which social and natural systems interact dynamically.[4] In particular, Davoudi and colleagues suggest four domains to assess the resilience of a socio-ecological system:

1. social learning capacity ("to achieve preparedness");
2. resistance to disturbances ("being persistent and robust");
3. ability to absorb disturbances ("being flexible and adaptable"); and

4. movement toward a more desirable trajectory ("being innovative and transformative"), stressing the importance of coupling characteristics of social systems with those of natural ones.[5]

While Davoudi and colleagues remind us of social and ecological systems' interdependence in urban resilience, Alan Kwok and colleagues unpack social resilience itself.[6] They point out that social resilience is a complex, multidimensional concept, spanning individual, community, and systems levels, and with myriad corresponding attributes. Like Davoudi and colleagues, they also point to the ways social resilience is both an outcome and a process. Building on Susan Cutter and colleagues, Douglas Paton and John McClure, and Philip Buckle, Kwok and colleagues further distinguish between *cognitive* and *structural* dimensions of social resilience.[7] The structural dimension pertains to the specific features of a social entity (e.g., demographic characteristics and available resources in a city), while the cognitive dimension has to do with people's perceptions of and orientations to their social environment. Through an analysis of disaster researchers', managers', and policymakers' definitions of social resilience, Kwok and colleagues propose core attributes of social resilience, organized by these cognitive and structural dimensions. Of particular relevance to our current analysis, these include collective efficacy, community inclusiveness, connectedness between networks, and social support, for the cognitive dimension; and collaborative processes, knowledge, skills, and social networks, for the structural dimension. Taken together, social resilience unfolds as individuals come together to work on common goals, sharing resources and support in such a way that members develop a sense of shared values and a sense of their collective problem-solving potential.

Along these lines, here we focus on social resilience not just as the capacity for people, groups, and communities to cope with contingent and unpredictable circumstances but also, importantly, as the flexible and dynamic web of connections arising through collaboration. *If resilience is a capacity of institutions and individuals to respond to change, collaboration is a process by which this capacity is built.* More concretely, through collaboration, people meet shared goals by mobilizing material resources, sharing information and expertise, fostering social learning, and sharing decision-making power. Thus, the social web that binds actors across scales and sectors, facilitates collective action, even as individuals and groups within the system pursue unique goals. This mix of the collective and the particular are essential for resilient systems. For example, Daniel Aldrich argues that in the wake of disasters, the most resilient communities are those containing a mix of bonding (strong, more exclusive) ties, along with bridging ties (weaker, more inclusive) and linking ties (linking to institutional power).[8] From this perspective, there is still a wide-open call to investigate how social resilience is operationalized in practice by exploring mutual interactions among individuals to explain existing (and generate new) social learning processes.

METHODS

The project presented in this chapter identifies people and organizations currently working in climate adaptation to shed light on the several ways practitioners, activists, researchers, and officials establish and nurture various forms of collaborative practices to build resilience in response to climate change. For the project's purposes, stakeholders are those who impact and/or are affected by efforts to achieve climate adaptation or climate justice–related efforts in the Greater Boston metro area. The overarching research question driving the work was, *What are the existing collaborative connections between climate adaptation stakeholders in metropolitan Boston?*

The methodology for the research is as follows. An initial list of 280 climate adaptation stakeholders was built through a phased process, which began with a meeting of SSL community partners where attendees listed out names of stakeholders. The list that emerged from this first meeting was shared with additional key stakeholders via e-mail, yielding additional names for a core list of 188 stakeholders. We then shared this list of 188 names with a broader set of stakeholders, representing diverse sectors of the climate adaptation field in metropolitan Boston. Eventually, the stakeholder list grew to 280 names. Only stakeholders working within a five-mile radius of downtown Boston (figure 5.1) were included in the stakeholder list, with the assumption that physical proximity (e.g., ease of travel to meetings, shared interests tied to local projects) is an important factor structuring collaborations. Extending the stakeholder inclusion criteria beyond this local focus would have resulted in a list whose length would have proved onerous for survey respondents to review and respond to.

FIGURE 5.1. Municipalities included in the five-mile radius of downtown Boston.

Using Qualtrics (an online software platform to generate surveys), we launched the online survey with a roster of 280 stakeholders in mid-September 2020. Invitations to complete SSL's stakeholder mapping survey were sent out to all 280 actors on the stakeholder list. Respondents had the option to nominate additional stakeholders not included in the list of 280. This resulted in twenty-one additional names being added to the stakeholder list. In early November, when the stakeholder survey closed, 175 stakeholders responded to our survey. However, due to missing data and errors, the final dataset includes the responses of 169 stakeholders. The stakeholder networks discussed below are composed of the connections among these 169 stakeholders only.

The roster survey, consisting of the list of 280 climate adaptation stakeholders, asked respondents to indicate if they had a relationship with any of the stakeholders on the roster. The survey asked about two types of relationships: (1) collaboration on climate adaptation-related projects, and (2) collaboration in response to the COVID-19 crises. Respondents were also asked to rate the strength of their collaborative relationships using a scale of 1 to 5, with 1 being "weak relationship/seldom collaborate" and 5 being "strong relationship/frequently collaborate." Collaboration was defined as working together in order to achieve a shared purpose or outcome, including sharing information, knowledge, resources, and/or effort.

Survey responses were cleaned and imported into UCINET (a software platform for the analysis of social network data) to compute basic network statistics.[9] Network statistics include density (proportion of existing ties), centrality (to identify stakeholders who occupy central positions within the stakeholder network), and subgroup analysis (to identify subgroups within the larger stakeholder network that has a higher level of collaboration). The stakeholder network data were also imported into Visone (a software platform for the visualization of network data) to develop network visualizations for analysis and interpretation.[10]

PRELIMINARY FINDINGS

Stakeholder Characteristics

Fifty-eight percent of respondents were women. While respondents represented a range of ethnic and racial backgrounds, 75 percent of respondents identified as white. Seven percent of respondents identified as Black or multiracial, 10 percent identified as Latinx, and 4.7 percent identified as Asian (which included East Asian, Southeast Asian, and South Asian). Table 5.1 summarizes stakeholder characteristics related to their organizational affiliations and the nature of the work they did within the climate adaptation field. Of network participants, 32 percent were in the nonprofit sector, 25 percent were in the private sector, and 21 percent were in the public sector.

We classified twenty different role types designating the nature of the work done by stakeholders. The top roles are presented in table 5.1. Most prominently, they included academia (14 percent), government (14 percent), and engineering (14 percent) roles. These roles spanned resilience efforts, with physical (i.e., infrastructural) resilience being the most common type of resilience work pursued by stakeholders (39 percent). Environmental resilience work was pursued by the lowest percent of stakeholders, at 17 percent. Finally, the majority of stakeholders reported having collaborated with at least one other stakeholder in the network on COVID-19-related response (56 percent).

TABLE 5.1. Work and Organizational Characteristics of Stakeholders

	(N = 147)	
ATTRIBUTE	*N*	%
Organization type		
Foundation	4	2.7
Government (elected)	1	0.6
Independent	3	2
Labor union	1	0.6
Network	5	3.4
Nonprofit	47	32
Private sector	37	25
Public sector	31	21
University	18	12.2
Top roles		
Academic	20	13.6
Advocacy	10	6.8
Conservation	15	10.2
Development	10	6.8
Energy	9	6.1
Engineering	20	13.6
Government	20	13.6
Organizing	14	9.5
Resilience work		
Environmental	25	17
Physical	58	39.4
Social	30	20.4
Spanning or nonresilience work	34	23.2
COVID collaboration (Yes)	82	55.8

Figure 5.2 shows the network of 169 stakeholders who responded to SSL's stakeholder mapping survey. The nodes represent each of the stakeholders, and the lines represent the collaborative ties between them. With only 25 percent of all possible ties in the network present, the metropolitan Boston climate adaptation stakeholder network was connected but not densely so. On average, stakeholders were connected to 42 other stakeholders in the network (out of 169). Still, as is evident in the tangle of ties depicted in the

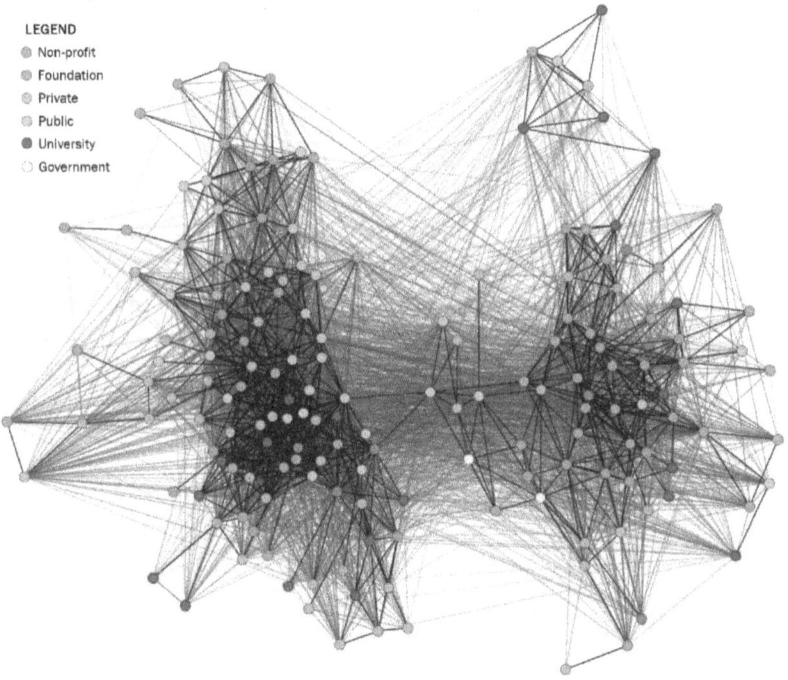

FIGURE 5.2. Climate adaptation stakeholder network map: Visualization by type of organization.

network visualization, the climate adaptation field is bound together in one large component. In theory, this would mean that knowledge, information, and other types of resources could flow to all members of the network—though a number of factors determine how easily certain actors or subgroups could access circulating resources.

The shades of gray of the nodes represents the type of organization that the stakeholder primarily worked in. The network is structured into two primary groups. These two groups reflect especially embedded sets of relationships, with higher levels of interaction among them than with other stakeholders in the network. Broadly, the two groups include: mostly grassroots stakeholders working through nonprofit organizations on the right side of the visualization (henceforth, the "grassroots" group), and a larger group of stakeholders from public and private sectors on the left (henceforth, the "institutional" group). The private organizations were mostly engineering firms, while stakeholders from the public sectors worked mostly for the city of Boston.

In figure 5.3 we present the same network while highlighting the distribution of race/ethnicity within the network. In this figure, we use only two categories: white and BIPOC (Black, Indigenous, and People of Color). While BIPOC stakeholders work in various sectors of the climate adaptation field, they are especially represented in grassroots organizations. With 25 percent BIPOC representation, there is still a significant improvement margin to increase diversity in the regional climate adaptation conversation.

Once more, we present the main stakeholder network in figure 5.4, this time differentiating the nodes by each stakeholder's type of resilience work identified within the broad realms of physical (e.g., of physical infrastructures development), environmental (e.g., development of green and blue infrastructures), and social (e.g., community-informed activities related to climate adaptation) resilience issues. A fourth category includes those individuals whose activities either span across these three primary realms or transcend them. The three main types of resilience work are distributed throughout the network. However, we point out a few notable patterns.

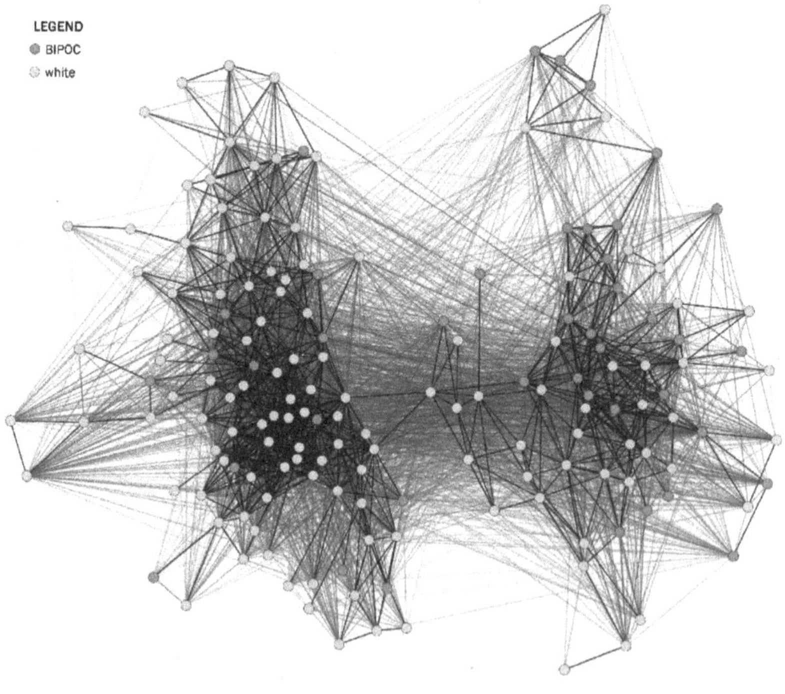

FIGURE 5.3. Climate adaptation stakeholder network map: Visualization by race.

First, a small subset of actors doing environmental resilience work cluster on the top part of the network's institutional side. With a few exceptions, stakeholders doing environmental resilience work are more peripheral to the network. Second, a large proportion of the network's institutional side are stakeholders working on physical resilience, including public and private sector stakeholders. In contrast, social resilience work is primarily pursued by stakeholders in the grassroots group, with a few stakeholders from the institutional side who do social resilience work pulling toward the grassroots side.

We should note again that the visualizations are organized to facilitate pattern identification. Despite some clear patterns, it is still the case that meaningful levels of collaboration exist among all stakeholders such that the grassroots and institutional sides are not completely segregated from each other. This becomes clearer when we examine the network of stakeholders who reported having the strongest levels (a rating of 5) of collaborative relationships with each other (figure 5.5). Here we see that while

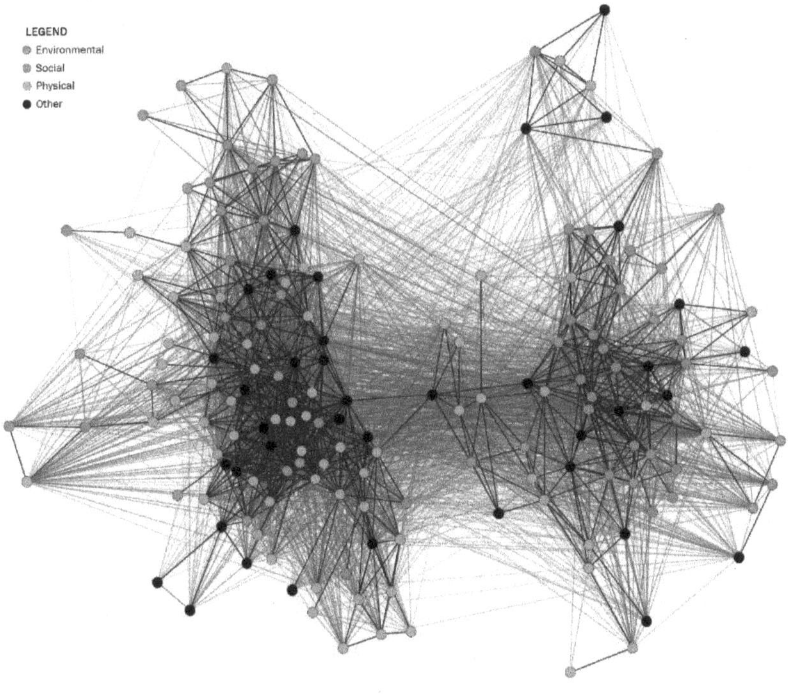

FIGURE 5.4. Climate adaptation stakeholder network map: Visualization by resilience work.

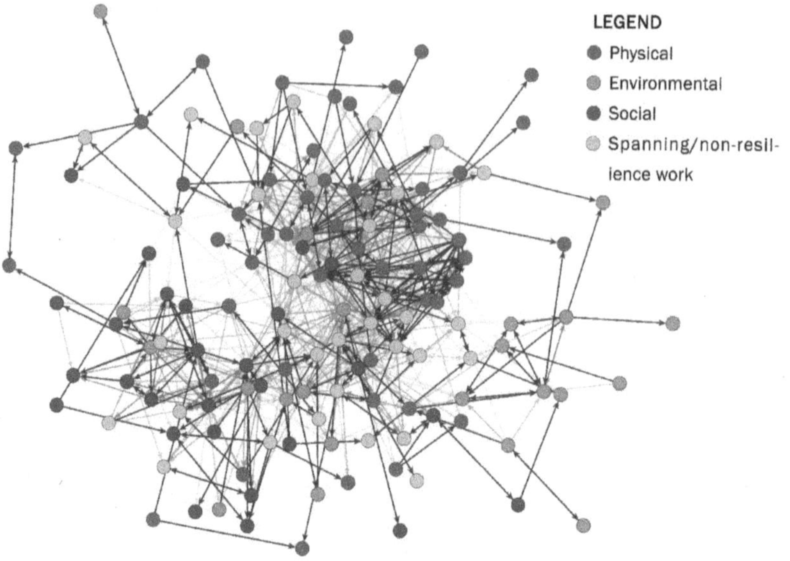

FIGURE 5.5. Visualization of the network among stakeholders who were the most highly collaborative.

resilience work types are distributed in a patterned way (e.g., social resilience stakeholders tend to appear closer together, and physical resilience stakeholders tend to appear closer together), in fact, this core network of highly active and strongly tied stakeholders span all resilience types, intersecting regularly.

COVID-19 Response Network

In our final analysis, we focus on the network of a group of eighty-two stakeholders who reported collaborating with other stakeholders in response to the crises that unfolded locally with the COVID-19 pandemic. In figure 5.6a we see that while women and men are about evenly distributed in the COVID-19 response network, women played a particularly prominent role within the network. This is confirmed by the greater numbers of connections, on average, among several of the women stakeholders in the network (shown by the size of the nodes). To use the technical language of social network analysis, figure 5.6a specifically depicts "in-degree centrality." Degree centrality is a measure of the number of ties an actor has. The more ties someone has, the more "central" or powerful they are within the network. In-degree centrality specifically measures the number of incoming times to a node (shown by the direction of the arrow on a line). In other words, it is a measure of the number of ties that are directed toward a given actor. This is an indicator of importance or prestige, since high in-degree scores suggest that the stakeholder is sought after for collaboration.[11] The stakeholders with the highest in-degree scores in the COVID-19 network were primarily women. This raises questions about the gendered nature of crisis response in the specific case of COVID-19, which heavily mobilized certain types of care work.

When examining the COVID-19 response network focusing on resilience, some notable insights emerged (figure 5.6b). In the larger climate

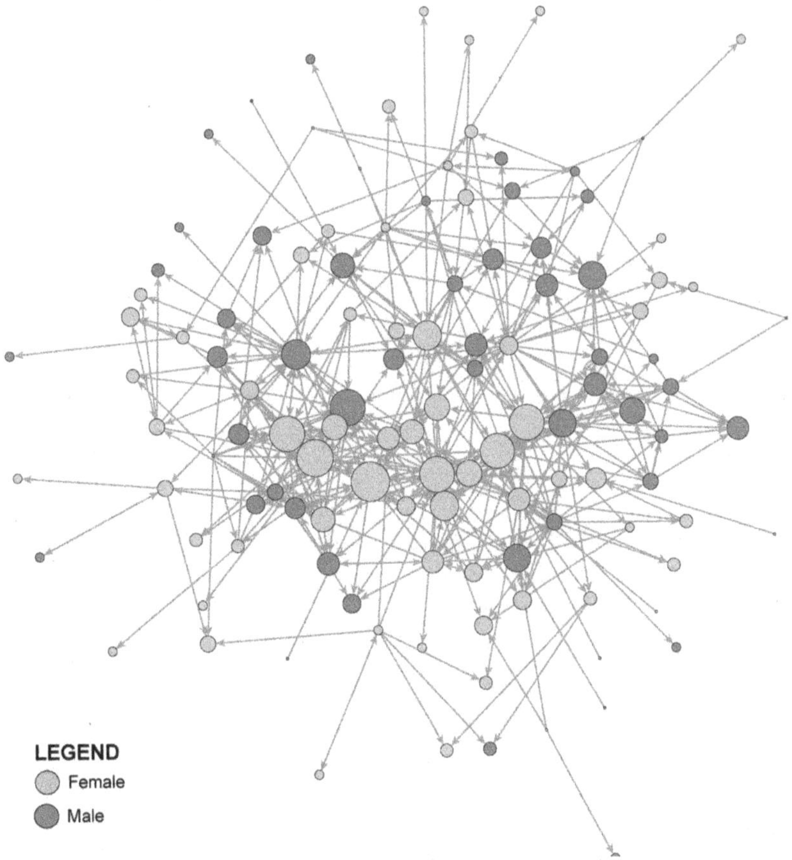

FIGURE 5.6A. Stakeholders' collaboration in response to the COVID-19 crises: Visualization by gender.

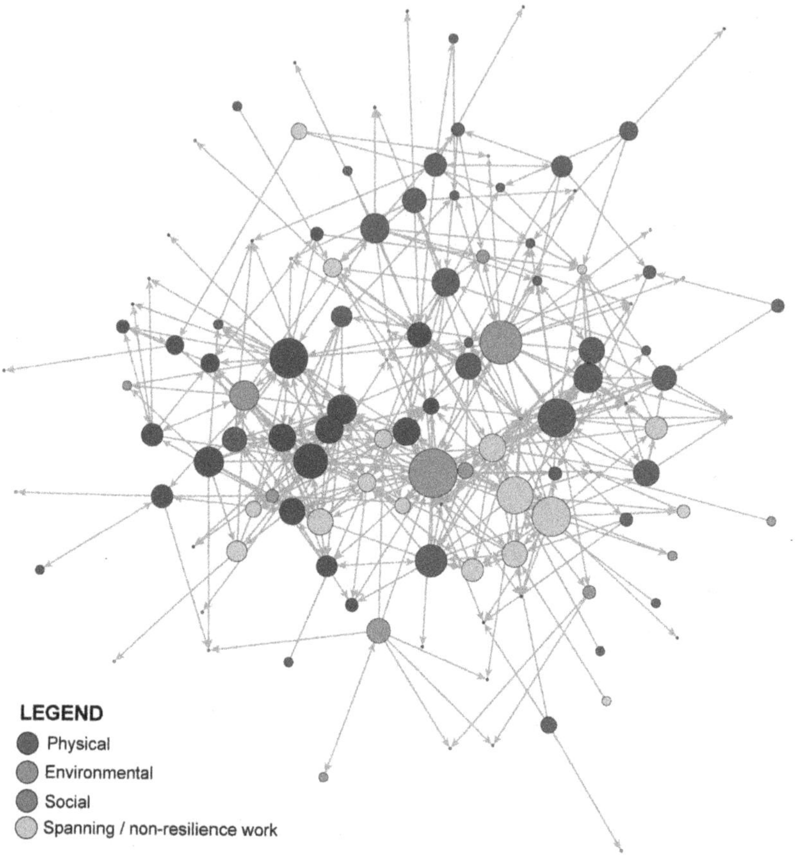

FIGURE 5.6B. Stakeholders' collaboration in response to the COVID-19 crises: Visualization by type of resilience.

adaptation stakeholder network, as well as the smaller network of the stakeholders with the strongest ties, environmental resilience stakeholders were positioned more peripherally within those networks. In the COVID-19 response network, however, two environmental resilience stakeholders were the most central stakeholders, as measured, again, by in-degree. This runs counter to the expectation that, for example, social resilience stakeholders would be the most central given that the COVID-19 precipitated urgent needs related to health, job loss, food, housing, and child care. Without a doubt, social resilience stakeholders are prominently represented in the COVID-19 network, with several stakeholders playing evidently central roles within the networks. And, of course, social service organizations outside of the climate adaptation field played prominent roles in COVID-19

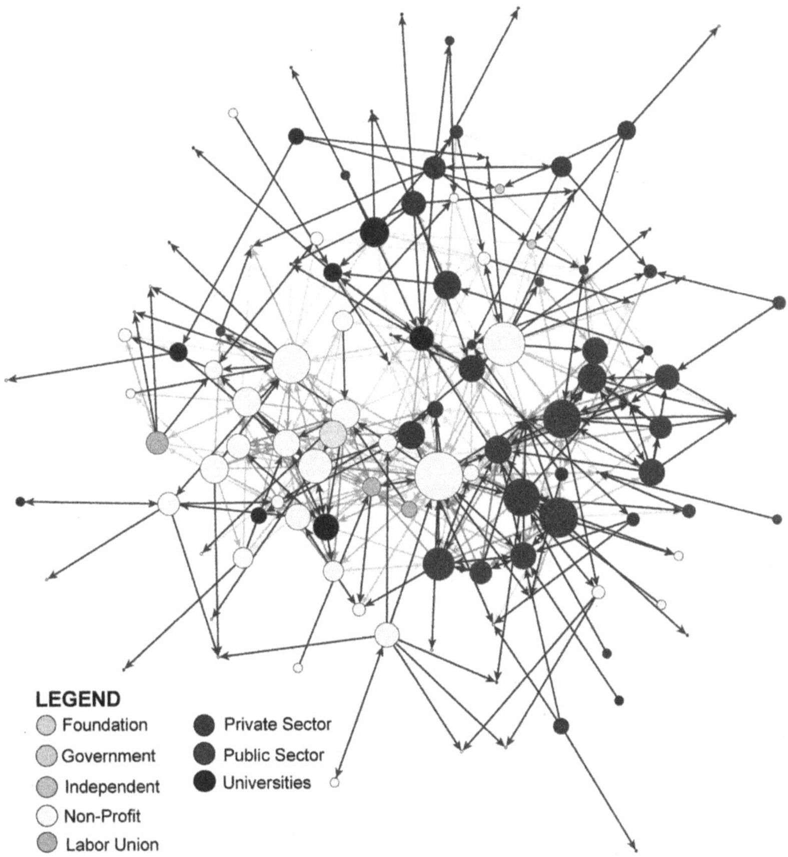

FIGURE 5.6C. Stakeholders' collaboration in response to the COVID-19 crises: Visualization by type of organization..

response. But in this network physical resilience stakeholders and stakeholders whose work spans or goes beyond resilience goals also collaborated on COVID-19 response.

As shown in figure 5.6c, a considerable majority of those who responded to the pandemic were in the nonprofit and public sectors, with the private sector less central to the COVID-19 network than how they were positioned in the other networks assessed here. All in all, a slight majority of metropolitan Boston climate adaptation stakeholders responded to health, economic, and social crises through collaborations that went beyond the specific resilience work they typically do. While more research is needed to understand the sorts of collaborations and resources that flowed through these collaborative ties, the climate adaptation field—particularly nonprofit and public actors—proved to be flexible in response to the COVID-19 crisis.

DISCUSSION

In this chapter we provided a snapshot of the collaborative connections that have emerged in response to climate adaptation efforts in metropolitan Boston in order to help us think about social dynamics that are interacting with the ecological changes being wrought by climate change. Earlier we introduced a framework developed by Davoudi and colleagues to assess the resilience of socio-ecological systems. Understanding the metropolitan Boston climate adaptation field as such a system, we can ask: (1) How is the system's social learning capacity being built? (2) Can the system persist in the face of disturbances? (3) Can the system adapt in the face of disturbances? and (4) Is the system moving in a transformative and innovative trajectory? This way of looking at resilience emphasizes "process" and brings our attention to the role of human intention and interaction with ecological systems. We contrasted this socio-ecological view of resilience with engineering or ecological notions of resilience, which, we argued are more "ends" oriented. But we also show that the metropolitan Boston climate adaptation field contains within it markers of both process-oriented and ends-oriented climate adaptation practices, creating social and institutional structures that advance certain resilience agendas over others (e.g., physical resilience agendas over social resilience agendas). This begs the question: What ultimate *goals* are metropolitan Boston climate adaptation collaborative practices trying to achieve?

While further research is needed to better understand the implications of stakeholder network analysis, we can draw some initial insights.[12] First, the metropolitan Boston region features meaningful levels of collaboration among stakeholders from different backgrounds and affiliated with various public and private institutions. Individuals taking part in these various forms of collaboration appear diverse in terms of know-how and professional experiences. However, there are many missing connections in the metropolitan Boston climate adaptation network. This low level of interconnection can point to a number of issues in the local climate adaptation field. One of the drawbacks of sparse networks like this is that information flows less efficiently. This can result in efforts that are underrealized, duplicative, or at cross-purposes, as people work on projects without the benefit of knowledge about similar efforts in distant parts of the network.

More interconnection also makes for more robust networks that don't easily break apart—with people or groups becoming completely disconnected from each other—in the face of disaster. This undermines the ability for the system to persist, robustly, in the face of disturbances (see Davoudi and colleagues' points 2 and 3 above). The largest cluster—an institutional one composed of a mix of engineering and planning firms, government groups, and universities, and predominantly white—seems to advance a resilience agenda through public-private partnerships that apply new ideas from research to develop innovative physical infrastructures. Through this greater emphasis on physical infrastructure, the institutional cluster advances an idea of resilience based on resisting or absorbing disturbances generated by the short- or long-tern effects of climate change. Within the institutional portion of the network, a smaller cluster of stakeholders advances a similar agenda focused on constructing ecological infrastructures or protecting natural sites.

This institutional part of the network appears to have fewer connections to the grassroots cluster mostly composed of community organizations, with higher BIPOC representation, advancing a resilience agenda based on collaborations spanning education, community development, community organizing, and social programs. Compared to the institutional cluster, the grassroots cluster advances the social learning capacities of the metropolitan Boston climate adaptation field. These social learning practices can enhance preparedness through community organizing, which challenges status quo resilience actions carried out by the institutional cluster. They may also, independently, develop social programs (through community development) focused on potential coping mechanisms to climate change. What we see in these maps, then, are resilience silos. On the one side, means—including knowledge production, economic resources, technical know-how—are deployed to produce very tangible outcomes. On the other side, means seem to be used to foster intangible outcomes mostly related to social cohesion processes around climate change. The existence of metropolitan Boston resilience silos raises the questions of whether the climate adaptation field is currently using the many available means and resources toward common goals, and why or why not.

What do these findings suggest for our capacity to cope with unknowable and unpredictable futures, whether climate change-related or not? The COVID-19 pandemic has forced us—locally and beyond—to consider whether and how individuals and groups can collaboratively act in the face of unpredictable circumstances. Our findings here suggest that a pursuit of social resilience goals related to the pandemic was activated across sectors and actor types. The climate adaptation network dynamically organized to advance social resilience and, in the process, possibly developed new structural possibilities for the climate adaptation field overall. This provides a compelling example of resilience as a process. To meet social resilience needs that emerged because of a non–climate crisis, climate adaptation stakeholders redirected collaborative resources, thereby transforming the climate adaptation network. Future research could assess the extent to which these new activities have modified the structure of the overall climate adaptation stakeholder network, such as adding new connections, strengthening existing ones, or reframing the nature of stakeholders' work.

The network backbone built mainly around topics unrelated to COVID-19 represented a reliable social infrastructure to sustain existing and expand new mutual help mechanisms. Once again, a follow-up discussion based on this analysis might highlight essential lessons learned. Initial areas of discussion include whether emergency collaborative actions have been able to address COVID-19 related needs and, moreover, whether day-to-day social infrastructures and operations are organized to respond in a timely manner to unknowable and unpredictable challenges.

CONCLUSION: MOVING FORWARD

This chapter highlights the broad set of individuals' current collaborations in the Boston metropolitan region to face climate challenges. Drawing on different theoretical ideas about resilience, and in particular social resilience, we explore the existing and potentially changing structures of climate adaptation practices. While this type of inquiry might open ground for critical analysis of the positives and negatives of existing climate adaptation practices, we advocate for the stakeholder network mapping to serve as an intervention tool. By understanding the nature of collaborative practices, the agendas behind their work, and the sorts of structures that these practices and agendas lead to, we may identify the need to create new connections (and perhaps de-emphasize others) in order to build a metropolitan

Boston climate adaptation field that better integrates different resilience agendas.

Re-evaluating and rethinking the use of means toward specific ends, rebalancing the distribution of available funds to support network connections, and fostering collaborations with the highly diverse stakeholders involved might be some promising areas for discussion and action moving forward. In this vein, we note how other chapters in this book point to the need for deeper public discussion of overlooked issues whose implications and interconnections are not fully addressed. For example, the urgent need to better understand public health in processes of urban transformation (see the "Health" chapter) and to find ways to curtail development in the face of injustice in disenfranchised communities (see the "Affordability," "Economy," and "Equity" chapters).

NOTES

1. Crawford S. Holling, "Resilience and Stability of Ecological Systems," *Annual Review of Ecology and Systematics* 4, no. 1 (1973): 1–23.
2. Simin Davoudi, Keith Shaw, L. Jamila Haider, Allyson E. Quinlan, Garry D. Peterson, Cathy Wilkinson, Hartmut Fünfgeld, Darryn McEvoy, and Libby Porter, "Resilience: A Bridging Concept or a Dead End? 'Reframing' Resilience: Challenges for Planning Theory and Practice; Interacting Traps: Resilience Assessment of a Pasture Management System in Northern Afghanistan; Urban Resilience: What Does It Mean in Planning Practice?; Resilience as a Useful Concept for Climate Change Adaptation?; The Politics of Resilience for Planning: A Cautionary Note," *Planning Theory and Practice* 13, no. 2 (2012): 299–333), https://doi.org/10.1080/14649357.2012.677124.
3. Davoudi et al., "Resilience."
4. Simin Davoudi, Elizabeth Brooks, and Abid Mehmood, "Planning Practice and Research Evolutionary Resilience and Strategies for Climate Adaptation Evolutionary Resilience and Strategies for Climate Adaptation," *Planning Practice & Research* 28, no. 3 (2013): 307–22. https://doi.org/10.1080/02697459.2013.787695; Todd Swanstrom, *Regional Resilience: A Critical Examination of the Ecological Framework,* 2008, working paper, no. 07, https://www.econstor.eu.
5. Davoudi, Brooks, and Mehmood, "Planning Practice," 311.
6. Alan H. Kwok, Emma E. H. Doyle, Julia Becker, David Johnston, and Douglas Paton, "What Is 'Social Resilience'? Perspectives of Disaster Researchers, Emergency Management Practitioners, and Policymakers in New Zealand," *International Journal of Disaster Risk Reduction,* 19 (2016): 197–211, https://doi.org/10.1016/j.ijdrr.2016.08.013.
7. Susan L. Cutter, Kevin D. Ash, and Christopher T. Emrich, "The Geographies of Community Disaster Resilience," *Global Environmental Change,* 29 (2014) : 65–77, https://www.sciencedirect.com/science/article/pii/S0959378014001459; Paton Douglas and John McClure, *Preparing for Disaster: Building Household and Community Capacity* (Springfield, IL: Charles C. Thomas, 2013); Philip Buckle, "Assessing

Social Resilience," in *Disaster Resilience: An Integrated Approach* (Springfield, IL: Charles C. Thomas, 2006), 88–103.

8. Daniel P. Aldrich, *Building Resilience: Social Capital in Post-Disaster Recovery* (Chicago, IL: University of Chicago Press, 2012).
9. Borgatti, Stephen P., Martin G. Everett, and Linton C. Freeman, *Ucinet for Windows: Software for Social Network Analysis,* 2002, https://pages.uoregon.edu/vburris/hc431/Ucinet_Guide.pdf.
10. Ulrik Brandes, and Dorothea Wagner, *Analysis and Visualization of Social Networks* (Berlin: Springer, 2004), 321–40, https://doi.org/10.1007/978-3-642-18638-7_15.
11. Robert A. Hanneman and Mark Riddle, *Introduction to Social Network Methods: Table of Contents,* 2005, http://www.faculty.ucr.edu/~hanneman/nettext/.
12. Since the writing of this chapter, this project has evolved with additional phases, including stakeholder interviews and stakeholder mapping convenings. These additional research methods allowed individual and collective interpretations of the maps included in this chapter. Results from these additional research phases are not included in this chapter.

LEADERSHIP

CHAPTER SIX

LEADING WITH DESIGN: CULTIVATING URBAN EXCELLENCE

ANNE-MARIE LUBENAU

"Make no little plans . . ."
—Daniel Burnham, "Stirred by Burnham, Democracy Champion," *Chicago Record-Herald,* October 15, 1910

Boston has demonstrated that it has the ability to do extraordinary things. As the city implements its first comprehensive plan in fifty years, there's a once-in-a-generation opportunity to draw on its history, culture, and leadership to craft and advance a collective vision for a city that is equitable, resilient, and beautiful for generations to come. The design community can leverage its collective talent and expertise to shape the city's vision for the future and position Boston as a global leader for innovation and creative solutions to twenty-first-century urban issues.

Boston is blessed with a rich cultural history; a distinctive physical, natural, and manmade form; and a strong tradition of leadership and innovation. Founded 1630, the "city upon a hill" has long been a place of high ambitions, a New World city founded on Puritan principles that valued education and hard work, and the tradition of the collective commons and decision making of the New England town hall meeting.[1]

Over the course of its nearly four-hundred-year history, the city has proven to be extraordinarily resilient, responding to shifting economic, political, and social conditions. Boston has consistently been a leader, from its early days as a port of international trade and site of the nation's first college, across the river in Cambridge (Harvard, 1636), to a manufacturing center during the industrial revolution, and more recently as a center for business and finance, education and medicine, and technology. It is home to Boston Latin School, the oldest public school in America (1635), and Boston Public Library (1852), the first free municipal library in the country. Today the city of Boston is home to more than thirty-five colleges and universities that attract and generate talent and ideas.[2]

The city's legacy incorporates a remarkable number of ambitious and visionary investments in public space and infrastructure that offer insight into the ongoing evolution of American cities. It includes extensive filling and grading that transformed a narrow peninsula and series of hills and islands to create the footprint of today's city. Green spaces such as Boston Common, America's first public park, and the 1,100-acre chain of parks that make up the Frederick Law Olmsted–designed Emerald Necklace demonstrated the value of investments in open space and public realm. Boston Harbor Association (now Boston Harbor Now) led the decades-long cleanup of Boston Harbor and reclamation of the waterfront and creation of a thirty-nine-mile Harborwalk. The city is also home to some of the

TABLE 6.1. Boston's Infrastructure Legacy

1634	Boston Common
1710–1721	Long Wharf
1830	Boston and Lowell Railroad
1837	Public Garden
1848	Boston Public Library
1857–1894	Back Bay Infill and Development
1878–1880	Emerald Necklace
1897	Tremont Street Subway
1910	Charles River Esplanade
1960s	Government Center
1979	Faneuil Hall Market Place
1985	Boston Harbor Project
1990	Southwest Corridor
1991–2008	Rose Fitzgerald Kennedy Greenway
2018–present	Northern Avenue Bridge Reconstruction

Boston's investment in public infrastructure spans nearly four hundred years and includes internationally renown places inextricably associated with the city's identity such as Boston Common and the Emerald Necklace.

FIGURE 6.1. Recent visionary investments include replacement of the elevated Central Artery expressway with an underground roadway and the Rose Kennedy Greenway, a seventeen-acre linear park that connects downtown neighborhoods with each other and the waterfront. Kyle Klein Photography, courtesy of the Greenway Conservancy.

nation's earliest and most celebrated preservation and historic redevelopment efforts, such as the South End and Faneuil Hall Marketplace. Boston has also been the site of bold and innovative transportation projects such as the Massachusetts Bay Transit Authority—"America's first subway," the Southwest Corridor greenway (1989 Rudy Bruner Award silver medalist), and the Central Artery Project or "Big Dig," now known as the Rose Fitzgerald Kennedy Greenway.

This tradition of innovation and leadership is reflected in the breadth and depth of Boston's professional design community. It includes architects, landscape architects, urban designers and planners, and leading firms that work nationally and globally. Boston's rich design heritage includes notable architects and landscape architects such as Henry Hobson Richardson, Frederick Law Olmsted, and the modernist Josep Lluís Sert. The region is home to internationally renowned schools and the first programs in architecture (MIT, 1865), landscape architecture (Harvard, 1900), urban

FIGURE 6.2. Boston is home to an extraordinary professional design community, including leading schools of architecture and planning, award-winning firms with global practices, and the Boston Society for Architecture, one of the nation's oldest AIA chapters. Paige McWhorter, courtesy of Boston Society for Architecture.

planning (Harvard, 1923), and urban design (Harvard, 1960) in the country. Founded in 1867, the Boston Society of Architects (now Boston Society for Architecture), is one of the oldest and largest American Institute of Architects (AIA) chapters in the country.

Yet, despite these resources and precedents, there is a collective sense of frustration about the lack of progressive design and development in the city and a clear vision for its future. *For many in the arts and the design community, there is the perception that the weight of history, along with the city's conservative and risk adverse culture, has constrained creativity and innovation.*

This perception has an impact on not only the city's physical form but also Boston's ability to address the critical issues facing it and many other American cities. These include aging infrastructure and an inadequate and outmoded transportation system; climate change and sea level rise (Boston is ranked fifth among U.S. cities at risk after Miami, New York, New Orleans, and Tampa[3]); rapidly increasing housing costs and demand, especially for affordable and middle-income/workforce housing (see chapter 1); and growing economic and amplified racial disparity (see the two chapters that follow).[4]

During former mayor Martin Walsh's administration, the city and mayor participated in several national initiatives focused on climate change and equity. Boston was one of the Rockefeller Foundation's "100 Resilient Cities." Mayor Walsh led a U.S. Conference of Mayors task force on income inequality together with mayor Bill de Blasio of New York City. He also made a commitment to design excellence and inclusive planning and development processes. In his 2015 address to the Greater Boston Chamber of Commerce, the mayor advocated for "world class design," challenging "developers to reach for more inspiring architecture."[5]

A series of planning initiatives led by the Walsh administration signaled a shift toward a new way of thinking and approaches. *Imagine Boston 2030*, the city's recent comprehensive plan; *Boston Creates*, the city's first cultural plan; and the appointment of Karilyn Crockett as the city's first chief of equity offer potential models for a new way of doing business. The approaches reflect the former mayor's commitment to inclusiveness and transparency, and the desire to engage residents of Boston in planning the future of their city and to inject the planning process with creativity and fun.

Boston is in the midst of an "urban moment." In a rapidly changing and increasingly global market, cities must compete for resources and talent. Quality of place is increasingly important,[6] creating demand and a higher market value for places that offer a variety of housing options, walkability and convenient public transportation, a vibrant and diverse arts and culture scene, and outdoor recreation and public spaces. As it approaches its four hundredth birthday, the city of Boston is poised at a point of inflection. Like many older American cities, it is experiencing a renaissance, attracting new residents and businesses and undergoing an unprecedented amount of new development.

New, progressive mayoral leadership is in place with Michelle Wu, and a number of long-term planning initiatives are underway. Cities change, whether we like it or not. And many cities are becoming more deliberate and intentional in dedicating resources to projects and policies that enhance their unique characteristics and quality of place. How can we create an enduring sense of place that embraces the past, present, and future? What is it the city of Boston wants to be? *How can Boston cultivate a civic culture that aspires to urban excellence?*

Boston is not alone in this challenge. As *New York Times* architectural critic Michael Kimmelman suggested at a 2014 forum at Harvard University, "Cities are the story of the twenty-first century."[7] Cities across the country and the world are struggling to respond to increasingly rapid economic, environmental, social, and technological changes. There are many ideas and resources to draw on, and much can be learned from the experiences of other cities from across the United States.

With those in mind, following are six recommendations for action:

- Foster a culture that values design and planning
- Cultivate a civic dialogue about design and its role in shaping the future of the city
- Engage and empower the community in planning and visioning
- Leverage local, national, and global talent and resources
- Advocate for and sponsor projects that demonstrate and support design excellence
- Nurture political leadership that understands the critical connection between design of the built environment and quality of life

FOSTER A CULTURE THAT VALUES DESIGN AND PLANNING

Cities that offer a distinctive identity are anchored in their own unique social and physical context will be the leaders. For some cities, like Chicago, a culture of urban excellence seems to be embedded in their DNA. For others, like Philadelphia or Chattanooga, the focus on quality design and development is a more recent evolution. Attitudes toward design and planning differ among cities, influenced by history, culture, and leadership. They are often the product of a combination of circumstances and factors—planned and unplanned—which coalesce and evolve over time.

The underlying history of a city—the environment, people, and events that shape its economy, culture, society, and place—has an indelible influence on attitudes toward planning and design. While we can't go back and change history, understanding its impact can provide a powerful tool for interpreting the cultural and physical landscape. It can also create the foundation for trust, essential to initiating a conversation about planning for the future. Not surprisingly, planning and preservation efforts often result from the loss or threat of loss of a historic sense of place, as was the case with urban renewal in Boston and Philadelphia. Many cities have recognized the value of their historic inheritance, in cultural as well as economic terms, and have developed planning policies and development strategies that capitalize on them.

Among American cities, Chicago is most closely associated with ambition and architecture. The legacy of Daniel Burnham and Edward Bennett's *Plan of Chicago* plays a central role in the city's attitude toward design and planning, and Burnham's statement "make no small plans" still resonates in the city's ongoing efforts to be bigger, better, and bolder than anyone else. Chicago's legacy is intertwined with architectural legends such as Daniel Burnham, Louis Sullivan, and Frank Lloyd Wright, and the city continues to be fertile ground for professional talent. The bold ambition and competitive spirit that fueled Chicago's economy and rapid expansion also shaped its physical form and early attention to progressive planning and design. Grand projects such as the 1898 World's Columbia Exposition and the 1909 *Plan of Chicago* and accompanying *Wacker's Manual,* which educated school students about city planning and Chicago's aspirations, provided an early blueprint for development and helped to embed a culture that valued design and planning into the city's fabric.

Not many cities can claim an architectural heritage like Chicago's. Yet it is possible to affect change in attitudes and culture of design. For example, the Philadelphia story is still unfolding. The concurrence of a number of events—the election of mayor Michael Nutter to two terms beginning in 2008, along with the emergence of grassroots advocacy for better design, and education and planning efforts led by the University of Pennsylvania, nonprofits, and philanthropy—contributed to a shift in attitudes towards planning in the city. In the words of Alan Greenberger, the former deputy mayor for economic development and planning, "The City is moving towards a point where the culture of design has embedded itself."[8]

CULTIVATE A CIVIC DIALOGUE ABOUT DESIGN AND ITS ROLE IN SHAPING THE FUTURE OF THE CITY

A design literate and engaged community is an essential ingredient. The culture of the community has a significant impact on a city's attitude toward design. More often than not, cities that have well-educated, environmentally oriented, and engaged populations that understand the connection between the built environment and quality of life are more likely to take an interest in the big picture. In some cases, such as Chicago, this culture was shaped over time by the city's history and evolution, and design is considered an essential part of civic life rather than an elitist activity. In other cases, such as Philadelphia, it is the result of deliberate efforts to raise awareness and encourage public engagement and dialogue that in turn created demand for political leadership focused on systemic planning reform.

Cultivating civic dialogue in any form requires platforms for the exchange of information and ideas as well as public input and discourse. These include forums and programs such as exhibits, events and lectures, research and publications, and competitions, not to mention a robust communications strategy. Encouraging dialogue about design requires technical expertise and resources such as strong academic and professional communities as well as people and organizations that have capacity to take the lead in organizing efforts.

In Philadelphia, Mayor Nutter ran on a platform that included reforming the planning and development system, in large part in response to a series of initiatives that created the demand for change. The Design Advisory Group, an all-volunteer organization emerged with the goal of building design consciousness in the city by providing "an independent and informed public voice for design quality in the architecture and physical planning of the Philadelphia region." The University of Pennsylvania's PennPraxis, a nonprofit community outreach arm of the School of Design, turned its attention on planning, developing *A Civic Vision for the Central Delaware* with substantial public input and launching PlanPhilly. AIA Philadelphia opened the storefront Center for Architecture + Design across the street from the convention center, which hosts chapter offices, the nonprofit Community Design Collaborative, and space for public exhibits and forums.

In Chattanooga, Tennessee, a series of planning initiatives and public investments focused on design and environmental sustainability helped to reposition the city from the most polluted in America (in 1969) to a national leader in sustainable development initiatives. The process began in 1984 when the local Lyndhurst Foundation and Chattanooga Venture initiated a community visioning process focused on investing in quality-of-life amenities and the downtown area. A series of public workshops hosted by the Planning and Design Studio, a university-based community design center, in a storefront venue led to the creation of Vision 2000 and the later 21st Century Waterfront plan. Over a twenty-year period, Chattanooga leveraged an initial $120 million in public-private investment into $1.5 billion in private development. Five principles guided process of planning and implementation: a clear regional vision, public participation in planning, a one-stop design center, portable planning for neighborhoods, and design excellence.[9] Over time, the Design Studio became part of regional planning services, housed with other regional planning offices at a new Development Resource Center and funded by city and county government.

In Boston, the Rudy Bruner Award for Urban Excellence partnered with Northeastern University to curate and cohost *Inspiring Design: Creating Beautiful, Just, and Resilient Places in America* for the spring 2021 Open Classroom. The fourteen-week speaker series brought together leading voices in architecture and urban design, planning and development, education, public policy, and civic leadership to share examples of innovative projects and initiatives and discuss how the experience and lessons learned from them can inform and inspire current and future efforts in Boston and other cities.

ENGAGE AND EMPOWER THE COMMUNITY IN PLANNING AND VISIONING

An educated and engaged community leads to demand for better design and support for policies and projects that demonstrate excellence. There have been subtle shifts in the design and planning practices toward more inclusive, community-driven design processes that generate a collective vision, values, and goals, and place-based solutions. In a time of shrinking public funding for urban development, new and innovative development approaches are emerging from public/private partnerships and multidisciplinary collaborations, in contrast to the top-down, large-scale redevelopment efforts of the prior century.

The emergence of nonprofit community design centers, architectural organizations, and social impact design over the past fifty years has contributed to changes in practice, including an increased focus on public engagement in design and planning, that are benefiting cities. Independent and university-affiliated community design centers such as Texas-based buildingcommunityWORKSHOP with offices in Dallas, Houston, Brownsville, and Washington, D.C.; the Community Design Collaborative in Philadelphia; and the Albert and Tina Small Center for Collaborative Design at Tulane University School of Architecture in New Orleans are involved in citywide planning, sponsoring activities and projects that empower residents and community participation.

Architectural organizations such as the Chicago Architecture Center, San Francisco Bay Area SPUR (with offices in San Francisco, Oakland, and San Jose), and Copenhagen's Danish Architecture Center offer prominent

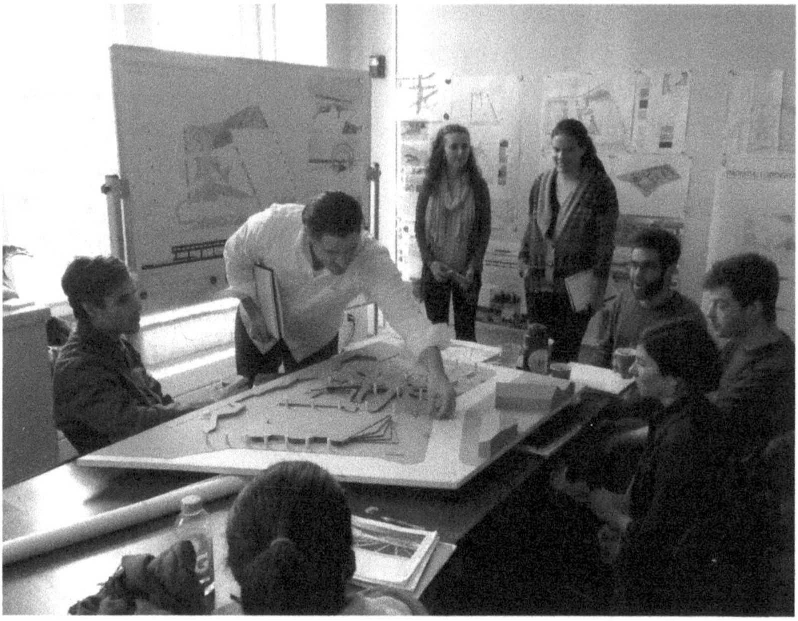

FIGURE 6.3. Nonprofit community design centers such as the Albert and Tina Small Center for Collaborative Design at Tulane University School of Architecture in New Orleans engage and empower local residents in design and planning initiatives and projects. Image: Emilie Taylor Welty, courtesy of the Albert and Tina Small Center for Collaborative Design at Tulane University School of Architecture.

downtown centers that host exhibitions, public forums, and tours that educate and engage the public and promote civic dialogue about urban issues. Across the United States, chapters of the American Institute of Architects have followed suit, opening and operating storefront spaces promoting architecture and design in cities including Boston, New York City, Philadelphia, and Seattle.

Cultivating relationships with the media and keeping dialogue about design and planning issues in the public consciousness is important. Few cities today are fortunate to have architectural critics who serve as valuable interpreters and advocates, such as Pulitzer Prize winners Inga Saffron of the *Philadelphia Enquirer,* Blair Kamin, formerly with the *Chicago Tribune,* and Mark Lamster of the *Dallas Morning News*. New, alternative approaches are required, particularly in an era of diminishing resources for traditional journalism. In 2018 Christopher Hawthorne, the former architecture critic for the *Los Angeles Times,* became the city's inaugural chief design officer,

FIGURE 6.4. Architecture organizations such as the Chicago Architecture Center increase understanding about the role of design and planning in cities with public programming, including educational exhibits, events, and tours hosted in prominent downtown storefront facilities. Image Steinkamp Photography, courtesy of Chicago Architecture Center.

the first such position in an American city. In Philadelphia, PlanPhilly, an innovative initiative started by PennPraxis and now hosted by WHYY, serves as a portal for online information focused on the built environment, with seasoned journalists collecting, curating, and writing articles. The Bloomberg CityLab, NextCity, and PLANetizen provide platforms for sharing stories about local, national, and global policies, practices, and projects.

LEVERAGE LOCAL, NATIONAL, AND GLOBAL TALENT AND RESOURCES

Building awareness of issues and community dialogue via communications is critical. It requires resources—capacity, expertise, and funding. Fortunately, there are a growing number of local and national funders and programs focused on design, cities, and cultivating civic dialogue and leadership within the profession, community, and public officials. Academic institutions, especially those with community-oriented service programs, play an equally vital role. Established national programs such as the Enterprise Rose Architectural Fellowship and Harvard Loeb Fellowship build capacity, cultivate leadership, and foster cross-disciplinary collaboration and connections between designers and communities. The Mayors' Institute on City Design, National League of Cities, and Urban Land Institute's Rose Center for Public Leadership connect mayors and their teams with resources to help them address design and development issues in their cities. The Bruner Foundation's Rudy Bruner Award for Urban Excellence offers examples and detailed case studies about transformative urban development that illustrate the economic, environmental, and social impact of design.

Increasingly, particularly in a time of diminishing government funding, change is being driven by philanthropic organizations. Foundations such as Ford, Rockefeller, and Surdna are pursuing national agendas focused on equitable urban development. Programs such as Bloomberg Philanthropies' Mayors Challenge, the Knight City Challenge, and the Rockefeller Foundation's 100 Resilient Cities encourage collaborative, innovative approaches to twenty-first-century issues such as climate change as well as leveraging information sharing and technology.

Foundations are also playing important roles in their respective cities. Investments from Barr Foundation in Boston, the Kresge Foundation in Detroit, the William Penn Foundation in Philadelphia, and the Heinz Endowments in Pittsburgh have been instrumental in building local capacity for advocacy and engagement, increasing interest in design and planning, and advancing strategic projects and systems change. This philanthropic support is critical, especially in older legacy cities grappling with complex challenges such as population loss and inadequate public resources.

In Philadelphia, the William Penn Foundation funded multiple, concurrent initiatives that fostered change, including the creation of PennPraxis at the University of Pennsylvania and key projects and programs such as *A Civic Vision for the Central Delaware* and PlanPhilly. The foundation also provided support for establishing the AIA Center for Architecture + Design, expanding the Community Design Collaborative, and launching the city of Philadelphia's Citizens Planning Institute.

Multiple philanthropic organizations were critical in reshaping the latest renaissance of Pittsburgh. The Heinz Endowments, the McCune Foundation, the Richard King Mellon Foundation, and others provided funding to nonprofits such as the Community Design Center of Pittsburgh, the Green Building Alliance, Riverlife, and Sustainable Pittsburgh to advance community engagement, design excellence, green building, riverfront planning, and sustainable development. In 2004 the Heinz Endowments convened the Pittsburgh Civic Design Coalition, an alliance of design advocates whose goal was to make quality design central to the revitalization and development of the Pittsburgh region as a world-class, distinctive, vibrant, and compelling place. The coalition sponsored a civic design learning exchange trip to Chattanooga with thirty Pittsburgh leaders, hosted mayoral candidate forums focused on design, and authored editorials and provided public testimony on major development projects, including a new riverfront casino.

ADVOCATE FOR AND SPONSOR PROJECTS THAT DEMONSTRATE AND SUPPORT DESIGN EXCELLENCE

Investing in civic projects that demonstrate and leverage the value of design is critical. Community-driven planning processes are essential to developing a collective vision. Equally important are implementation of public policies and civic projects that illustrate commitment to progressive planning practices and design excellence.

By the conclusion of his second term in 2015, Mayor Nutter's administration had completed the Philadelphia2035 comprehensive plan. It was preceded by Imagine Philadelphia 2010, a two-year community-based process that identified a set of goals and values that guided the comprehensive plan. In 2010 the city launched the Citizens Planning Institute to "empower citizens to take a more effective and active role in shaping the future of their neighborhoods and of Philadelphia through a greater understanding of city planning and the steps involved in development projects."[10] By October 2022, the program graduated more than 700 citizen planners, including community leaders and residents from more than 130 neighborhoods. Projects such as renovating Dilworth Park in front of City Hall and the new Race Street Pier on the Delaware River reflect the city's renewed attention to urban design, while the Water Department's innovative Green Cities, Clean Water plan illustrates a creative approach to managing stormwater runoff and pollution and an aging sewer system.

In Greenville, South Carolina, a series of planning initiatives spanning more than one hundred years has resulted in a distinctive urban center and increased civic pride. Planning investments included a 1907 *Beautifying and*

Improving Greenville (by Boston-based Kelsey and Guild Landscape Architects) that offered a civic vision and proposal to create a park along the waterfall and river running through the center of the city. Later, in 1974, the city engaged Lawrence Halprin & Associates to prepare *An Urban Diagnosis for Greenville* that focused on downtown and streetscape improvements that enhanced its urban character. In the 1980s and 1990s visioning and master plans by RTKL and Sasaki led to the creation of award-winning Falls Park on the Reedy in 2004 (2015 Rudy Bruner Award Silver Medalist). Integral to its success was advocacy by mayor Knox White for the replacement of an automobile bridge constructed directly over the falls, with a striking pedestrian suspension bridge (designed by Miguel Rosales of Boston-based transportation architects Rosales + Partners) that has become the synonymous with the identity of the city. In 2022 the city of Greenville celebrated the opening of Unity Park, a new sixty-acre venue that completes the 1907 civic vision while addressing the city's history of racial segregation and environmental injustice, as well as the more recent threats of climate change and gentrification.

The city of Boston has utilized design competitions to engage local, national, and international design talent in new development. An invited competition that solicited design proposals for a new municipal building in Roxbury in 2008 attracted the Dutch firm Mecanoo, which partnered with Boston-based Sasaki on the winning submission for what became the Bruce C. Bolling Municipal Building. The city and the Boston Society for Architecture collaborated on a series of design competitions, including Boston Living with Water in 2014, in partnership with Boston Harbor Now, which solicited creative design solutions for addressing sea level rise at three sites, and the Boston Northern Avenue Competition of Ideas in 2016, which sought proposals for a new, multimodal twenty-first-century bridge to replace the deteriorated 1908 structure spanning the channel between downtown and the Seaport District.

NURTURE POLITICAL LEADERSHIP THAT UNDERSTANDS THE CRITICAL CONNECTION BETWEEN DESIGN OF THE BUILT ENVIRONMENT AND QUALITY OF LIFE

Strong, visionary mayoral leadership is instrumental. It's critical to have public leadership that believes that design is important and understands how design makes a community better. The value of leadership is reflected in commitments to long-range planning and policies, the hiring and empowerment of qualified staff, and investments in public spaces, buildings, and infrastructure. Support for good design comes from senior levels of the city, including elected and staff positions, and in particular the mayor.

Perhaps no American mayor is better known for his visionary leadership and passion for design than Joe Riley, who served as mayor of Charleston, South Carolina, from 1975 to 2015. His focus on revitalizing the city's downtown and waterfront and his attention to balancing preservation and new development helped to transform Charleston into a global cultural destination.[11] Riley is a founder of the Mayors' Institute on City Design, a national leadership initiative of the National Endowment for the Arts in partnership with the U.S. Conference of Mayors. Created in 1986, it offers technical assistance workshops with leading design experts to "prepare mayors to become chief urban designers of their cities." As Riley observed, "Whatever income strata you are or education level, you still are nourished by something that you feel looks nice. And that's what great cities in the world have always done—always cared about their built environment."[12]

In Chicago, mayor Richard Daley was instrumental in inspiring the creation of Millennium Park (2009 Rudy Bruner Award Silver Medalist). In just two four-year terms mayor Michael Nutter led the shift to a more inclusive and transparent planning and development system in Philadelphia. Over three terms, from 1994 to 2006, mayor Tom Murphy guided Pittsburgh through its transformation from a struggling postindustrial city to a leader in green building and riverfront development.

Over its history Boston has been fortunate to have several mayors, including the late Thomas Menino, who have been concerned with investment in infrastructure, neighborhoods, and the urban realm. Mayor Menino initiated development of Bruce C. Bolling Municipal Building (2017 Rudy Bruner Award Silver Medalist)—a new mixed-use development integrating Boston Public Schools headquarters, community meeting space, retail, and transit—after bringing the idea to a 2006 Mayors Institute on City Design session. In 2010, during Menino's final term in office, the city of Boston opened the Office of New Urban Mechanics, a new program housed in City Hall focused on civic research and design that now includes the Boston Housing Innovation Lab. After leaving office, Menino cofounded Boston University's Initiative on Cities, which focuses on urban research and teaching.

FIGURE 6.5. The award-winning Bruce C. Bolling Municipal Building—a complex integrating Boston Public Schools administrative headquarters, community meeting space, locally owned retail, and public transit, designed by Dutch firm Mecanoo and Boston-based Sasaki—is the product of international design competition sponsored by the city of Boston and illustrates the power of public leadership to advance design excellence. Image: Anton Grassl / ESTO, courtesy Sasaki.

NEXT STEPS: CREATING A CIVIC CULTURE OF DESIGN EXCELLENCE IN BOSTON

Fostering a change in culture does not happen overnight, or in a year or even five years; it takes time to incubate. It requires vision and leadership, along with concerted, patient effort. It demands the investment of time and resources in building collaborative partnerships and engaging the community to build awareness and cultivate civic dialogue about the value of design.

Boston is fortunate to have many of the essential ingredients in place. The city has a rich historical legacy, a vibrant cultural and intellectual community, and a strong economy. It has world-class design and planning schools, firms, and professional organizations, including the Boston Society for Architecture (and the legacies of *ArchitectureBoston,* the Community Design Resource Center, and Learning by Design in Massachusetts). Boston is home to MASS Design Group, the 2022 AIA Architecture "Firm of the Year," which is renowned for its international community-engaged design practice.[13] Journalists such as Robert Campbell, Renée Loth, and

Rachel Slade have been committed to writing about the built environment. The philanthropic sector is stepping up, with support for civic and planning initiatives from the Barr Foundation, the Boston Foundation, and others. There are nonprofit and academic organizations focused on urban development, such as the Lincoln Institute for Land Policy, the Harvard Loeb Fellowship, the Metropolitan Area Planning Commission, the Rudy Bruner Award for Urban Excellence, Boston University's Initiative on Cities, and Northeastern University's Kitty and Michael Dukakis Center for Urban and Regional Policy. Existing systems and mechanisms, such as the Boston Planning and Development Agency and the Boston Civic Design Commission, can be strengthened. And once-in-a-generation, large-scale development projects such as the Allston Interchange/Beacon Yards site, the Northern Avenue Bridge, and Suffolk Downs offer the opportunity to set a high bar for design excellence in new infrastructure, mixed-use, and public realm projects.

Most importantly, Boston has political leadership committed to design excellence and to creating an inclusive and economic, environmental, and socially equitable community. This is not something to be taken for granted, and could change in the next election cycle. Now is the time to leverage Boston's remarkable legacy and resources to establish and advance a collective vision for Boston as a world-class equitable, resilient, and beautiful city. In order to do this, we need to:

- LEAD: Position the design community as leaders with the Boston Society for Architecture as a key convener. Engage Mayor Wu's new administration and support and amplify its commitment to and investment in design excellence and planning reform. Ensure that the commitment becomes an essential and integral part of every mayor's platform.
- ANCHOR: Embrace and build on Boston's unique and evolving cultural heritage and community as a global leader to develop an ambitious, distinctive, and inclusive vision for the city. Highlight the city's legacy of investment in public infrastructure and civic amenities to increase advocacy and support for continued public and private leadership and investment. Involve local design firms to share their connections and work on progressive initiatives and projects elsewhere in the world to inspire new approaches in Boston.
- ENGAGE: Increase and sustain civic dialogue and advocacy about design with interdisciplinary, cross-sector activities and programs that

educate and involve more elected leaders, businesses, for-profit and nonprofit organizations, neighborhoods and residents, and design, development, and planning professionals.

- COLLABORATE: Partner with local and national government, nonprofits, foundations, businesses, and educational institutions—especially those that share an interest in quality of life, design, and the urban environment—to leverage collective talent and resources and increase influence and impact.
- LEVERAGE: Identify and sponsor strategic events, initiatives, and projects—design charrettes and competitions, public forums, and workshops—that demonstrate and leverage the power of design. Build on the success of the Boston Living with Water international design competition, the city of Boston Housing Innovation Lab and Urban Housing Unit (uhu) roadshow (see chapter 1), the Boston Society for Architecture's Allston Interchange/Beacon Yards and Suffolk Downs urban design workshops, and the Community Design Resource Center's neighborhood projects.[14]

With a new mayor, the city is at a turning point, possessing resources many other cities would envy. Now is the time to harness Boston's collective energy and resources and activate the community to work together toward a shared agenda and vision. This kind of opportunity comes along only once in a generation and is not to be missed.

NOTES

1. "We shall be as a city upon a hill, the eyes of all people are upon us"; John Winthrop, 1630, New-York Historical Society Museum and Library, "John Winthrop's 'City Upon a Hill' Sermon and 'An Erasure of Collective Memory,'" December 5, 2018, https://www.nyhistory.org/blogs/21991-2. These ideas were informed by lectures by Alex Krieger as part of the fall 2011 "Cities by Design" course that I audited as a 2011–12 Loeb Fellow at Harvard Graduate School of Design and the following book: David Hackett Fischer, *Albion's Seed: Four British Folkways in America* (New York, Oxford: Oxford University Press, 1989), 13–205.
2. Boston Redevelopment Authority, "Boston by the Numbers Colleges and Universities," bostonplans.org, October 1, 2022, http://www.bostonplans.org/getattachment/3488e768-1dd4-4446-a557-3892bb0445c6/.
3. Tran Viet Duc, "Which Coastal Cities Are at Highest Risk of Damaging Floods? New Study Crunches the Numbers," The World Bank, August 19, 2013, https://www.worldbank.org/en/news/feature/2013/08/19/coastal-cities-at-highest-risk-floods.
4. Alan Berube and Natalie Holmes, *City and Metropolitan Inequality on the Rise, Driven by Declining Incomes*, Brookings, January 14, 2016, https://www.brookings.edu/research/city-and-metropolitan-inequality-on-the-rise-driven-by-declining-incomes/.

5. Mayor Martin J. Walsh, "Address to the Greater Boston Chamber of Commerce," Greater Boston Chamber of Commerce, September 24, 2015.
6. This concept was first brought to my attention through conversations with Richard Florida in Pittsburgh in Spring 2000 in connection with "Competing in the Age of Talent: Quality of Place and the New Economy," a paper he wrote and published in January 2000 with support from the Richard King Mellon Foundation, the Heinz Endowments, and Sustainable Pittsburgh. The following article highlights themes from that report: Richard Florida, "Competing in the Age of Talent," *Greater Philadelphia Regional Review*, Summer 2001, https://creativeclass.com/rfcgdb/articles/2000-Competing_In_The_Age_Of_Talent.pdf.
7. Michael Kimmelman, "The Politics of Public Space," February 6, 2014, Radcliffe Institute for Advanced Study, Harvard University.
8. This quote is taken from my notes from conversations with Alan Greenberger during his visit on February 22, 2010, to Pittsburgh to speak as part of the Community Design Center of Pittsburgh's 2009/10 Design Excellence Lecture Series.
9. This information is drawn from *Design, Community, and Quality of Life: Report from Chattanooga*, a report written by Christine O'Toole and published by the Pittsburgh Civic Design Coalition in 2005 documenting the trip to Chattanooga on October 27–28, 2005. I participated in the trip as one of seven members of the coalition that included leaders of the American Institute of Architects Pittsburgh Chapter, the Carnegie Mellon University Urban Lab, the Community Design Center of Pittsburgh, the Green Building Alliance, The Heinz Endowments, the Pittsburgh Department of City Planning, the Riverlife Task Force, and Sustainable Pittsburgh.
10. Philadelphia Citizen Planning Institute, "About," accessed October 1, 2022, https://citizensplanninginstitute.org.
11. Spencer Elliott, *Charleston Continues Best City Streak: Why This South Carolina Spot Is an American Favorite, Forbes*, October 6, 2021, https://www.forbes.com/sites/forbes-global-properties/2021/10/06/charleston-continues-best-city-streak-why-this-south-carolina-spot--is-an-american-favorite/?sh=7703d42142fe.
12. Debbie Elliot, *One of America's Longest-Serving Mayors Steps Down*, NPR, January 9, 2016.
13. Other Boston-area firms or legacy firms that have won the AIA Firm of the Year Award include Payette (2019), Leers Weinzapfel Associates (2007), Cambridge Seven Associates (1993), Benjamin Thomson & Associates (1987), Kallmann, McKinnell and Wood (1984), Sert Jackson and Associates (1977), Shepley Bulfinch Richardson and Abbott (1973), Hugh Stubbins and Associates (1967) and The Architects Collaborative (1964).
14. The five steps—lead, anchor, engage, collaborate, and leverage—are adapted from recurring themes gleaned from the Rudy Bruner Award for Urban Excellence's thirty-five-year investigation into urban development. The themes are summarized in a paper I wrote with Robert Shibley, dean of the University at Buffalo's School of Architecture and Urban Planning, for the 54th International Making Cities Livable Conference in 2017. Anne-Marie Lubenau and Robert Shibley, "Creating Excellent Urban Places: Learning from the Rudy Bruner Award," Rudy Bruner Award for Urban Excellence, October 2017, https://www.rudybruneraward.org/wp-content/uploads/2016/07/IMCL-Paper-170913_Lato.pdf.

ECONOMY

CHAPTER SEVEN

POWER, THE ECONOMY, AND INTERDEPENDENCE

A CONVERSATION WITH MARIA ELENA LETONA, JAMES JENNINGS, IMARI K. PARIS JEFFRIES, AND MARIE-FRANCES RIVERA

This conversation was convened by Marie-Frances Rivera (she/ella), president of the Massachusetts Budget and Policy Center on February 18, 2021. She was joined by Imari K. Paris Jeffries (he/him), executive director of King Boston[1]*; Maria Elena Letona (she/ella), PhD, director of philanthropy, learning, and evaluation at Episcopal City Mission; and James Jennings (he/him), PhD, professor emeritus, urban and environmental policy and planning at Tufts University.*

Almost a year into the pandemic, we were struggling together to make sense of the paradigm shift that COVID-19 had thrust on us. During this dialogue we were holding a duality: how to make sense of this moment while acknowledging and addressing long-standing realities about the challenges and opportunities in the City of Boston, our Commonwealth, the nation, and the global struggle for economic and racial justice.

The political winds were shifting in Boston. Days before this conversation, the U.S. Senate confirmed former Boston mayor Marty Walsh as U.S. secretary of labor, at which time then city council president Kim Janey became the first female, Black mayor of Boston. This then created the conditions that ultimately led to former city councilor Michelle Wu becoming the city's first Asian American female mayor of Boston.

The conversation was edited for clarity.

MEL (MARIA ELENA LETONA): My name is Maria Elena Letona. I am an immigrant from El Salvador. I have lived in the city of Boston since 1984 and attended UMass Boston. So I have seen the city change quite a bit in the past few decades. I have directed two people of color–led base-building groups. And for many, many years have considered myself an organizer, a person of the community, an immigrant, and a woman of color. I'm really looking forward to our conversation today.

JJ (JAMES JENNINGS): I'm James Jennings, a professor emeritus at Tufts University. I've been in Boston since 1978. I'm Afro-Boricua, and worked in both Black African American and Latino communities on a whole range of community development issues and housing issues. Most recently, I was part (and still am part) of an assessment of fair housing for Boston. I will say a few words about that because it encapsulates how different Boston is today than when I came in 1978.

IPJ (IMARI PARIS JEFFRIES): I'm a transplant, but I feel like I grew up here. Like many Black folks who didn't see college as an option, I ended up joining the army and got stationed in Massachusetts and lost my Southern accent and made this place my home. And so Boston feels like a home to me. It's probably the longest place that I've ever lived. I'm forty-nine years old and have been here since I was eighteen. I have had an opportunity to raise my children here, my youngest, who's going to be a sixteen-year-old, and my other two, my two daughters are almost twenty and twenty-seven. So this is a special place to me and I'm excited to be with you all today.

MFR (MARIE-FRANCES RIVERA): I'M currently the president of the Massachusetts Budget and Policy Center (MassBudget), and I lived in Boston for over a decade. I'm on the younger side of the intergenerational spectrum here. I grew up here in Massachusetts, in a Gateway City,[2] New Bedford. Like James, I'm also a proud Afro-Boricua, very proud. I currently live in Roslindale and have lived in a lot of different parts of the city. Through my work at the Hyams Foundation, I did a lot of great work with Maria Elena, who was the trustee.[3] I got to learn a lot about different neighborhoods, including Chelsea, Massachusetts. When we think about the Greater Boston area, it also includes places like Chelsea and Revere.

Let's launch in. This is a question that Maria Elena posed to me several times before. "What time is it?" Meaning, what moment are we in right now in the city of Boston? Today, we're starting our conversation in the mist of converging crises: the racial, economic, environmental crises that we find ourselves in have existed for decades and come from a centuries-long history in Massachusetts, our nation, and globally. Now we have this paradigm shifting public health pandemic. With that, what moment are we in here in Boston? What are your reflections?

JJ: I'll take the first crack at this. I think that we are at a sort of crossroads. *Boston, as I think almost everyone knows, has one of the most racist histories in the country.* That challenge has not been resolved, but some opportunities have been emerging. These opportunities, if they can be interconnected, can move the city forward. Not just for people of color, they could move the entire city forward. The COVID-19 pandemic is certainly not an opportunity, but what it did is it uncovered racism and how it manifests itself. Racism is not just prejudicial attitudes. It's also something in the system, something in the structure, something in what government does or does not do. While the pandemic has revealed certain truths, those of us in this room have always been aware that racism is a problem. But many times those observations have fallen on people with no real interest in hearing that narrative.

MEL: First, we need to credit Grace Lee Boggs with that expression, "What time is it on the clock of the world?"[4] She's the beautiful soul that coined that expression. I do think it's a beautiful question to ask ourselves every now and then. I see the moment we're living in as a crossroads. When you reach a crossroad, it's about making a choice. What are the choices we're going to make? Are we going to go *this* way or are we going to go backward? There are choices in front of us. For us to make better choices, knowing our history is a very good place to start. So we're aware of the things that no longer serve us. Knowing our history is part of it.

Understanding power is super important at this moment, too. Getting a grasp on power and how power operates structurally and its impact on our lives. That requires paying attention. Paying attention to the signs, what are we reading, et cetera. For example, the COVID-19 pandemic really shows in real time how interconnected we are. This may be the first time in human history that the entire world has been in quarantine for two years; that's huge. There's deep interconnection there. It is not enough to vaccinate Boston. If you don't vaccinate the rest of the state, if you don't vaccinate the rest of the country, if you don't vaccinate the rest of the world—that's the only way that we're going to get to feeling safe again.

It's also the interconnection in how we craft our lives. I remember at the very beginning [of the pandemic] how keenly aware people became of so-called frontline workers, the people we need to maintain a certain quality of life, whether it's having access to food or other basic necessities. At *this* moment, hope has sprung from all these mutual aid networks. The interconnectedness of the world is something to keep in our minds and hearts as we decide which choices we're going to make moving forward.

While it's a difficult road ahead, I'm very hopeful about the moment that we are living in. We have many women of color that are serving on our Boston City Council. Going back to my and James's time in Boston, there was a moment of incredible hope when the Rainbow Coalition got together and came very close to electing Mel King as our first Black mayor of Boston.[5] Even then, there were decades of advancement for some, the very few, and stagnation and going backward for many of us. The naming of "us," for me, is important to do. The "us" are the poor, working-class people of color, we're majority Black and Latinx. It is, for me, very important to name who is on the losing side of the choices that we make. So, while those of us that have been around for a while may feel hopeful, on the other hand, we're wondering if we are going to make the right choices going forward. That, to me, remains to be seen. That is very tied to power.

IPJ: I have seen Instagram memes that have popped up, and I saw one that said, "I wish I would have known I was in the good old days, so I could enjoy the fact that I was in the good old days." That meme struck me. As I've been listening to folks like Reverend William Barber,[6] who is leading the Poor People's Campaign and is on the NAACP board, among other things, he and other folks, other activists, have framed this moment in time as living in the Third Reconstruction. The other two reconstructions are after the Civil War and the second being when Black World War II veterans returned up until the end of the civil rights era of the late '60s early '70s.[7] Now being this third moment in time with three pivotal spheres: an emergence of political and elected spheres, economic spheres, and social spheres.

I have witnessed this reconstruction in the post-Obama era in Boston: congresswoman Ayanna Pressley unseating a long-standing white male incumbent to win her congressional seat;[8] Suffolk County district attorney Rachael Rollins emerging. We have secured some wins.[9] This emergence of elected officials coupled with civic leaders in this moment that I've seen really operate and do things from Segun Idowu, executive director of the Black Economic Council of Massachusetts to you, Marie-Frances, many people have emerged, both civic and elected leaders.[10] I see us talking about the suing of the City of Boston alleging its contracting system discriminates against businesses owned by people of color to pushing a narrative around economic justice.[11]

The pandemic is revealing a desire for us to acknowledge the social aspect of our humanity as well. If you ask people what they want, more than ever they want to be together with other people. Our desire to be in relationship with other people is tied to economic justice, it's tied to safety and belonging. For example, there are very few liquor licenses awarded to venues owned by people of color. That's an economic justice issue, but it's also a spatial, safety, and social justice issue. If there's only seven liquor licenses/entertainment licenses issued to businesses of color, there's only seven establishments where brown bodies can eat food and nourish their soul and feel safe.[12] It's both a spatial justice and an economic justice issue, simultaneously.

I'm hopeful because we're in this moment of the Third Reconstruction. We have better language to explain our reality. When an elected U.S. president during their acceptance speech talks about and uses the words "systemic racism"—that's a moment.[13] People are increasingly bold in what they are saying. Twenty-four months ago, if you said "systemic racism" in a meeting, it would get really awkward, and people would stop talking. Now you see the unlikeliest folks saying it. I mean we were in a meeting just last week and they were saying it: systemic racism. They were throwing it around like it was, how you say, dinnertime or something. Like let's grab a cup of coffee. People were talking about it like that.

That's why I'm hopeful. It feels like I have contextualized this moment for us. I contextualize a lot of things, positive things. I mean it's not perfect, but a movement in this reconstruction frame makes me feel hopeful because there are a lot of things happening. And what Dr. Jennings's and Dr. Letona's points were is that we have an opportunity to get this right this time and actually complete the reconstruction because of the pandemic. Because people have had to sit still. And maybe that's one of the extra drivers that, I hate to say, was necessary to complete this one.

MFR: Do either of you want to respond?

JJ: Not really respond, more like a friendly amendment. I agree there are opportunities. Though, recall that during the first two reconstructions there was immediate pushback, and there will be immediate pushback to this opening of opportunities. As was mentioned earlier by Elena, power is not going to disappear from the hands of the wealthy and shift to working-class people or to workers with very little wages. There is going to be some pushback. What's interesting to me is that the pushback may have a different rhetoric to it. As you stated, "Black Lives Matter," "systemic racism," these terms are more commonplace. We must make sure that those terms don't simply become accepted symbolic language. We must put substance behind that symbolic language.

A quick example that comes to mind is the philanthropic world in Boston and Greater Boston, Massachusetts, and nationally. About ten to fifteen years ago, there was this theme in the foundation sector, among our foundation leaders, that nonprofits must be bigger. They have to be meaner; they have to be leaner. Some of us said that narrative misses the boat in terms of the needs of people at a grassroots level. This thinking has tremendous implications for how foundations do their work and support communities. The notion of "if you can't measure it, it's not worthwhile" needs to be pushed back on. We're all *just* numbers. That's going to be challenged.

MEL: I wanted to add to the power piece. It is so related to you mentioning foundations, James, I was also going to go there. It is not that I have the right answer. But I believe the power is exerted when it's organized. The more institutionalized that power is, the better it can advance an agenda and to push back the way that James was talking about.

So, what do I mean by this? I think it is great to have more Black leaders, like you were saying, Imari. Absolutely. That Marie-Frances is now leading MassBudget,[14] right on! That's an institution. And when I look around, I see the context shaping our lives is the corporate landscape. Corporations are not in our hands. The media landscape is also very powerful; it is not in our hands. There are all three levels and three branches of government, which are not in our hands. So, these institutions, corporate boardrooms, everything that's happening there is about making decisions. That's power. They're making choices in those rooms every single day. They are affecting what we think, what we buy, everything.

For me, at this moment, just like the response from the grassroots in 2020 to what happened with the police brutality, the murder of George Floyd and others—it was a moment that philanthropic foundations began mobilizing some resources to Black-led movement organizing. However, that commitment needs to be for the long haul. It cannot be this year because, "Oh my God, I feel badly about that and to make myself feel better I'm going to put some money into this this year." No, no, no, no. It's got to be the kind of commitment that over the long term you invest in a truly Black-led power infrastructure that can move the communities' agenda. So, the community at some point can say, "We are in charge of our lives. We are self-determined now. We don't have all these other structures around us writing us off, not ever having a seat at their tables." For me, the power piece is very important. And the Black officials that we have elected—if they don't have solid organizations keeping them accountable, then they are very quickly going to start saying yes to other interests that are also asking to meet with them. Interests that are also seeking to influence their campaigns and the decisions they're making. Power, to me, is important to pay attention to.

MFR: Maria Elena, you talked about the Rainbow Coalition and when Mel King ran for mayor of Boston. The other moment that we're in is that mayor Marty Walsh has left the City of Boston to work for the Biden administration as U.S. secretary of labor. There are several women of color—including Kim Janey, who's going to be taking over as the interim mayor of Boston, and others—who are who are running.[15] Let's link this back to the economic power piece. Do you feel same type of movement that Mel King helped to galvanize at that moment in time along with others happening today? Do you feel like there are more things that we should be doing? Political power, economic power, corporate power, it's all linked at the end of the day. You need to build political power to make sure policies are in place to ensure families are economically secure in *all* of Boston.

MEL: Yes, I don't know how my friends here feel, but it's going to be interesting. We have Boston city councilors Michelle Wu (now mayor), Andrea Campbell, and Annissa Essaibi George who have all declared. People have different opinions about how they have served their neighborhoods. For those at a district level everyone has their opinions. Their people know whether those members have represented their interests well or not. I'm very certain that we will end up with a woman of color as the next mayor of Boston. I will be happy for that. But it remains to be seen. I really cannot play the fortune teller right now. I am very happy that we have this many women of color running. That doesn't mean it's going to be very easy for those of us in the community to get solidly behind one of these candidates.

JJ: What we must try to avoid is the old thing: a politics based on a piece of the pie. We want a progressive agenda to be the dominant narrative as we move forward. I would have been pessimistic ten to fifteen years ago, but now I have a little bit of optimism because people are beginning to talk more with each other. For example, health advocates are talking to environmental justice people, to the business folks, to educators, and that interconnection didn't happen before in Boston. But it's happening now. Recently, I was part of a Zoom with the Urban League, which was very well attended. And when people were asked, "How do we go forward with the notion of intersectionality?," it's not just in that forum; it's in other forums. So, there's a possibility to begin seeing again what Mel King and his team were able to do with the Rainbow Coalition when he ran for mayor in 1979 and 1983.

MEL: I was organizing at the grassroots level not very long ago and I do think that something supremely hopeful was already happening. We were bringing together many organizations that were working with different populations in different neighborhoods and they were coalescing in state-wide networks to advance housing justice and environmental justice. It felt qualitatively different to me from the way that we were organizing in the early 2000s. To me that's very hopeful, because that's power. Communities coming together through our organizations, to me that equals power. That is where we need to invest. Investing in individual leaders is great, don't get me wrong. But what is the power behind and around the leader?

Look at me. At some point people knew me. I had great titles, executive director of Neighbor to Neighbor and executive director of Centro Presente.[16] People really wanted to talk to me, but the power was not me. The power was *actually* the organization, the people, and what we were doing together. I left those two positions, and now nobody's calling me. I'm fine with that, by the way! But that's what I mean about understanding power, and very few of us get to be a Van Jones, or those speakers that can ask for thousands of dollars because they're inspiring.[17] Most of us do what we do in the political arena because we have an organized base around us. Unless, of course, you're a researcher or an academic or at MassBudget. You're putting out ideas into the world. You're organizing ideas. *When you're organizing people, the strength, the real source of your influence, is the organized base.*

IPJ: I agree. I do feel like we're organizing differently . . . especially compared to the 2000s. There's a Segun Idowu, there's a Sheena Collier,[18] there's a Willie Bodrick,[19] and others. There's some of us leading the Massachusetts Budget and Policy Center, and there are folks building organizations centering Black joy, right? That feels different to me. In this moment in time, I think we know more, and we articulate a better understanding around systemic racism than we did before.

Even with this, folks who are way younger than all of us are just not here for it. I'm definitely not a young person, but just listening to young people—there was a nicety in which we approached things that millennials are just not doing. This is the generation that, as my daughter says, "They're too shy to ask for two packets of ketchup but will burn the building down to fight for defunding the police." The way in which folks who are younger than us respond to things is different. This also feels like a time where we understand that we need more than one NAACP, the way that we interrogate racism is through a myriad of NAACPs.

We also must build institutions that last. We're trying to build our institutions to last because, in all our optimism, it's still a long fight. We're not going to dismantle four hundred years of racism in twenty-four months. We need organizations that can stand the test of time to hold elected officials accountable, because our institutions have always been shaky. We didn't have the power, at least the institutional power, to hold individuals accountable. So they didn't need to listen to us.

MFR: Exactly! It's about institutions that are led by, supported by, and inclusive of people of color. We need people in these institutions who understand—that in a city that is so racist, so unequal in terms of income—how white supremacy operates. And that, for everybody to have positive well-being and be economically secure, there are just things that we need to dismantle. We do need to have our own institutions and organizations, whether they are base-building groups or think tank organizations like MassBudget. Another area I wanted to cover is policy. Let's dig into that a bit more. James, at the top you mentioned some of the Fair Housing work that you've been focused on. Could speak to that?

JJ: For the last five years, I've been working with a group called Community Advisory Committee on Fair Housing[20] with the City of Boston, with representatives from the Department of Neighborhood Development and the Boston Housing Authority. Over the years, we've had a lot of debates. Finally, we're at a point where the city has accepted the draft of a complete report. It approaches fair housing with the theme of intersectionality. Fair housing is not just housing. It's everything that's connected to housing. In 1968, that was the intention of the fair housing law.[21] When you look at judicial decisions since 1968, clearly fair housing was to be approached as an intersectional policy.

I'm very excited about the possibilities, but a particularly exciting victory was won in 2020. For the first time in Boston post–World War II, fair housing language was incorporated into the zoning regulations by the Boston Zoning Commission.[22] We're going back and forth on how to fully implement this. But if you look at the new zoning regulations, they clearly state that big projects, like Suffolk Downs, for example, will no longer be permitted or allowed to even go before the zoning commission until the Boston Planning and Development Agency ensures that certain fair housing requirements have been met.[23] And so I was shocked, pleasantly shocked, when the city agreed to city councilor Lydia Edwards's proposal to do this and the momentum it generated. Of course, the devil is in the details, but I think this is a very, very important event. As a matter of fact, *Shelterforce* magazine featured this in one of their newsletters. So that's why I said earlier that maybe I'm more of an optimist today than I used to be. That's a big victory, but little victories, if they can be connected, can help develop the narrative that our elected officials must abide by.

MEL: Marie-Frances won't be surprised that I think one of the most important policy areas is taxes. Over the past few decades, since the 1980s, inadequate tax revenue has had a direct impact in our communities and on the level of anger and frustration that people feel across the board. Our quality of life has really deteriorated. It's true. It is because we have completely dismantled the way that government supports people, families, and communities.

Many of us feel that government has this key responsibility of taking care of the social well-being of all of us. It's not there. We have incredibly aging infrastructure. I would have never thought that the United States had the kinds of conditions where a storm would leave people dying or without water, electricity, heating, day in and day out. We have an aging infrastructure that has not been kept up, that has not been taken care of. We have these fights every year with the state budget, where fewer resources are made available for the things that we need, and we care about—schools, healthcare, you name it. So how do we get to a collective understanding that my well-being is very tied to your wellbeing? In a healthy, loving, sustainable community, I put into the collective coffer what I can. We all do. And then we'll receive from that.

The only mechanism we have for that at the structural level is government. Government has the power to tax us. With that money it can then give to the society. But that entire system has been hijacked by corporations.

They're hardly paying into taxes. We're going to continue to be in dire straits in terms of funding adequately the things that we all are fighting for. For me, tax policy is an incredibly urgent priority. It's not that easy to organize people around a tax policy the way that it is for housing, for example. People understand taxes in a more indirect way when it comes to the importance of things our taxes pay for.

MFR: The work of advocating for progressive tax policies to fund all the things we need is really helping to draw connections with people. Educators, parents, and students already know that our school buildings are falling apart and don't have adequate ventilation. People know that the MBTA trains and buses don't always run on time, are rusty, and don't have enough personnel to operate them safely. People see the potholes. The disinvestment, especially in under resourced communities, is glaring. My continued work, the work of Maria Elena and many others, is to say that it's all linked to the taxes. That we must all pay our fair share to fund all the things—housing, education, transportation, mental health supports—we need to be collectively healthy and well. In addition, we want people to make good wages and have benefits so that they're able to have their well-being and their families' well-being taken care of that way. We need investments in the public good and to guarantee decent wages and benefits and even guaranteed income for those who are not able to work for any period of time. That's collective care.

Let's dig deeper into public investments though. One thing that became glaringly obvious during this pandemic is that there are things that government does and invests in that are harmful. Having the conversation and building power to shift resources away from things that are harming people is critically important as well. Families for Justice as Healing has been doing transformational work on this, with women who are incarcerated and formerly incarcerated saying, "Actually don't build that new women's prison. Do not use city dollars. Do not use state dollars. Do not use federal dollars for that. We have ideas for how we can better spend our public dollars."[24] Continuing to elevate this message and build out the systems so that everyday folks *actually* have a say in what we spend our tax dollars on is going to create that real change.

MEL: In Massachusetts, we have one of the oldest water and sewage systems in the nation. And we're not paying attention to it. One day, something is going to go wrong, and who knows. We're not investing in repairs and upkeep.

In regard to the wage piece, again, if we go back to the 1980s, Ronald Reagan and that entire Republican generation ushered in an economic model that really preferences the private sector over the public sector in taking care of public needs. It all started there. So what happened over time is that the United States became a two-tiered service economy, with not a lot of union jobs or manufacturing jobs that could send your kids to college like in previous decades. We had lots of people in the lower rungs of the service sector—including many immigrants. Then people with the degrees, like the engineers and other white-collar professionals. It is disingenuous to say that to address our current economic situation that people simply must go to school and get a degree. It is not right. I go back to the pandemic. Who became the most important, essential workers in the pandemic? Many of our essential workers in grocery stores and other core jobs did not have college degrees or were not paid very well. While this was happening, the Bezos of the world simply got richer.

The fact is that we don't care to pay these "essential" workers a living wage with benefits. The fact is that we don't care that those workers are unionized. We just say, "Go to college." Then graduates get saddled with debt? No, we need a better way to think about how to lift the economic well-being of most people.

We need an economy not just with doctors, lawyers, researchers, and nonprofit managers. We need all of us. We need to deeply honor and be in deep gratitude for the people that are making peanuts right now. They are the *essential* workers. I'm getting on my high horse, but I get angry.

JJ: I actually have been looking into what you just touched upon. What is the return for schooling and education? I've been looking at census data, IPUMS data, controlling for race, ethnicity, age. We know this, when you go beyond the high school diploma to one year of college, associate's degree, bachelor's—the racial gaps for average salaries are enormous. To say to a young person today "You know, you've got to get to college because you're going to make more money" isn't the whole truth. We also must add that we live in a system that has a racialized gap in Boston and in Massachusetts. I'm glad that you raised that because that's also part of an old way of thinking. "Oh, they just need to get to school. They just need to graduate, and everything will be fine." There are academics who have pushed that line for decades in Boston. I'm not going to mention any names, but for decades they pushed that line in terms of resolving Black and Latinx youth unemployment.

MEL: You know how many white people get to be middle-class with factory jobs? Nobody was telling them, "Get a college degree." They were unionized, they were paid well. (There have been racist unions, by the way). This to me gets at the very core of the injustice, the ugliness, and the pain. Even unions are freaking racist. But back in those days, nobody was telling those white folk to go to college. They were doing quite well, thank you very much, with one wage earner, not two. With one job they could go buy their home *and* send their kids to college. That's how they bought homes. A lot of these people were not professionals. They were working-class people that had the social support that allowed them to get to the middle-class status without thinking that they had to pay $100,000 for a college degree.

MFR: James, can you take it one step further with the fair housing work that you're doing? Because you talked about it in a technical sense, but in a real sense, how can it help people of color to be able to afford safe and stable housing?

JJ: We looked at the issue of homelessness, which in a lot of narratives is not connected to fair housing. It is, and there's a sizeable homelessness issue in the Boston public school system. If we don't deal with the issue of the thousands of children who are homeless in the Boston public school system at any point in the year for the last several years, that really is a violation of fair housing. It is a violation because they have no access to quality, affordable, and clean housing for their families. We had a debate with the city about overcrowding, as we felt they were misinterpreting the numbers. The highest rates of overcrowding are in the Asian American community, then the Latinx, and then Black. But those three groups are much higher than whites who are not Latinx. If you define "fair housing" as Mayor Walsh first proposed, that's really just about building more so the price goes down; that's missing the point. You have to solve for overcrowding, because that is a fair housing issue.

When you look at the information that just came out around the business contracts, you know, we are less than 1 percent of all contracts with the Blacks, as I recall, and less than 1.5 percent of Latinx. If people of color in Boston are being denied the wherewithal to be economically productive, they will not be able to afford certain types of housing. The other thing that the former mayor initially proposed (and he backed up from this, which is why I said I'm a little optimistic) is the definition of "affordability." They said, "This is not a fair housing issue, James and company." The definition of "affordability" is important, as it can either include or exclude people who need housing most. We know that the median income of Blacks in Roxbury, for example, is way lower than the median income of someone living in another part of the city, or another part of the state. So, if you define "affordability" based on this sort of metadata, you're saying to a lot of poor working-class households, especially in communities of color, that we're going to put you in a big bucket. Your median income is $42,000 per year but we're going to put you in a bucket for affordable housing where people are earning $80,000 to $100,000 per year. So, getting the definition of "affordability" shifted was another battle that we won. Believe it or not, there was one person in the city, who was one of the point people for the city, who said health has nothing to do with fair housing. "That's not what we're here for." Those are the little battles that we had to go through over the last three or four years. I'm glad you asked that question because some of us want to push the envelope around fair housing to address gentrification and displacement.

MFR: Imari, let's talk about the work that you've been cobuilding at King Boston around reparations and defining what local reparations can look like. Explain how you are centering community voice as a way to define what reparations mean in the twenty-first century for Bostonians.

IPJ: Dr. Letona, you were talking about things that occurred during the Reagan era, and I think multiple things were happening simultaneously. On the one hand, we saw different reforms happen. On the other hand, we saw the subtle deterioration of the public good. "Private is better than public; private schools better than public schools; private transportation is better than public transportation; private college is better than public." These things happen simultaneously. So, it's like when you look at my right hand, you don't see what my left hand is doing. It's part of how we've been socialized around what's good—it's quite subtle. Folks couldn't pay attention to these things because we were paying attention to policy. And, suddenly, they were socializing us into other ways of being. Those ways of being have been dangerous and detrimental and have diminished our confidence in the public good, which is the currency of our democracy. *It's like they've done their job, we have been psychologically socialized to think the public is not as valuable as the private.*

The same can be said with higher education. It has shifted away from knowledge for the sake of the public good to this neoliberal, commodified way of getting a college degree so you can get a job. Everything is neoliberalized. It's like they make college accessible but simultaneously neoliberalized it. We've commodified students as customers versus seeing education as an opportunity for knowledge expansion.

The idea of reparations is not just coming up with reparation policies. What happens oftentimes is we create policies that are not accessible to people or that people don't trust. We just don't trust them. Some people don't trust our public education system because they are not healed from the 1974 federal court ruling by Judge Garrity on busing, so they're not buying into any neighborhood walk-zone shit.[25] They're not going to do it, because we've never had a reparations conversation around redlining and its interconnections with school quality. They're not going to buy into walk-zone schools, they're just not.

So how do we approach engaging in a reparations conversation? I'm not only talking about slavery but reparations for redlining, reparations for public education crisis, reparations for transportation catastrophes. How do you look at a reparations approach that builds trust? Truth and reconciliation as a part of policy change, it's an essential part of policy change. Otherwise, you're not going to get people to buy into it. You don't get into a fight with your partner, come home with flowers and candy, and say forget about the argument. I could be unkind to you and bring flowers and candy, and then it's going to be good. That's unhealthy. But we do this with policy solutions. We continue to have good policy approaches but without a reparation or repair framing. So we can continue bringing flowers and candy without addressing the challenges and then wonder why people don't engage in things that sound like great ideas, and in many cases are brilliant ideas.

The Boston Human Rights Commission is a great venue for these reparations conversations, for these truth and reconciliation conversations around these progressive policies, which are in many cases effective but won't get the buy-in that we need to implement and move them. It's more of an approach, less about any specific policy. There are people a lot smarter than me on the policies, but we need to understand that we're constantly being socialized to not believe or not buy into the things that are actually healthy for us.

The other positive thing is there are Black-led organizations that are addressing the psychological and the socialization part of racism in ways that the NAACP did back in the old days. Those organizations should be beside a Massachusetts Budget and Policy Center that does policy analysis.

FIGURE 7.1. Photograph of the King Boston memorial titled *The Embrace*. The sculpture was installed on Boston Common, where in 1965 Dr. Martin Luther King, Jr., called Boston to live by its highest ideals. The Common—America's first public park—has a vibrant four-hundred-year-old history and a tradition of civic gatherings. The new memorial will spark public conversation about how to advance racial and social justice in Boston today. *The Embrace*, Hank Willis Thomas and MASS Design Group. Commissioned by Embrace Boston, the Boston Foundation, and the Collection of the City of Boston. Image courtesy of Mass Design Group.

They should be beside an arts organization, and they should be beside a BIPOC-led higher education organization and a BIPOC-led housing justice organization. We need as many institutions as possible at this time that are built to last. I'm tired of an Alianza Hispana, a Freedom House, and others not having the support they need and keep disappearing. When I started in the sector at twenty-one years old, there were like forty-five thriving Black and Latinx organizations. There's like ten now. There was a bunch of them. When I first came to Boston, there was so many leaders, there was Concilio Hispano in Cambridge, gone.

MEL: Teatro Latino in the middle of Chelsea, gone.

IJP: Yep. We just didn't build with the long-term in mind. We felt we just didn't have the capacity to do it. I've gotten mentored to believe the opposite of that. I feel affirmed when I hear, "Foundations are responsible. Don't believe that mess; build organizations that are built to last."

MEL: The reparations piece, I would love to have another conversation and learn more from you. It's very beautiful the way you talked about it. I have never heard it that way, and I really want to learn about it because I had a very narrow understanding of reparations. My first reaction was, "Hey, anything that redistributes wealth I am thoroughly for."

IJP: Yes, exactly, reparations from redlining! There are whole generations of Black and Brown families that were redlined out of their homes—government was part of it, the real estate and banking industries. Marie-Frances and I were at an event, and the head of Bank of America was there, and I was like, "Man, there's a reparations conversation you have to have, because there's a direct benefit off the backs of brown people and their homes that you took away." We don't have to go back to tracing our ancestors to slavery. You could go back to redlining or to the 1974 Judge Garrity ruling in Boston, and there are reparations to pay. There's a justice conversation to have.

NOTES

1. King Boston is a program of the Boston Foundation working closely with the City of Boston to create a living memorial and programs honoring the legacy of Dr. Martin Luther King, Jr., and Coretta Scott King, and their time and work together in Boston.
2. "About the Gateway Cities," MassInc, accessed July 2022, https://massinc.org/our-work/policy-center/gateway-cities/about-the-gateway-cities/#:~:text=The%20Legislature%20defines%2026%20Gateway,%2C%20Springfield%2C%20Taunton%2C%20Westfield%2C.
3. The Hyams Foundation is a private, independent foundation with a mission of increasing economic, racial, and social justice and power within low-income communities, focusing on Boston and Chelsea, Massachusetts.
4. Grace Lee Boggs (1915–2015) was an American author, social activist, philosopher, and feminist.
5. "The Honorable Melvin King," The History Makers, accessed July 2022, https://www.thehistorymakers.org/biography/honorable-melvin-king; Mel King, *Chain of Change: Struggles for Black Community Development* (Boston: South End Press, 1981).
6. "William Barber II," Wikipedia, last modified on March 27, 2022, https://en.wikipedia.org/w/index.php?title=William_Barber_II&oldid=1079596299.
7. Reconstruction (1865–1877), the turbulent era following the Civil War, was the effort to reintegrate Southern states from the Confederacy and four million newly freed people into the United States. Second Reconstruction (1946 and 1963) was a period of the civil rights movement when African Americans began to win significant victories against racist policies and laws in the United States. During this period, African Americans finally received legal guarantees of rights that had been granted during the original Reconstruction, which followed the American Civil War.
8. Katharine Q. Seelye and Matt Flegenheimer, "Ayanna Pressley's Victory: A Political Earthquake That Reflects a Change in Boston," *New York Times*, September 5, 2018, https://www.nytimes.com/2018/09/05/us/politics/ayanna-pressley-massachusetts-elect.html.
9. Rachael Splaine Rollins (born March 3, 1971) is an American lawyer and politician

who is the U.S. attorney for the District of Massachusetts. Rollins was formerly Suffolk County district attorney in Massachusetts, which includes the municipalities of Boston, Chelsea, Revere, and Winthrop. Rollins was the first woman to hold the office of Suffolk County D.A. and the first woman of color to serve as a Massachusetts D.A. In July 2021, president Joe Biden nominated Rollins to be the U.S. attorney for the District of Massachusetts.

10. The Black Economic Council of Massachusetts serves as the chief advocacy organization for Black businesses across the Commonwealth. Its mission is to advance the economic well-being of Black businesses, organizations, and residents through advocacy, business and leadership development, and strategic partnerships.
11. WBUR News and Wire Services, "Federal Complaint Filed against Boston over Lack of Contracts with Black- and Brown-Owned Businesses," WBUR, Radio Boston, February 17, 2021, https://www.wbur.org/news/2021/02/17/black-latinx-business-contracts-boston-discrimination-complaint.
12. In Boston, liquor licenses can sell for as much as $500,000 between private sellers. Critics say those sales happen within an arcane system that often can shut out new businesses and restaurant owners of color. Now several Boston city councilors are pushing to add two hundred new liquor licenses with the hope most will go to underserved neighborhoods such as Mattapan, Hyde Park, and Roxbury. Sydney Boles and Tiziana Dearing, "Boston City Counselors Push to Add Hundreds of New Liquor Licenses," WBUR, Radio Boston, April 11, 2022, https://www.wbur.org/radioboston/2022/04/11/boston-alcohol-bars-restaurants-licenses.
13. "Transcript of President Elect Joe Biden's Victory Speech," Associated Press, November 7, 2020, https://apnews.com/article/election-2020-joe-biden-religion-technology-race-and-ethnicity-2b961c70bc72c2516046bffd378e95de; the transcript reads, "I believe it is this: Americans have called on us to marshal the forces of decency and the forces of fairness. To marshal the forces of science and the forces of hope in the great battles of our time.

    The battle to control the virus.
    The battle to build prosperity.
    The battle to secure your family's health care.
    The battle to achieve racial justice and root out systemic racism in this country.
    The battle to save the climate.
    The battle to restore decency, defend democracy, and give everybody in this country a fair shot."

14. MassBudget is a leading think tank advancing equitable policy solutions that create an inclusive, thriving Commonwealth; see https://massbudget.org/.
15. Stephanie Murray, "Every Boston Mayor Has Been a White Man: Will 2021 Change That?," *Politico*, January 27, 2021, https://www.politico.com/news/2021/01/27/boston-mayor-white-2021-462794.
16. Centro Presente's Legal Immigration Services Department provides a wide range of affordable services and programs that are crucial to the Latin American immigrant community.
17. In 2021, Amazon CEO Jeff Bezos donated $100 million to philanthropic chef Jose Andrés and CNN commentator Van Jones, who were designated inaugural recipients

of his Courage and Civility Award. The money was earmarked for charitable causes but otherwise came with no strings attached.

18. Sheena Collier is the founder and CEO of Boston While Black.
19. Rev. Willie Bodrick, II, J.D., M. Div., fourteenth senior pastor (2021–present) is the talented, enthusiastic, and anointed senior pastor of the historic Twelfth Baptist Church in the Roxbury neighborhood of Boston. The Twelfth Baptist Church, born in 1840, is the oldest direct descendent of the African Baptist Church, which was founded on Beacon Hill in Boston, Massachusetts, in 1805. Over the years, preachers from the pulpit of the Twelfth Baptist Church have preached of a common faith united in exploring what it means to be a people of God through the saving power and leadership of Jesus Christ. They have proclaimed the Bible as the true, divine, authoritative, infallible, inspired word of God.

    Throughout its history, the Twelfth Baptist Church has served as a forum for champions of human rights and dignity such as William Lloyd Garrison, Frederick Douglass, Rev. Leonard A. Grimes, Rev. George Washington Williams, Rev. Dr. Martin Luther King, Jr., and others.

    From the antislavery cause of the 1800s through the civil rights movement to the present day, the Twelfth Baptist Church fostered a commitment to spiritual guidance and social action in the Greater Boston community.
20. Fair housing is the right to choose housing free from unlawful discrimination. Federal, state, and local fair housing laws protect people from discrimination in housing transactions such as rentals, sales, lending, and insurance.
21. The Fair Housing Act (Title 8 of the Civil Rights Act of 1968) introduced meaningful federal enforcement mechanisms. It outlaws the refusal to sell or rent a dwelling to any person because of race, color, disability, religion, sex, familial status, or national origin.
22. Boston Planning and Development Agency, "BPDA Board Approve Fair Housing Zoning Amendment, December 17, 2020, https://www.bostonplans.org/news-calendar/news-updates/2020/12/17/bpda-board-approves-fair-housing-zoning-amendment.
23. Suffolk Downs is a former racetrack in East Boston and Revere. The Thoroughbred horse track opened in 1935 and was sold in 2017 to HYM Investment Group. The large mixed-use project has been permitted for up to 10.5 million square feet of new development on approximately 109 acres. The multiphased proposal includes a forty-acre publicly accessible open space system and retail centers near the MBTA transit stations.
24. Families for Justice as Healing is led by incarcerated women, formerly incarcerated women, and women with incarcerated loved ones. Its mission is to end the incarceration of women and girls; see https://www.justiceashealing.
25. On June 21, 1974, U.S. District Court judge W. Arthur Garrity, Jr., found Boston's schools to be unconstitutionally segregated, instituting a plan of forced busing between some of the city's poorest (and most racially divided) schools.

EQUITY

CHAPTER EIGHT

SOCIAL JUSTICE AND URBAN ENVIRONMENTAL POLICY

A Framework for Achieving a Racially Equitable Boston through Design

THEODORE C. LANDSMARK

Boston has a long-standing and well-earned national reputation as a "racist" city. The region is known for discouraging diverse and talented people of color from being educated in and settling here as professionals and residents, even though immigrants contribute significantly to the economy and culture of our region. Boston's universities, research centers, and media resources have documented Greater Boston's racial disparities and the potential long-term negative implications such disparities will have on our region's competitive economy. Planning, design, and building resiliently play significant roles in shaping intentional social justice strategies to reverse our poor reputation for racial injustice, and the provision of opportunities for diverse populations to succeed in New England.

Engaging underrepresented communities in design processes reveals an awareness of potential unintended consequences, preparing public agencies and developers to implement investment strategies that can fairly compensate underserved communities for their losses. Diversifying planning and development staffs can help overcome the long-time elitism and systemic racism of the design professions, to enable planning teams to better incorporate divergent views into project development, as when mobility impaired persons help develop access plans, or when residents cite potential environmental injustices as roads or energy facilities are placed in their neighborhoods. Incorporating diverse local voices into regional planning decisions prepares future generations to be actively engaged in shaping their own futures as stakeholders invested in maintaining the economic and social strengths of their communities.

There is little to no direct evidence of overtly racist efforts to harm people of color and people of limited financial means through our environmental design and building processes. Planners, engineers, and builders are usually required to find the most direct, efficient, and cost-effective ways to solve problems in the built environment. But *our policies and practices are often a manifestation of systemic injustices that produce disproportionately negative impacts on poor people and people of color who live in lower-cost areas.* This is the essence of *institutional racism*—policies that seem neutral on the face of it can perpetuate injustices of diminished air quality, greater risks of flooding, heat accumulation, and reduced access to services. Whether deemed compensation for loss, redress, or reparative justice, we have long provided offsets for environmental damages, whether through eminent domain takings, air rights offsets, the Marshall Plan, or global reparations. As designers, we can do better in redressing the unintended negative impacts of our work.

Where do we want to be when Boston celebrates its four-hundredth anniversary in 2030? This chapter proposes initiatives toward a paradigm shift in Boston's racial relations, within a context that emphasizes the region's larger environmental justice issues. New public policies, educational initiatives, and private financing mechanisms to incentivize more environmentally and socially beneficial design and building processes are needed. These must be linked to more accountable ethical practices in order to overcome decades of negative impacts on our built environment to achieve social justice through design. *Enough is enough.*

COMMUNITY-BASED VISIONING TOWARD RACIAL JUSTICE IN GREATER BOSTON

While there is an emerged consensus that uncomfortable conversations are now required to address deep patterns of racial injustice across New England, we also need to realize that cleansing dialogues alone will not right the imbalances of racial justice across our region. We must also envision what justice will look like and define and apply tools and specific strategies that actively address our embedded inequalities. We must be willing to hold ourselves accountable for achieving measurably improved quantitative and qualitative racial justice outcomes.

Data analysis of the distribution of existing environmental planning resources and networking charts are useful tools drawn up by Boston's primarily white academics, universities, and foundations, but the region will need far more than such broad commitments to environmental justice for real progress toward social justice to be achieved. Such next steps require thoughtful facilitated community-wide *visioning processes* similar to, but perhaps larger than, the 2015 youth-focused *Imagine Boston 2030—A Plan for the Future of Boston* process that queried over fifteen thousand residents on their visions for Boston in 2030. There is a need for renewed diverse community policy engagement in laying out shared plans, procedures, and responsibilities for distributing financial, educational, and social resources. Visioning helps develop collective wisdom and establishes shared goals and projected outcomes, enabling policymakers and citizens to hold each other accountable for achieving measurable outcomes. The success of a visioning process is dependent on mutual accountability. Incentives will need to be implemented to encourage disparate institutional commitments to convene and work together, as successful shared Boston initiatives have collaborated in the past to reduce youth violence, provide summer jobs, or address COVID-care disparities.

ENVIRONMENTAL JUSTICE STRATEGIES CAN DEVELOP METRICS AND TOOLS FOR ADDRESSING BOSTON'S RACIAL INJUSTICES

Improving our environments, understood broadly not just as our relationship to the natural world but also as the political and social relationships nested within that symbiosis, is the defining issue of our time. Growing economic inequities and racial disparities in climate-based vulnerabilities require action to be centered in the confrontation of systemic injustices in human social organization. Achieving environmental justice also inevitably means engaging and preparing an emerging generation of workers of color to be employed in the green economy needed to address the challenges of climate change. In an era of accelerating climate change and increasing disruptions of all kinds, responding to the grand challenges of sustainability and resilience requires an integrated understanding of technology, data, and human literacies and an explicit connection with social, economic, and racial justice.

ACHIEVING RACIAL, SOCIAL, AND ENVIRONMENTAL JUSTICE

The effects of systemic racism in Greater Boston can take many forms. Quantitatively we have documented disparities in Black/white net worth ($8 versus $247,500 in 2017), driven largely by redlining and a lack of Black access to funds for home ownership and capital accumulation. Behind the harsh quantitative disparities are *qualitative* social practices that have systematically diminished access by people of colors to the region's vast educational and economic resources. As design injustices have placed roadways and toxin-producing laboratories and pollution hazards in inner-city Black and Brown residential neighborhoods, our challenge as planners and policymakers is to overcome these recurrent injustices through intentionally strategic actions that build a more equitable Boston.

Goals

Recognition of Racism and Goal Setting

Progress will be made toward achieving racial justice in New England when we:

- Openly acknowledge the hurt we have imposed on others unlike ourselves;
- Select data to address our disparities for setting specific metrics of improvement;
- Set timelines for achievable outcomes that close disparity gaps;
- Take defined public and private sector steps toward meaningful justice interventions, including reparations;
- Accept that there is a need for mutuality of forgiveness among the perpetuators and victims of the injustices;
- Recognize that healing will take time and effort; and
- Accept that accountability of all parties needs to be defined and implemented through specific procedures that may include reasonable sanctions.

Over the past half century, Americans have agreed to wear seat belts, reduce smoking, adopt ethical standards for financial investing, and expose sexual and child abuse in some of our longest-standing social institutions; we have legally sanctioned same-sex unions, identified environmental injustices, and adopted a national health care system. Approaching Boston's four-hundredth anniversary, we need to acknowledge that our regional policies addressing racial equality have trailed our demographic changes, potentially contributing toward a declining long-term attractiveness as an educator and employer in a competitive global economy.

ON BEING A BLACK PLANNER IN BOSTON

I am an African American lawyer, urban planner, and design educator. I was raised by a single parent in public housing in East Harlem before moving to Boston, where I have practiced law, built and managed real estate, worked for several mayors on educational and social justice initiatives, and served for seventeen years as president of the Boston Architectural College. I have served on the boards of the Boston Planning and Development Agency (BPDA), Massachusetts Bay Transportation Authority (MBTA), and various museums, and chaired national accreditation organizations.

These experiences can obscure how it actually *feels* to be an emerging design professional of color in New England. A Black or Brown person in Boston carries a daily emotional burden of isolation and disengagement from social mobility that whites rarely feel. No white colleague has ever expressed to me a perceived need to "get dressed up" in order to shop on Newbury Street, to live in the right "comfortable" neighborhood, or to be ready with an explanation as to why one might be driving a nice car. With few role models to consult, we become used to incessant microaggressions in elevators; at sports, museum, or concert events; or waiting to enter a restaurant. Well-meaning professionals told me that architectural firms would not support my internship path to licensure, so I worked instead for the Boston law firm that represented those exclusive design firms.

When I arrived in Boston in the early 1970s with three Yale degrees, such racial microaggressions were common, and a group of young Black professionals dominated by Blacks who had attended Boston's colleges and universities gathered regularly to commiserate over the "weirdness" of our white colleagues. While most of those young Black colleagues emigrated to other "more welcoming" cities with clearer career ladders for diverse

FIGURE 8.1. Civil rights lawyer and activist Ted Landsmark (author) captured by photographer Stanley Forman in the April 5, 1976, protests over the busing crisis at City Hall Plaza, Boston. Titled "The Soiling of Old Glory," the image captures teen Joseph Rakes (*left*) using an American flag to attack Landsmark (*right*), who was passing by for a meeting in City Hall. The image was awarded the 1977 Pulitzer Prize for spot photography.

professionals, I stayed in Boston because I believed that career growth prospects here were, and are, greater than in other American cities with similar but less-well-recognized systemic racial disparities. Even after being attacked by an American flag-bearing teenaged antibusing protestor on Boston's City Hall Plaza, I insisted that the attack was not personal but instead reflected deep-seated inequities supported by New England's elected officials and corporate leaders, reflecting a culture of hierarchical systemic racism.

ACKNOWLEDGING THE ROLE OF RACE IN SHAPING BOSTON'S HISTORY AND CULTURE

As an emerging planner I was hardly alone in recognizing Boston's patterns of racial and gender exclusion. Court orders to address such exclusions have mandated changes in local public housing, educational, policing and public safety, fire, and transportation agencies. During a half century of public service, I have seen numerous Boston-area institutions issue antidiscrimination and anti-racist statements declaring their commitments to increasing racial equity by reaching out to include the city's diverse populations across their organizational activities. These commitments have been sporadic, unmonitored, and unfulfilled. University faculties, real estate and law firms, media, commercial builders and design firms, finance and tech industries, social clubs, and cultural institutions remain managed almost exclusively by middle-aged white men. *For all our self-possessed confidence and globally marketed liberal intellectual reputation, Boston, as the regional capital of New England, can be startlingly small and provincial.* The population of the Greater Boston region is equivalent to the population of Brooklyn. Boston has proven to be aggressively tribal and insular, with various ethnic groups clustered in neighborhoods that rarely interact collaboratively with our "downtown" financial, commercial real estate, tech, university, and legal communities.

The city's demographics have evolved significantly, with Boston's population having grown by nearly 10 percent from 2010 to 2020 (58,000 new residents), with steady percentage declines in both our Black and white populations, offset by significant increases in diverse new immigrant Asian and Latinx residents. We welcome immigrants, and in Boston today, 29 percent of residents are first-generation Americans. Traditional Black/white racial social and economic dichotomies are being subsumed by more complex interrelationships among ethnic groups, yet the net worth disparity between white and Black families is at a ratio of thirty thousand to one ($247,000 versus $8). Nevertheless, recurrent patterns of institutional racism have perpetuated a long-standing New England legacy of perpetuating anti-Semitism and anti-Asian, and anti-Black discrimination.

As a half-century Boston resident, I saw a significant turning point in Boston's racial policy history in 1983 with the departure of mayor Kevin White, who had used city funds to defend against NAACP-filed lawsuits challenging Boston's patterns of public sector racial discrimination. The two final candidates were Black state representative Mel King and a Rainbow Coalition he had assembled, and South Boston representative Ray Flynn, who had opposed busing. Flynn won, and quickly appointed to senior positions the largest number of women and people of color in the city's history—the deputy mayor, treasurer, health commissioner, schools superintendent, elections commissioner, housing director, and others formed a diverse cabinet of policymakers committed to implementing significant racial changes in the city's public resource allocation policies. Flynn's appointments set a precedent for demonstrating that people of color could achieve success as public sector managers, a precedent rarely seen even today in Greater Boston's private sector. Few knew that as a teenager Flynn had hitched weekend truck rides to Harlem to improve his basketball skills, and had developed cross-racial friendships throughout Boston. Mayors Thomas Menino and Marty Walsh continued and expanded Flynn's racially focused policies to transfer developer wealth from downtown to Boston's neighborhoods of color, directing new funds toward school programs, public facilities, and social services.

Today, Boston has a high bond rating, a rapidly growing population, greater demographic diversity, and human, cultural, and educational services envied by other American cities of comparable size. At the same time, Greater Boston has become one of the most economically segregated regions in the United States, with high rates of gentrification, resegregating schools, and a decayed transportation infrastructure managed outside the city's jurisdiction. We are among the most educationally segregated regions in the United States. Our housing costs are among the highest in the nation, public transportation is disorganized, our job opportunities favor whites-dominated highly educated technology and finance, and racially diverse low-paid hospitality workers. Our economic leadership, once dominated by local enterprises, have been supplanted by global firms using Boston's local university, financial, and high-tech resources to expand their global footprints. These disparities paint conflicted visions of what the city could be when Boston reaches its four hundredth anniversary in 2030. Economic and social equity remain unrealized goals across our entire region.

EDUCATIONAL PATHWAYS TOWARD RACIAL EQUITY

Today, the majority of Boston's high school valedictorians are people of color, and many are from first-generation families where English is not the primary language. Our educational policies have enabled us to feel good about sending talented young children of color to suburban white METCO schools while underinvesting in schools in the Black and Latinx neighborhoods.[1] Inner-city schools have improved substantially, while white parents enroll their children in quasipublic charter schools. The numbers of Black and Brown local students enrolled in major colleges have actually declined as universities have replaced American people of color with international students. Our private universities pride themselves on making offers to local students of color, while disinvesting in advising and first-generation student support systems to enable those students to persist to graduation and entry into the region's professions.

Data indicate that change in overcoming racial injustices throughout New England has been slow, begrudged, and prone to facing intransigent white resistance. The Greater Boston region in 2020 is as residentially segregated as we were in 1990, although people of color are now more widely dispersed. Zoning, redlining, and financial investment strategies have perpetuated racially segregated residential and commercial real estate investment segregation. Our major development, legal, financial, banking, university, health care, technology, cultural, and other professions have minimally more people of color employed in management positions as in 1975.

SOCIAL CHANGE IN THE PUBLIC SPHERE

If we are to be truly resilient as a growing region of smart, hard-working, long-term residents and diverse new arrivals, we need to make an honest assessment of our strengths and needed areas of potential improvement in the next decade and dedicate ourselves to planning and implementing deep structural changes in our policies and practices concerning economic growth and development, inclusivity, access to resources, and how we close the gaps between what we believe and what we actually do.

Social change theorists have posited strategies for change that rely on data analysis and collaborative action. Northeastern's Beth Simone Noveck, for example, has compiled the following skill sets as essential to activists' implementing effective social change:

- Problem definitions that stress urgency, engage real people, and are resolvable;
- Data-analytic thinking that comprehends the breadth, complexity, and nature of the problem;
- Human-centered design that draws on the advice of those being assisted;

- Collective intelligence that adopts participatory approaches to utilizing shared community resources and assets;
- Rapid evidence reviews that scan for best ideas and alternative models of action;
- Powerful multi-sectoral partnerships; and,
- Measuring what has and has not worked.[2]

Such a rubric lays out procedures for addressing urban problems in comprehensive ways that draw on currently available statistical data. They are an introduction to the complexities policymakers face in developing fair, ethical, racially aware solutions that may also require knowledge of the historical, socioeconomic, and cultural roots of the problems being addressed, which in fairness may require the introduction of reparations and healing policies that are not always readily quantifiable.

What is often missing from academically based, theoretical approaches to urban problem solving is a deep understanding of how race has skewed and distorted data sets in much data-gathering and analytical sociological research over the past century, and how data-driven quantitative approaches to problem solving too often excluded the voices and analyses of people of color in making their own determinations of what interventions may actually produce qualitative improvements in their lives. We need to invoke approaches to generating solutions that involve both quantitative economic and sociological data, and decolonialized, qualitative, on-the-ground engagement and solution design with those stakeholders who are most affected. In this context, the principles laid out by Erica Chenoweth's 2011 *Why Civil Resistance Works*, linked with the tangible design interventions possible within a "Just City" rubric (see below), would help Boston find a way toward being a model of a city that has confronted racism directly and taken positive steps to address the issue.[3]

COMMUNITY ENGAGEMENT AND PLANNING

A "Just City" Framework for Racial and Environmental Equity in Boston

"Just Cities," a concept propounded by Susan S. Fainstein in *The Just City*, counter "the ideological triumph of neoliberalism [that] has caused the allocation of spatial, political, economic, and financial resources to favor economic growth at the expense of wider social benefits" by "combin[ing] progressive city planners' earlier focus on equity and material well-being with considerations of diversity and participation so as to foster a better quality of urban life within the context of a global capitalist political economy."[4] "Just Cities" addresses the principles of education, professional practice, and public accountability, which lighten the environmental burdens on the economically, racially, and socially disadvantaged while better preparing dense urban environments for the diverse community-based needs of the mid-twenty-first century, embedding social justice concerns into urban planning, development and design.

"Just City" principles provide for:

Acceptance—belonging, empathy, inclusion, reconciliation, respect, tolerance, and trust;
Aspiration—creative innovation, delight, happiness, hope, and inspiration;
Choice—diversity and spontaneity;
Democracy—conflict, debate, protest, and voice;
Engagement—community, cooperation, participation, and togetherness;
Fairness—equality, equity, merit, and transparency;
Identity—authenticity, beauty, character, pride, spirituality, and vitality;
Mobility—access and connectivity;
Power—accountability, agency, empowerment, and representation;
Resilience—adaptability, durability, and sustainability;
Rights—freedom, knowledge, and ownership, and
Welfare—healthiness, prosperity, protection, safety, and security.

Two of the most essential qualitative principles for transforming Boston's approach to increasing equity are transparency and the initiation of honest dialogues leading to change.

BUILDING EMPATHY AND TRUST

Trust evolves within a context of truth telling, respect, shared values, honesty in thought and action, mutuality of responsibility, and fulfilled commitments. Following centuries of grossly unequal distributions of resources and wealth, as in efforts to develop racial reconciliation, empathy and trust have begun to be built, over extended time periods, through facilitated dialogues and networking focused on building understandings across perceived racial and class lines.

Trust building across the many Boston-area research and nonprofit stakeholder institutions and the limited number of communities they tend to study (primarily Roxbury, Dorchester, North and East Cambridge, East Boston,

Chelsea, and Chinatown) is essential to repair decades of extractive university and nonprofit analyses undertaken by well-educated white researchers on underresourced communities of color. *Communities have too often been seen as research subjects rather than as active participants in community-centered capacity-building processes.* The studies and analyses have produced vital data and learning for all involved (which data has not always been shared with members of the communities even as funding sources have accumulated this extracted data), while generating few discernible direct benefits for those communities. This academic research has infrequently been translated into achievable public policy actions.

Many factors account for this failure of translation from analysis into policy-driven action, and high among these has been the absence of honest dialogue among the participants about the shared responsibilities of policymakers, researchers, and communities in implementing practices that produce improved community outcomes. Effective research must be participatory, inclusive, and intended to build community capacity for self-assessment and action using available resources. Research by activist academics such as Rebecca Riccio and Lily Song of Northeastern University's School of Public Policy, and Toni L. Griffin of the Harvard Graduate School of Design's Just City Lab, as well as organizations such as Boston's MASS Design Group are addressing this lack of capacity building and community empowerment.

Facilitated racial dialogues, conducted region-wide over an extended period, leading toward tangible reparative and healing interventions could produce new community links with universities and major nonprofits. Such dialogues could begin a measured transfer of power to younger generations who would learn to work comfortably with experienced leaders, and would diminish the implicit racism of intergenerational class distinctions. Dialogue surfaces divergent opinions and uncomfortable truths, and helps explain why certain decisions *must* be made on a timely basis. Inclusive, honest, and sometimes difficult dialogue helps overcome short-term reservations about essential longer-term choices (e.g., why seemingly expensive infrastructure investments can avert significantly more expensive restorative interventions and potential losses later). Remediative dialogues provide the opportunity for marginalized people and communities to be heard in their own voices, and to gain agency in future decision making. Such dialogues are time-consuming, potentially contentious, often uncomfortable, and must be well and fairly facilitated.

Difficult conversations are essential. As planners and designers of the built environment, we need to use improved dialogues to (a) address issues outside our comfort zones, and recognize our stereotypes about our community-based clients; (b) begin to replace our biased and often economically driven assumptions about community-based clients; (c) reach out to better understand our clients as individuals; (d) explore new non-colonializing perspectives on who our clients are; and (e) create opportunities for making positive contacts with a wider range of Boston's increasingly diverse residents through building language and cultural bridges to people different from ourselves. We must ask for example, why Muslims, of any color, are rarely seen in local marketing firms' depictions of typical Bostonians. Why do we turn a blind eye toward the perpetuation of ethnic invisibility? *Why is Boston so often portrayed in our design representations as young, white, and male, even though our demographics are increasingly constituted of women of color?* Why are we ageist, and why do we rarely depict people with disabilities in our renderings of Boston's future?

Racial reconciliation dialogues are not new to Boston—the National Conference of Christians and Jews, various religious groups, and mayor Martin Walsh initiated such dialogues over the past quarter century. LeadBoston, a sponsored program of this type that has been in action over the past three decades, serves as a successful model for bringing together diverse people and viewpoints around racial healing. These frameworks and their outcomes can be useful precedents for the work that lies ahead.

Dialogues must begin with a surfacing of what we believe our own identities are, and how those identities relate to the identities of those whom we perceive to be different from ourselves. We can apply "systems justification theory" to these challenging conversations to ask how we can overcome the propensity that we have to justify their existing biases and stereotypes.[5] In this regard, we, as planners and designers, need to demonstrate patience in listening to "marginalized," community-based people without being assertive about potential built environment solutions based on our educated and experiential expertise. If even as few as 5 percent of Boston-area residents were to be active participants in such dialogues, the impact on planning and ethical decision making around resilience and the future of the region could dramatically build empathy and trust.

SPECIFIC STRATEGIES TO ACHIEVE RACIAL AND ENVIRONMENTAL JUSTICE THROUGH COMMUNITY-BUILDING

Transparency in communications and visibility of processes catalyze the perception of credibility and trust in any successful planning process, and are prerequisites to wide public engagement. Facilitators of transparent and effective community dialogues must ask, "What do we want to achieve, and how will we *know* we have gotten there?" All stakeholders need to be well-informed about answers to these questions, in all the languages (linguistic and digital) and formats (print, digital, and face-to-face in laundromats, hair salons, and other places where people gather) the stakeholders rely on in their normal communications.

Working with Greater Boston's diverse communities to include them in empowering processes needs to go beyond listening, developing empathy, and being inclusive in planning processes to include the following three key things.

Asset mapping resources is essential, as the process enables affected communities to see their strengths and needs in an objective and comparable light, and informs planners of less visible community resources that can be built on. Asset mapping provides an accurate baseline for assessing whether intentional diversity initiatives have actually achieved progress toward an articulated equity goal, rather than merely uncovering existing but underutilized community strengths.

Education, mentoring, and *capacity-building* are core tools of inclusive planning processes. Not every community resident needs to fully understand all the complexities of the real estate or climate change infrastructure investment processes, but well-informed residents are more likely to be supportive of disruptive investments (new sewer lines, digital infrastructure, the demolition of unsafe residences, etc.) than are residents who feel excluded from knowledge of such processes. Few of our planning clients have had opportunities to work with, and learn from, professionals who look like them, and as well as providing services, we have an obligation to train the next generations of diverse planners and builders by introducing our clients to the field, providing training opportunities through our trade associations and universities, and engaging them in processes that achieve demonstrable positive outcomes. Simple updating signage and notices on construction sites, for example, can keep a community's children engaged with how new physical improvements may affect their lives.

New collaborative roles for universities, cultural institutions, hospitals and other nonprofit institutions help share responsibilities for education and economic growth. Successful private corporations are rarely dependent on their places of origin—they come and go from the places where they were founded and grew. Local stakeholder-anchored institutions instead tend to be major nonprofits and cultural institutions that often derive their core brands from the places where they are based. These organizations have symbiotic relationships with their local communities through employment, ticket sales, real estate investments, and educational programs, and they are long-term civic assets for the cities that host them. Thoughtful new town/gown relationships are emerging. The University of Pennsylvania in Philadelphia, Columbia University's campus in Harlem, the University of Minnesota in Minneapolis, Arizona State in Phoenix/Tempe, and Mills College in Oakland have, through intentional planning and school-wide collaboration, enhanced economic development, increased job opportunities, provided educational benefits, and brokered mutually beneficial working relationships with adjacent communities. In Richmond, for example, a twenty-year partnership between city government and Virginia Commonwealth University and Virginia Union is providing workforce development, mentoring for adults, employer-offered apprenticeships, procurement assistance, and STEM education for middle schoolers to address issues of racial equity. The delivery of high levels of in-kind services then exceeds the value of mere cash contributions to the city, drawing on the institutions' missions and core values.

Greater Boston hosts the largest concentration of fine nonprofit institutions in the world. Our multiple universities, museums, public service entities, hospitals, and spiritual organizations are aggregated into the smallest land area of any American city, providing a wealth of services while benefiting from substantial tax exemptions for their land holdings. For generations, Boston was culturally rich, and tax-revenue poor, and payments in lieu of taxes (PILOTs) were introduced to try to recoup the value of municipal services provided, such as fire protection, policing, public transit, street cleaning, and public education for nonprofit staff to support the success of these not-for-profit entities. The institutions often objected to paying these pilots, or paid significantly less than requested.

At the outset of the PILOT programs, the city's ability to calculate what fair contributions might be were fairly crude, depending primarily on land assessments. Today, algorithms are available to determine what the real contributions and uses of city services might be, and an understanding has developed that what the institutions contribute to city residents and area workers could be far greater if the contributions were made in services more intrinsic to the institutions' missions than in mere cash contributions to Boston's general fund. What Harvard, the Institute of Contemporary Art, Massachusetts General Hospital, the Boston Symphony, the Museum of Science, or the Trustees of Reservations can contribute to Greater Boston's residents in the form of direct services in line with their missions could be far greater than the value of a cash contribution, while making the institutions greater stakeholders in the future of the area's residents, and gaining the support of nonprofit boards.

If Boston were to de-emphasize nonprofit cash contributions to the city through unfilled payments in lieu of taxes and increase expectations of in-kind contributions to meet the city's needs, innovative practices, including the provision of career-focused educational certificates and badges to city residents, could be considered. Arts, cultural, science, health, and environmental education could supplement public school offerings to a greater extent than has been the case. This form of continuing and extended education would increase the educational and employment capacities of young and older residents, and could provide a point of entry into a range of opportunities in higher education, technical trades, resilience and sustainability, health, and childcare employment where universities already have demonstrated strengths.

ENVIRONMENTAL JUSTICE AND THE ACADEMY

Within the past decade a more diverse cohort of environmentally sensitive students, community advocates, millennial architects, and technologically advanced commercial building owners has emerged. The impacts of environmentally damaging policies on economically disadvantaged communities have been better quantified by data modelers, highlighting the inherent inequalities of existing hierarchies of who determines what is built. Northeastern University professor Jennie Stephens's *Diversifying Power: Why We Need Antiracist, Feminist Leadership on Climate and Energy* points to organizations that have identified racial injustices, and organizations that have developed approaches to redressing these injustices.[6] Such groups have initiated programs that provide *recruitment* to reach members of underserved communities and promote solar job opportunities; *experience* for new workers in this field; *readiness* in working with industry leaders to provide relevant job training; *referrals* to connect job seekers to the industry; and *retention* services to keep these new workers within the industry.

Environmental designers have long proposed solutions to societies' loss of meaningful connections to our environments. Conservationist Rachel Carson's *Silent Spring* (1962) initiated a movement of American sensitivity to our environment. Architect Bernard Rudofsky's *Architecture Without Architects* (1964) challenged modernist tropes that our best buildings should impose a designer's will on environments without regard to natural factors. Landscape architect Ian McHarg's *Design with Nature* (1969) highlighted our deteriorating relationships with our coasts due to environmental changes. Michigan professor Dr. Bunyan Bryant's *Environment Advocacy* (1990) raised awareness of the racial aspects of environmental injustice in a way that spurred a movement to address urban racial environmental inequalities and supremacist impositions of waste and heat and diminished resources on people of color. Former vice president Al Gore's *An Inconvenient Truth* (2006) brought a policymaker's perspective to how climate change and environmental injustice damage disadvantaged communities around the world. Professor Jennie Stephens's *Diversifying Power* (2020) points to ways of spreading authority for making environmental decisions among a wider range of affected women, people of color, and other generally excluded groups. Overall, global weather-related environmental crises have brought attention to widespread environmental injustices.

INVESTING IN HUMAN INFRASTRUCTURE AS COMMUNITY CAPACITY BUILDING

Recent scholarship on social change has focused on how institutions work, evolve, break down, and are reinvented through investments in both capital and human infrastructures. Harvard professor Erica Chenoweth, for example, focuses on nonviolent domestic movements for change such as antiracism, climate change, and immigrant rights movements, concluding that civil resistance efforts have been more successful at bringing about lasting social change over the last century than have violent or precipitous efforts at democratization. This research, in conjunction with work by Northeastern University's professor Daniel Aldrich on the effectiveness of building community resilience through investments in *human* infrastructure, indicates that the combined efforts of external protest and awareness building, and internal community-based capacity building of social structures, can effectively initiate and succeed at implementing social change toward racial justice. To reach a scale of effectiveness, such community building depends, in part, on supporting communications mechanisms and tangible capital improvements that require funding from outside the affected communities. "Outsider" financial support for strategic approaches to raising awareness and for the need for social change is essential to consciousness raising, and to mobilizing activities to confront racist policies and practices. These investments work in tandem with financial reparations, mentoring, reconciliatory dialogues, training, visible design and environmental interventions, and other community-based "insider" approaches to implementing and sustaining changes in attitudes, policies, and practices. Such "outsider" financial support can be obtained through multiple investment strategies.

PRIVATE SECTOR ENGAGEMENT AND PUBLIC/PRIVATE FINANCING

Individual initiatives in education, employment, or access to entrepreneurial financing are important immediate steps toward justice and must be pursued, but justice also requires systemic and syncretic approaches to social inclusion and change. We will not achieve a just city merely by documenting and cataloguing disparities, complaining about and protesting them, and demanding governmental action to overcome them. The disparities are the result of private sector actions, cultural patterns, and overt racism by powerful stakeholders protecting their perceived exclusive rights to access public and private resources, from education to networking access to financial investments to employment to housing to shared recreation. These factors are intimately interconnected.

Private sector involvement must include priority areas for new corporate taxes, such as the implementation of funding from Robin Hood funds that are directed at employers with fifty or more employees working in the city, including online workers. These funds, rather than simply being rolled into general operating revenues, would be specifically targeted for:

- Education and training of city residents (30 percent of whom are immigrants);
- Health supports (40 percent of Boston residents now receive care from neighborhood health centers);

- Affordable housing funding;
- Culture and cultural institutions engaging all populations;
- Environmental justice; and
- Small business development.

CREATING FINANCING MECHANISMS FOR REPARATIVE JUSTICE

In this regard, it may be time to create new financial instruments that raise new capital and provide tax shelter for investments in the form of reparations for past racial injustices. Such reparations have been paid out to Japanese internees, Jewish Holocaust survivors, and South African victims of apartheid. A serious discussion of the development of new financial instruments for reparations investments could lead to the generation of funds for residential home down payments, start-up investments in small businesses, scholarships for underrepresented people of color in professions from which they have been habitually excluded, tools for increasing digital access to educational resources, physical investments to overcome past environmental discriminations, and the like without raising taxes on taxpaying citizens who may be resistant to paying reparations.

When new capital has needed to be raised, transferred, or exploited to meet immediate needs for twenty-first-century economic growth, entrepreneurs within the American financial system have invented and won Securities and Exchange Commission, Treasury, and IRS support for new instruments that make such capital transfers possible. Among these have been speculative instruments that have risen and imploded in value, most of which have been designed to benefit individual investors and not the public at large. These have included derivatives, nonfungible tokens, block chain arrangements, special purpose acquisition companies, air rights valuations, Qualified Opportunity Zones, and cryptocurrencies. Most of these have used tax code openings to create incentives for wealthy individuals and institutional entities to invest in profitable or tax-sheltering activities. Public-focused instruments are overdue.

A corollary to such private financing could include raising the community compensation requirements for private commercial real estate developers in "hot" markets such as Boston to contribute more directly toward local education, job training, health improvement, and affordable housing development in underserved communities.

ENLARGING OUR NETWORKS

Relationships shape policies. As members of the professional built environment community, we have been perpetuating a centuries-old Boston class structure that excludes new arrivals, women, and minorities from real access to managerial power, and from the benefits that accrue therefrom, including access to higher education, career growth opportunities, wealth accumulation, home ownership, access to diverse forms of leisure, and private sector success. This depends on denying that racial, gender, and class segregation not only exist but are comparatively worse in New England than in other industrially and technologically advanced parts of the United States. We need to open our networks to wider ranges of diverse professionals. How and whom we admit to our best public schools and local colleges is a key to such expansion, and our admissions and retention efforts must focus more on providing opportunities for recently arrived Boston residents.

Achieving racial equity in Greater Boston requires systemic approaches to creating openings in informal social networks that are the pathways to inclusive power. Formal planning entities such as the BPDA (Boston Planning and Development Agency), the Urban Land Institute, Boston's Green Ribbon Commission, the New Urban Mechanics, A Better City, the Boston Society of Landscape Architects, the Boston Society for Architecture, the Chamber of Commerce, public radio, and the *Boston Business Journal* can expand partnering with community groups and local media to enlarge networking and information sharing opportunities.

A more radical approach to enlarging our networks could include the inauguration of region-wide public service gap years for Boston area high school and college students, focused on bringing together young people, as City Year does, for shared public service work on issues of resiliency and racial justice.

PUBLIC SECTOR HUMAN FACTORS DESIGN INTERVENTIONS

Public agencies and foundations are increasingly introducing programs to overcome past racial inequities that have led to current wealth generating disparities. First-time home buyer assistance, homeowner maintenance programs, changes in procurement practices, small business loans, rental housing supports, college loan forgiveness, and breaking down requests for developer participation into parcel sizes manageable by smaller developers and the like are laudable and essential tools for furthering racial equity. We know too little about how previous similar efforts fared. Did financially supported aspiring design students from the 1980s enter design and development careers? How did the increase of Boston's population at twice the rate of new housing production affect neighborhood gentrification? Do human-centered designs actually work?

Public planning and community-focused agencies such as the BPDA that provide job training, career support, and benefits to enhance social equity need to hold their funded entities accountable for achieving tangible outcomes for the intended recipients of those programs. Program access is important; so too are demonstrable benefits consistent with the opportunities provided, for example, graduation rates are as important as first-year scholarships; worker placement in jobs is as important as job training; and recycling capital within communities is as important as supporting small business start-up loans.

EXPAND PARTICIPATORY BUDGETING

Since the mid-1970s, Boston has sought to overcome its inability to fully address social equity needs due to its lack of a local income or sales tax and its high percentage of tax-exempt property by creating new taxable land and real estate investment on the South Boston waterfront and in selected other Boston neighborhoods. The Boston waterfront, which had been occupied for decades by abandoned railroad freight yards, was a rare piece of open real estate that could generate billions of dollars of corporate real estate taxes to fund needed social services throughout the city. It was, in effect, the opportunity to invent highly lucrative new tax revenues without displacement.

Participatory budgeting is an approach to engaging groups of residents in making decisions about the allocation of small portions of a municipal budget. While the amounts being allocated may be small within a larger budget, participatory budgeting generally engages youths in understanding the challenges in making difficult and fair decisions that affect real people. In Boston, beginning in 2014 (and in Cambridge up through 2021), participatory budgeting linked the Mayor's Youth Council, the redevelopment authority, and youth training resources in a shared educational process that equips diverse participants to become neighborhood leaders. As successful collaboration depends in part on having a stable and openly collaborative public funding base (including building strong bond ratings and multiyear budgeting models), the wider use of participatory budgeting becomes a tool for building diverse capacities in allocating public resources.

REGIONALIZE OUR PLANNING AND RESOURCES

Boston acting alone, without regional collaboration, cannot solve regional problems of housing affordability, public transportation, environmental justice, health care availability, food insecurity, or educational access. Decades of debate have not resolved the question of what incentives are needed to provoke collaboration across our excessively large number of small municipal jurisdictions. Some have argued that a substantial weather-induced crisis is necessary to bring cities and towns together around shared goals, while others have suggested that forceful state intervention is most effective. Massport, the MBTA, and regional parks systems have been formed successfully, as have smaller public safety compacts. The political vicissitudes of bringing cities and towns together is certainly a challenge, and regionalism is addressed elsewhere in this volume (see chapter 3), but if Boston were structured geographically and politically, as are other major American cities such as New York, Atlanta, Chicago, Houston, Phoenix, and Atlanta, the "city" would aggregate the shared needs of all municipalities within Route 128, with a focus on Boston, Brookline, Cambridge, Chelsea, Everett, Malden, Medford, Milton, Newton, Quincy, and Somerville (i.e., communities served by MBTA rapid transit).

What's clear is that there must be a weakening of resistance to local home rule that enables variations in design and planning approaches to address regional homelessness, environmental injustice, gentrification, and class discrimination, driven by a public sense that addressing such needs provides tangible local benefits.

With a regionalization of planning procedures, we learn from the diverse cultures now growing within the region to set different priorities for development, to honor elders and families, to increase institutional humility, to better understand the needs of working-class communities, and to reduce unnecessary ego-driven personal competition to assert and prove our talents. In short, we learn to cooperate and collaborate better with communities unlike our own, as the BPDA as a planning agency has begun to do over the past half decade.

DESIGN PROFESSIONALS' SELF-REFLECTION ON DIVERSITY AND EXCLUSION

Facing Our Elitist Career Pathways into Environmental Design

When we reflect on ourselves as planners, designers, developers, builders, and implementers of change in our climate-challenged and often racially unjust built environment, the image we see is appallingly inequitable. Greater Boston prides itself on being a center of higher education and professional learning, and a mecca for the education of architects and planners. As mentioned by Anne-Marie Lubenau in chapter 6, the Boston region has the largest per capita number of schools and professional firms of any city. Greater Boston hosts some of the most respected, innovative, and professionally engaged design and urban planning schools in the world, yet this creativity has largely excluded from leadership Americans of color and women. Our design and planning schools tout their commitments to diversity, but fewer than 10 percent of their students, faculty, and alumni are from American Latinx or Black communities.

Efforts to increase the diversity of the design and planning professions have been a dismal failure. Most of the diversity touted by design and planning schools is based on having admitted substantial numbers of international students of diverse backgrounds, relatively few of whom work on Boston's racial and class issues, preferring instead to focus on issues in their home countries. While school heads have historically denied such an assertion, they compete for these international students because they require little or no financial aid and are not deterred by Boston's reputation as a city that is unwelcoming to people of color.

Domestic diversity in America's design schools has remained flat or declined for a decade or more. While the percentage of Hispanic and Latinx students enrolled nationally in professional architecture programs (17.9 percent) tracks closely with the percentage of this population in the United States (21 percent), only 8.5 percent of licensed architectural professionals are from this "largest American minority" population. Concurrently over the past decade, only 5 percent of students enrolled in architecture programs accredited by the National Architectural Accrediting Board have been African American, and only 1.9 percent of these African Americans are women.[7] Forty-four percent of all architecture schools have no Black faculty to mentor and inspire these students, the majority of whom are enrolled in historically Black colleges and universities. The number of Black or African American students enrolled nationally in urban planning programs actually declined by 50 percent between 2009 and 2017, while the number of Latinx students in such urban planning programs declined nationally by 40 percent.

In a New England region known for marketing its welcoming inclusivity, the actual number of professional planners, designers, and builders or color is pathetically small. Fewer than 5 percent of Massachusetts's licensed architects and urban planners are African American or Latinx, and those numbers are lower in other New England states. There are, for example, 122,000 licensed architects in the United States, about 7,500 of whom are registered in Massachusetts. Of those Massachusetts architects, in 2020, fewer than fifty were African American. Similar dismal numbers are present for urban planners, commercial real estate developers, and private contractors capable of operating at a scale sufficient to build a fifty-unit affordable housing development. The Boston Society of Architects' book *20 on 2020* (2005) raised these issues two decades ago, with negligible responses from New England's professional design and education communities.

How do we redress this disparity between the need for diverse designers and planners and the productivity of our New England schools in filling this need? In addressing the region's dearth of diverse design professionals, it is time for design and built environment schools to work together around recruitment, domestic marketing, sharing faculty, revamping curricula, providing advising and internships, promoting licensure, and nurturing cohorts of diverse young professionals. Just as art and music schools in Philadelphia and Boston have come together to share their resources, so too could Boston's schools share their built environment educational resources to create a region-wide matrix of feeder schools (community and technical colleges, vocational high schools and community-based construction entities, all funded with public job training funds) to create a multitiered career pathway into various aspects of the professions. Positive networking could lead to a broader understanding of the multiple career paths available in design, from retrofitting buildings for resilience to creating new medical and accessibility devices for the health care industry to supporting the tech industry's environmental, energy, and Green Jobs employment initiatives. Institutional isolation about creating new initiatives could be replaced by demonstrable outcomes that would be attractive to industries and domestically diverse talent, drawing training resources into the region.

HOLDING OURSELVES FINANCIALLY AND SOCIALLY ACCOUNTABLE

Work to overcome racism and environmental injustice must be intentional and accountable. It must be directed toward achieving tangible strategic outcomes based on:

- Relevant research and case studies that assess the potential positive and negative outcomes of the intentional interventions; and
- Commitments to making reasonable disclosures of failures to reach intended outcomes, tied to recommendations for improved performance based on research-based findings.

Accountability for the planned and unintended consequences of planning decisions is essential. Too often, planning initiatives are announced and implemented, privately evaluated by private consultants or university researchers, and then held publicly accountable only later, when media send investigative reporters to examine the true effects of the decisions made. Regular public accountings for the effects of policy decisions leading to completed projects ("post-occupancy analysis") are essential to build credibility for decisions that are made and carried out collaboratively.

Quantitative and qualitative metrics need to be defined collaboratively at the outset of racial and social justice initiatives. Too often metrics are set by statisticians who rely on readily quantifiable data without regard to the qualitative expectations of those affected by the initiatives. When working to reduce crime and increase the sense of safety in a Dorchester neighborhood, city policymakers initially considered reducing traditional crime statistics in the area: assaults, drug arrests, gun seizures, and the like. Asking residents what they would like to see happen to feel safer elicited surprising responses: fewer needles in parks where children played and better lighting near where drug dealers were known to ply their trade. The city addressed both factors, quantitative measures of criminality and qualitative measures that reflected residents' feeling about safety. Crime rates were reduced, and neighbors felt that the city was responsive to their specific concerns. This same approach of asking diverse groups "What, if it were to happen, would enable you to feel as though Boston was becoming more racially just?" could elicit some surprising information about how residents feel as well as how they might view sometimes meaningful but invisible statistical improvements.

Community building is imperative. The development and implementation of these new financing mechanisms would require open discussion, and inclusive visioning about how the city raises and spends its revenues. Who should convene these public/private sector conversations about achieving racial and social justice through targeted investments and cultural dialogues? In the 1980s an informal group known as The Vault, constituted of business and public sector leaders from banks, clergy, higher education, corporations, utilities, and foundations, met regularly to assist the city of Boston in raising and distributing financial resources into public and neighborhood improvement efforts. In some American cities, the Chamber of Commerce or Urban Land Institute plays this role, while in others a newly elected mayor or a specially convened and outside-facilitated visioning group takes on this challenge. Throughout, there is an important role to be played by legal scholars and faith leaders whose credibility in facilitating ethical dialogues is an essential component of having participants speak their truths. What matters is that otherwise disconnected stakeholders in the future of the region coordinate their material planning, resource generating, community supporting, and spiritual activities to directly address the roots, consequences, and solutions to overcome racism.

There is not a strong body of evidence about how our failed efforts have informed changes in policies to direct designers and planners on what might be done differently, or better. Few people know, a half century later, why large window panels fell out of the glamourous Hancock Building, creating dangerous conditions in Copley Square. As practitioners within the built environment, we have done an extraordinary job of keeping our secrets to ourselves, to the detriment of the profession and the public at large. Unlike the self-assessing mechanisms found in law and medicine (through readily available platforms such as the *Yale Law Journal* and the *New England Journal of Medicine*), there are few public policy publications that go beyond celebrations of partial successes or critiques of badly planned or executed urban initiatives.

If we, as the built environment profession, are to achieve the public respectability of other learned professions, we need to be open and transparent about our failures. Such openness can help cast a light on the guild-like secrecy of our work processes, and help draw diverse new community-based practitioners into the field. What is needed is a full assessment of what might be done differently with each public project, and then, a year or three years later, a further assessment could be performed to see whether these "postoccupancy analyses" led to real improvements in public policy. As academics and policymakers, we are very good at knowing what to do with input data about programs, and not so good at demonstrating how we use longitudinal outcome data to actually improve our policies and practices. As policymakers, we can do much better in this regard, starting with open admissions of where we have failed or could have done better, and with the application of appropriate correctives by policymakers where we have failed. This accountability could lead to the construction of fewer pollution-generating and business-killing highways through marginalized communities of color, and to greater environmental justice throughout Boston.

To address this issue, our metropolitan region could create a new public/private regional accountability mechanism to monitor progress toward racial and gender equity in the built environment and related fields. Members of such a group could include representatives of the Boston Mayor's Office, the BPDA, Massport, the MBTA, the Boston Municipal Research Bureau, and the attorney general, one each from a public and private university, the governor's office, Metropolitan Area Planning Council (MAPC), the Lawyers' Committee, the Boston Foundation, community-based environmental groups, and the Federal Reserve Bank. The group could meet three times a year to monitor data provided by funded universities and research centers, and could issue public reports on progress toward defined goals for increasing participation in key industries: real estate, higher education, cultural institutions, health care, finance and banking, hospitality, and municipal employment. Today, such data collection and analysis are disparate and sporadic. Yet if we were in a region comparable in size to New England (e.g., the states of Georgia or Washington), such data collection and analysis could be managed by a single state agency. Greater Boston, with a population roughly the size of Brooklyn, could get this work done effectively if we are willing to work together. Data collection and dissemination would be followed by the development of strategies to move an equity agenda forward, publicly and accountably. The time for such shared action has arrived.

GOALS FOR IMPROVING OUR BUILT ENVIRONMENT

The proposed built environment paradigm shifts here would entail:

- Raising awareness of the climate and biodiversity emergencies and the urgent need for action among clients, collaborators, and supply chains, and advocating for the rapid systemic changes required to address the climate and biodiversity crises, as well as the policies, funding priorities, and implementation frameworks that support these changes.

- Initiating public discourse on the desirability of introducing regional, metropolitan area *public service programs* that would bring together high school and college students in paid and academically credited internships focused on addressing built environment resilience. Such internships could be paid for out of developer and public contributions to a fund specifically focused on shared learning and action to address our environmental crisis and to provide initial training for entry into green jobs. A component of this work would involve education to address environmental injustices.
- Addressing the disproportionate impact of these crises on disadvantaged and marginalized communities, and ensuring that all mitigation and adaptation efforts address the needs of all people. Evolving policies of inclusivity need to employ fair labor practices so that people of all backgrounds can participate in decision making about the future of the designed environment.
- Including life-cycle costing, whole life carbon modeling, and postoccupancy evaluations as part of our basic scope of work, to reduce both embodied and operational resource use, and adopting regenerative design principles.
- Upgrading existing buildings within our region for extended use, as a less-carbon-intensive alternative to demolition and new construction whenever there is a viable choice. Such upgrading would include proactively educating the public on the real costs of retrofitting residences and businesses to make them more environmentally resilient.
- Advocating to our public officials for detailed disclosure of material provenance and environmental impacts by resource extractors, manufacturers, and distributors, to accelerate the shift to low-carbon, nontoxic, and ethically produced materials, and eliminating waste while supporting a rapid transition to circular economies.
- Investing in research and technology development into urban resilience, sustainability, and environmental justice, guided by systems thinking, to further these goals, and sharing across industry sectors the tools, data, and strategies being developed on an open-source basis; we have too many talented consulting firm and university researchers whose work is limited in distribution by client-proprietary restrictions.
- Establishing climate change mitigation, biodiversity protection, and positive social impacts as the key measures of the building sector's

success alongside existing financial measures; working to redirect the mentality of the building sector away from maximizing short-term financial and tax returns toward more durable investment for the long term; setting clearly articulated climate mitigation goals for every project and communicating those goals to our clients; and changing the structure of awards programs to make such criteria the basis for recognition in architecture and urban planning.

WHAT INNOVATIVE PILOTS LIE AHEAD IN NEW ENGLAND'S SOCIALLY JUST DESIGN FUTURE?

How do we achieve ambitious and racially equitable goals for Boston's four-hundredth anniversary? These aspirations require rethinking design processes from a policy, as well as a conceptual and a physical, perspective. As a public official and university professional, I have been troubled by how few good public design ideas have been translated into pragmatic long-term policies that address racial disparities in our region. I have observed that systemic cultural changes in racial attitudes instead take place incrementally, and that what incentivizes changes are crises such as COVID-19 or natural disasters, or the implementation of successful pilot initiatives such as infant mortality programs.

Disparities in access to health care (e.g., AIDS, maternal health, or cancer screening), education, adequate affordable housing, sufficient food in poor and communities of color, small businesses financing, childcare availability, female employment, crisis preparedness and community resilience, access to technology, and infrastructure investment are extensively documented by universities and foundations, and brought to the clear attention of policymakers through local media. Yet despite such documentation, focused actions to address these disparities tends to be sporadic and unsustained. Planned pilot interventions and long-term accountability are required to bring about change in these racial equity parameters.

As planners, we know how to implement pilots, and this chapter calls for specific steps to begin this process. New England is undergoing a fundamentally transformative shift in our demographics as the area become more diverse, the economic bases supporting our economy have changed, and planners are positioned to reshape our cultural environment. There must be a desire to change toward integrating diversity into our vision for achieving an environmentally just region, incentives to invest in change, a willingness to be honest in self-evaluation, greater receptivity to new arrivals and inclusivity, a shared vision for our future, and honesty about how our past has shaped racial attitudes today. It is time to embrace and move beyond data analysis, academic discourse, and citations of disparities to implement compelling pilot programs and accountable actions that produce measurable transformations in Boston's racial culture. *Enough is enough!*

NOTES

1. METCO is the voluntary school integration program in Boston. It has grown to become the nation's largest voluntary school desegregation program. Each year, the state of Massachusetts provides the funding for approximately three thousand Boston students from racially segregated neighborhoods to enroll in suburban schools that are racially segregated.
2. Beth Simone Noveck, Solving Public Problems: A Practical Guide to Change our Government and Fix Our World (New Haven, CT: Yale, 2021).
3. Erica Chenoweth, *Why Civil Resistance Works* (New York: Columbia University Press, 2011).
4. Susan S. Fainstein, *The Just City* (Ithaca, NY: Cornell University Press, 2010).
5. System justification theory attempts to explain why members of disadvantaged groups may become accepting of their disadvantaged position.
6. Jennie C. Stephens's *Diversifying Power: Why We Need Antiracist, Feminist Leadership on Climate and Energy* (Washington, D.C.: Island Press, 2020).
7. Kendall A. Nicholson, Where Are My People? Black in Architecture (Association of Collegiate Schools of Architecture, August 2020), https://www.acsa-arch.org/resource/where-are-my-people-black-in-architecture/.

ARTS

CHAPTER NINE

EMBRACING ARTISTS AT EVERY TURN

KATE GILBERT

Boston is at a cultural crossroads, one that can solidify our status as a global city where we acknowledge our colonial past, honor our citizens' racial and cultural diversity, and project new ways of equitable living in the twenty-first century—but only if we embrace bold temporary public art made by artists as diverse as our citizens. As new buildings appear on Boston's skyline and edge our main streets at an alarming pace, attention centers on traffic impacts, the rising cost of living, gentrification, and, occasionally, climate change resiliency. Yet, we miss a critical component of our city and citizens' well-being: the human connection, wonder, and innovative thinking that arises from bold contemporary art. *If we are to become the global, dynamic city our leaders have purported, we need artwork that challenges our biases and reflects a diversity of opinions and cultures.*

Art, design, and policy leaders must fight against the homogenized and formulaic city planning that relies on data and market forecasts alone. Like Assembly Square in Somerville or the Seaport in Boston's Waterfront, these districts look as if plucked from an urban planning catalog. Overly contrived, they leave no place for complexity, independent thought, or choice. Practicing human-centered design, a problem-solving technique that centers people in the development process, values our citizens' needs and opinions, adapts to what is important to them, and envisions a Boston that respects all cultures, races, ethnicities, and sexual orientations takes time and resources. Luckily, there are willing practitioners in a parallel field that can inform the practice: artists.

Contemporary art bucks trends, celebrates ambiguity, questions our current reality, and puts humans at the center of experiences and decision making. Once imbued in our spaces, art and the spirit of its creators can infiltrate our minds and conversations, opening new vistas and possibilities. It is not until we focus on the aesthetic quality of life as an integral part of the lived experience that we can, and will, unlock Boston's potential: to become a public art city.

PUBLIC ART: EVERYONE HAS SOME

Travel to a major city across the globe, and you're bound to be met by art in the public realm that defines, and sometimes challenges, that city's culture. Be it the plaza-scale sculptures of Chicago, the street art of Buenos Aires, or social practice works inviting social exchange like Rick Rowe's *Project Row Houses* in Houston that emphasize cultural identity's impact on the urban landscape. Visit any one of the top ten most populous U.S. cities, and you'll find public artworks created by an endowed public art program run by a municipal group and fueled by a percent-for-art development program. Phoenix, which recently knocked Boston from the top ten list, boasts over

FIGURE 9.1. Janet Echelman's *As If It Were Already Here* suspended over the Rose Kennedy Greenway, Boston, May–October 2015. Commissioned by the Rose Kennedy Greenway Conservancy. Image © Melissa Henry courtesy Studio Echelman.

two hundred permanent works created since the Phoenix Office of Arts and Culture was established in 1985. Phoenix's collection includes a piece by Boston-area artist Janet Echelman, who still does not have a permanent artwork in her hometown despite her temporary ethereal work *As If It Were Already Here,* commissioned by the Greenway Conservancy in 2015.

Philadelphia pioneered the Percent for Art model requiring the inclusion of site-specific public art in new construction or major renovation projects when its Redevelopment Authority and Office of Arts, Culture and the Creative Economy were established in 1959. Since then, many development-catalyzed percent-for-art projects across the United States have become safe, meaning they've been proven or created in another city.[1] Characterized by swoops of polished steel exploding from the sky and often reminiscent of a flame or growing plant, these heroic gestures and feats of engineering popular in the late twenty-first century have already begun dating themselves. To be fair to the artists who have created tepid permanent works across the country, they often respond to archaic or unimaginative processes created by municipal groups afraid to rock the boat. Jurors who approve permanent commissions also add another level of unpredictability if they are not well-researched in the artwork's topic and site or are fearful of participating in constructive debate.[2]

Boston might be a lucky outlier. We do not have a development-funded percent-for-art program that could have littered the city with these "forever" testaments to artists' love of mark making or risk-intolerant jurors. (In 2017, then mayor Marty Walsh created Boston's Percent for Art program, devoting 1 percent of the city's annual capital budget toward embedding public art in municipal projects. A few excellent permanent projects by local artists have resulted, such as Napoleon Jones Henderson's *Roxbury Rhapsody* in the Bruce C. Bolling Municipal. The program pales in comparison to what it could be with 1 percent coming from new, private construction.)

Too often, permanent works that pay tribute to women, or LGTQIA+, Black, Indigenous, and communities of color—those that can offset the "stale and male" statues or "swoopy abstractions"—take the longest to be funded and created. Boston has some memorials that buck the tepid trend but took too long and significant political capital to realize. The *Puerto Rican Veterans Memorial* by Bob Shure, erected in 2013 in the South End, is the first U.S. monument to Puerto Rican veterans. It portrays a male in army combat uniform and a female in desert camouflage. It took Vietnam War veterans Tony Molina and Jaime Rodriguez, who first received permission from the City of

Boston to install a plaque honoring the 65th Regiment, over fourteen years to raise the necessary $400,000 and civic support to create the work.

Similarly, the *Boston Women's Memorial* on Commonwealth Avenue Mall by Meredith Bergmann honoring three noteworthy writers and contributors to social change in Boston—Abigail Adams, Lucy Stone, and Phillis Wheatley—took decades to conceptualize, fundraise for, and execute. The figures stand on the ground, not on pedestals as most monuments do, encouraging relatable humanness.

Were it not for the City of Boston leadership, members of the Frederick Douglass Sculpture Committee Community might still be fundraising for a figurative work of Douglass pointing forward from atop a stack of books. The monument to the great abolitionist and statesman with Boston ties was designed by California sculptor Mario Chiodo after drawings by celebrated local artist Paul Goodnight. They first presented their design to the Boston Art Commission in February 2009, and at the time of this writing, their GoFundMe page has raised $3,825. Between 2021 and 2022, former mayors Marty Walsh and Kim Janey contributed a combined $950,000, and the work is currently in fabrication.

The inverse occurs with permanent art projects commissioned by bottom-line-oriented developers on private property that move at warp speed. They can, and mostly do, sidestep community processes—not because they wish to install controversial works but because process equals time equals expense. The result is artwork devoid of context. At their best, they are selfie moments. At their worst, they are insensitive expressions that fight with their surroundings or unintentionally harm local heritage. As noted, money is also a critical factor in how quickly a piece of permanent public art is commissioned and installed. Well-intentioned citizens with influence can do significant damage in their benevolent rush to have one of their heroes memorialized or, more self-serving, exhibit one of their collected artists for market gain.

According to Cher Krause Knight's definition of "public art" in the 2014 *Oxford Encyclopedia of Aesthetics,* public art in its earliest form was the "human desire to translate ideas into tangible forms and share these with an audience larger than one's own immediate circle, with the hopes of satisfying aesthetic needs, instilling morals, teaching lessons, codifying history, swaying opinions, or securing allegiance."[3] It is therefore understandable given the near-propagandistic legacy of public art that "let us not offend" seems to be the motto of commissioners of permanent works. And with the complicated but necessary public process involved in permanent works, too often a work's radical, provocative statement or intentional ambiguity is smoothed over and, in the end, lacks teeth. It becomes that poorly defined "meh" art you walk by and never think twice about.

Be it by patrons, foundations, municipal programs, concerned citizens, or developers, Boston's visual identity is being shaped right now. These are the leaders who are making aesthetic decisions that are often uninformed by contemporary art knowledge. This same process also sets an unfortunate precedent for how we operate as a public. Too few examples of stunning projects, combined with an absence of developments that lack adequate public input, leave citizens defensive, dismissive, or skeptical of contemporary art, new ideas, and any kind of public process.

Creating temporary, contemporary public art that balances artistic risk taking with genuine community engagement, inclusive of diverse points of view, is not only an innovative way to increase a city's livability but also, taken one step further, it is a new form of activism, a way of practicing democracy in a time when we need to come together. It can help visualize our differences, make an "other" more approachable, pay reparations, and chart a new path forward as an open, unified Boston. As critic Patricia Phillips contends, art has the ability to interrogate notions of the "public" and encourage productive friction.[4]

THE CASE FOR TEMPORARY ART

Temporary public art—be it a sculpture, projection, mural, choreographed performance, facilitated conversation, or architectural intervention that lives in the public realm from a few days to a few years—can prove a model for shifting a city stuck in a closed, parochial, and racist mindset. The sheer promise that a temporary artwork will eventually "go away" lessens the content's scrutiny (though temporary works often require as much structural and material review and funding as permanent ones). But the temporality allows those in charge of permissions, from property owners to permitting officials, to move more quickly into the artist's "give it a try" mentality. They often become collaborators, advisers, and advocates with a vested interest in the artwork's success. As Phillips asserts, *temporary* "is not about an absence of commitment or involvement but about an intensification and enrichment of the conception of public."[5]

Once installed, temporary public art is an effective Trojan horse for broaching difficult conversations, inviting innovative thinking, and fostering a sense of possibility. With it, we create more opportunities and a platform for voices and a multiplicity of opinions not usually heard, especially those of Black, Indigenous, and artists of color who do not see themselves reflected in Boston's permanent public art collection. With temporary art, we can invite opinions we might disagree with but be comfortable exploring for a little while. Like the way we might rent a different movie genre one night just to "try something new" but return the following evening to our serial drama. It allows us to observe our complex reality beyond the oversimplified binaries that give us comfort as humans.

Commissioning more temporary public art instead of permanent pieces also lowers the barriers to entry, providing previously inaccessible opportunities for creatives from historically marginalized communities who have rich lived experiences to draw from but may not have had the skill building of their wealthy peers who attended art and architecture schools. When we create wildly imaginative, show-stopping temporary works of art in Boston that promote racial justice and fairness, we lead the way to more equitable and beautiful communities and perhaps even model new forms of democracy. Before building this utopic public art city, we must take a hard look at where we are now and how we got here.

BOSTON IS CLOSED

Boston is a closed city steeped in a celebrated colonial past. We are rich in innovative technologies but closed to experiencing novel cultural experiences and adverse to public expressions of joy—except when tied to a winning sports team. It is perplexing how our progressive sociopolitical values,—such as those that led Massachusetts to be the first state to legalize same-sex marriage in 2003—don't extend to experiences in the public realm. Unlike our Canadian cousins, we go inside during the winter. No carnivals or firepits to warm us. And in nicer weather, we flee to seaside retreats. We're emotionally reserved and seem to have perpetuated Puritan values when it comes to being fraternal in public spaces.

To wit, prepandemic Boston hosted over thirty parades in 2019, and, arguably, only two were inclusive. There were eleven religious processions for Catholic saints, seven celebrations of a nationality or culture (e.g., Haitian, Greek), five events recognizing a city or U.S. holiday (e.g., Independence

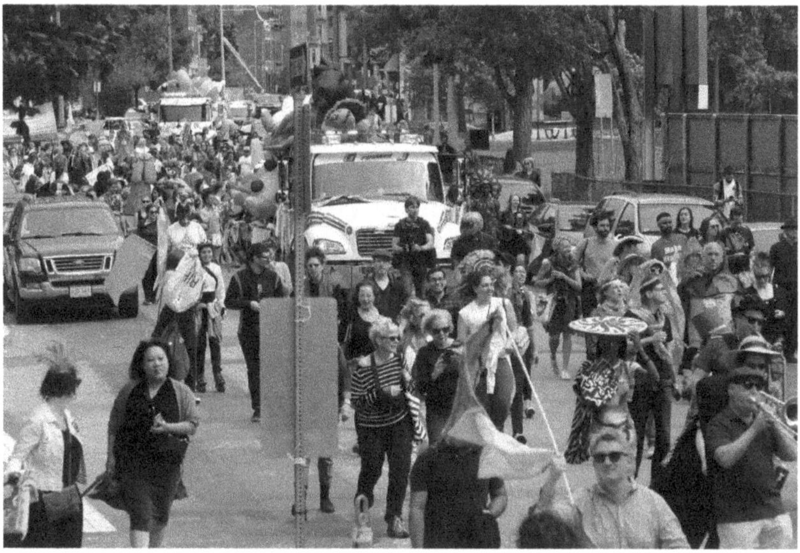

FIGURE 9.2. Nick Cave's "Joy Parade." Image courtesy of Dominic Chavez.

Day, Bunker Hill Day), four neighborhood-specific celebrations (e.g., Roxbury, Dorchester), one procession for LGBTQ pride, and one led by an artist, Nick Cave. Cave's "Joy Parade," produced by Now + There, an organization curating temporary and site-specific artwork in Boston, invited anyone, regardless of religion, zip code, or sexual orientation, to answer Cave's prompt, "What brings you joy?"

Add all this to Boston's historic, though slowing-changing, lack of substantial financial support for visual culture, and you have an inhospitable environment for creative thinking and cultural transformation. Despite the Commonwealth climbing to ninth in the nation in per capita arts spending, at $3.10 in 2022, we do not invest in cultural creators.[6] The exorbitant cost of living in Boston, coupled with a lack of venues for artists to showcase and practice their craft, makes Boston one of the least nurturing progressive cities for artists to thrive. While we foster some of the brightest and most empathetic young artists in our art and design colleges—like MassArt, the nation's only publicly funded independent art school—these culture shifters rarely stay in Boston. On the flip side, the global talent that flocked to our technology start-ups over the last two decades and who can afford to call Boston their home seek counterparts in the arts. They ask why their fields' vibrant, innovative creativity isn't matched by more daring visual arenas.

Dare we tell them authentic creative art exchange was last experienced at Mrs. Gardner's famed salons at the turn of the nineteenth century in her Fenway Court, now the Isabella Stewart Gardner Museum?

YES TO START-UPS—BUT NOT THE MESSY CULTURAL ONES

Boston was built and is sustained by staid, cautious habits that value measurable progress, conservative risk mitigation, and iterating on what is known and tested. It's why, as a population, we visit and invest in the venerable Museum of Fine Arts, Boston (MFA). Over 1.3 million people visited the MFA in 2019, which boasts an endowment of $605 million. In the same year, the Boston Symphony Orchestra, a bastion of orchestral heritage and experimentation since 1881, listed a $456 million endowment. Compare this to Boston Art and Music Soul (BAMS) Fest, a creative incubator and presenting nonprofit that breaks down racial and social barriers to the arts through an annual festival. In June 2022, BAMS Fest, with a 2019 revenue of $170,000 and no endowment, featured nineteen Afro-centric and Black artists on two stages with live mural arts at a free music festival. Over ten thousand predominately Black and brown Bostonians took up space and suggested how our historic Olmstead-designed Franklin Park could

FIGURE 9.3. A woman standing outside a beauty parlor waves to the participants in Nick Cave's "Joy Parade" as it moves from the South End to Upham's Corner on September 14, 2019. Commissioned by Now + There. Image © Faith Ninivaggi.

be reimagined as a site for "cultural movement on the front lines of racial equity, creative freedom and economic empowerment for Black creative entrepreneurs," as their mission suggests.[7]

If we keep investing in what is known or only take cautious steps to question and ultimately dismantle our history, we continue to underwrite our current closed culture. The result: more progressive minds will leave Boston for more attractive places. BAMS Fest will become yet another "remember when" example, like the Reclamation Artists or the Revolving Museum, two unconventional artist-led approaches to infusing artistic experiences in neglected areas of the city. The message to artists and culture entrepreneurs: we invest in technology and pharma start-ups but not in cultural start-ups. *The very habits of artists to live in ambiguity, take risks, question the status quo, and reflect back nuances of our lives are the characteristics we mine in business leaders but fail to support in cultural entrepreneurs.*

WE'VE DONE IT BEFORE

But we do know how to dream big and break patterns. And some once-concepts are now institutions. The move of the Institute of Contemporary Art (ICA), Boston, from a converted firehouse on Boylston Street to the Seaport in 2006 signified a radical move from exhibiting to collecting contemporary art. Already, the gender equality in the museum's collection far exceeds the MFA Boston's ratio. With an incredible fundraising effort and a motivated board behind executive director Jill Medvedow's vision, the ICA pioneered Boston's Seaport District. Today, it acts as a cultural anchor in this now-developed neighborhood. And their what-if growth mindset propelled them across Boston Harbor to a temporary outpost, the Watershed, in East Boston, offering art access in a predominately Latinx community where some resident's median income is only $15,757, or 18.4 percent of the Massachusetts median.[8]

The Big Dig, the decades-long project that replaced the hulking steel of the elevated I-93 that cut through downtown Boston with an underground highway, is an example of massive interdisciplinary urban transformation that was also born of necessity. Begun as a way to alleviate traffic congestion, the Central Artery/Tunnel Project completed in 2008 catalyzed a 1.5-mile park, the Rose Kennedy Greenway, investments in greater walkability, and connection to the Boston Harbor. It spurred street-level development that knits the harbor and the land back together. The Greenway Conservancy, the steward of the Greenway since 2013, has exhibited over fifty temporary and often participatory public art installations that shift narratives about public space. Today, Bostonians under sixteen years of age don't remember the days of navigating bumper-to-bumper traffic or the shadows and noise under the elevated highway. What similar darker underbellies of Boston's landscape and culture can we hope Bostonians two decades from now don't remember?

TODAY'S IMPETUS: INEQUITY

Amid a global pandemic caused by COVID-19, the wake of 2020's great cultural reckoning that resulted from George Floyd's murder and ensuing calls to address our culture of white supremacy, we have another opportunity to take a giant artistic leap. We must ask ourselves (and be ready for the answers): Whose culture are we preserving in our architecture, urban planning, museums, and public art? What is publicness in the twenty-first century? What are we doing to recognize, admit to, reckon with, and ultimately move beyond our colonial past? Simply put, how we present ourselves in visual culture has a profound impact on how we see ourselves.

Today, critics and artists alike are looking to protests, demonstrations, and local aid social services such as Boston Community Fridge at 672 Center Street in Jamaica Plain or Free the Vaccine for COVID-19, co-led led by the Center for Artistic Activism. Conversations about social and economic disparities are being aired in the most egalitarian locations—on our sidewalks and on the Internet. This form of art, socially engaged art, is akin to human-centered design. It builds on "new genre public art" as defined by Suzanne Lacy in the 1990s, which included "formerly marginalized populations and addressed matters of race, ethnicity, class, gender, and sexual orientation as well as the power structures attendant to them."[9]

Imagine if we harnessed that human desire to survive and support one another on a larger scale without bureaucratic planning processes. What would happen if we invited more public participation, processionals, picnics, and social gatherings led by artists in our streets, plazas, and roadways with more frequency and intention? It might make us question who is (still) in charge.

DISMANTLING THE SYSTEM AND A FEW ARTWORKS ALONG THE WAY

As we carefully choose the kinds of public art we commission in the future, we must also turn an eye to the works we continue to invest tax-payer money in cleaning and preserving. Nationally, the prevailing conversation about public art centers on removing permanent works that celebrate figures who've sown division and hatred, perpetuated slavery, and profited from the knowing destruction of people and lands. Much like how the victors write history, public art, especially permanent works, has historically been commissioned by those with wealth or power. And the #TakeDown movement isn't just affecting Southern U.S. cities.

Boston-area artist Hilary Zelson's *Bronze History Today* multimedia project of 2015 quantified our permanent bronze statues and their overwhelming lack of racial and sexual diversity. Men created 65 percent of Boston's artworks. Only one woman of color is listed as a sculptor. And the subjects of our bronzes? Men. Sixty-four percent of the subjects. So, yes, we are a city visually defined by dead white guys on horses. From these examples, we must ask and grapple with the questions: Whose culture are we preserving in the permanent works we display in Boston? Who are we unknowingly triggering with figures that represent oppression or disempowerment?

While we wait for more permanent works honoring Boston's Black, Indigenous, and people of color, what should we do with the blatant displays of racism and xenophobia still looming over us in our public statuary? Local artist Tory Bullock was successful in calling for the removal of the Emancipation Memorial near the Park Plaza installed in 1879. The work, a copy of the original by Thomas Ball in Washington, D.C., shows a newly freed enslaved person kneeling at Abraham Lincoln's feet. The shirtless man stays fixed on his knees forever, never fully realizing his freedom. Bullock gathered over 12,750 signatures calling for the work's removal and sparking a citywide conversation on race and identity in public art. The Boston Arts Commission removed the work on December 29, 2020, and today there's a call for temporary responses to sit atop the plinth where Lincoln once stood. This is a strong example of the power of temporary art to allow a diversity of responses to a conversation with no neat ending.

One individual, or a group of citizens, decided not to wait for a public process to remove another problematic figure in Boston's landscape. On the evening of June 9, 2020, the often-vandalized statue of Christopher Columbus in the North End Waterfront Park was beheaded. It was deemed too brittle for repair and permanently removed. This statue, installed during the bicentennial and never officially permitted or approved by the City of Boston, represents a symbol of cultural pride for some Italian Americans. For others, especially Indigenous Peoples, Columbus's figure triggers memories of oppressive and violent acts against their people and their land. What will replace the statue, if anything, is up for debate between whatever concerned citizens participate in city-sponsored conversations.

Too often, however, there is a lack of participation due to apathy. On February 28, 2020, a *Boston Globe* headline declared, "Boston Was Robbed of a Slave Monument," referencing Steve Locke's *Auction Block Memorial.* Locke's piece, developed within a city of Boston arts program, was an elegant yet hard-to-ignore proposal for a public memorial to those Africans whose trafficking and sale financed the building of Faneuil Hall. The proposal was for a roughly ten-by-sixteen-foot bronze plaque embedded in the ground and comprised of two rectangles—a smaller one representing the site of the auctioneer and a larger area for those being sold into slavery. It was to be warmed to a human body's temperature, 98 degrees Fahrenheit. It would have been the public's choice to step on, or over, the memorial to the brutal, inhumane industry of chattel slavery. Locke's concept, developed during a program with the city of Boston's Mayor's Office of Arts and Culture with City support, was criticized by the NAACP's local chapter, which was calling on the Mayor's Office to remove Faneuil's name from the hall. Sadly, the NAACP and Locke's similar priorities to publicly name the horrors of slavery could not be reconciled. With little public knowledge of the proposal and an administration held over the proverbial barrel, Locke withdrew his submission before a community process began. Imagine what allies could have rallied to speak with the NAACP, whisper in the mayor's ear, or publicly demand to learn more about the project if our city understood and appreciated contemporary art? What pain could Locke have been spared if Bostonians had been exposed much earlier to adventurous and provocative temporary public art?

One artist cannot lead a cultural shift. Nor can one vandal or one petition create a public art city. If we're to take bold steps in diversifying both who makes works of public art and the people or issues they represent, we must continue to hold accountable who curates, approves, and participates in the creation of works. And it's not just "those bureaucrats." It's all of us as citizens.

WHEN TEMPORARY LEADS TO . . .

Temporary public art quietly yet powerfully asks us to make individual choices or actions that affect the whole, as did Paul Ramirez Jonas's *Public Trust,* commissioned by Now + There, from August through September 2016. For twenty-one days during the 2016 presidential election, this free interactive traveling artwork asked Bostonians to consider the meaning of a promise in three different locations (Dudley, Kendall, and Copley Squares), ensuring a diversity of responses and the creation of social space through participation.

Using Ramirez Jonas's performance score, thirteen local artist ambassadors empathetically listened to 956 Bostonians, collected their promises at a custom "Promise Table," and together created a contract, an artwork, that participants kept after performing a ceremonial oath. The participant's promise (e.g., "I promise to be a better mom") then took center stage for five to fifteen minutes at a time on a sixteen-foot portable marquee, surrounded by promissory statements taken that day from headline news to provide context (e.g., "Volkswagen Promises an Electric Car," "Clinton Promises Immigration Reform," "Storms Tomorrow").

Regardless of age, status, or race, Greater Boston residents and tourists alike added to *Public Trust,* and their covenants live on in a book. Today, Now + There still hears from participants about promises kept—one man recently published his novel—and from the companies and political figures who added context (Volkswagen did produce an electric car, but Clinton never had her chance). More important than the promises kept was the collective questioning of our promises' integrity and an investigation into the potent speech act that holds a society together.

A final example of change sparked by a temporary Now + There project is Liz Glynn's *Open House,* installed from July through October 2018 at the end of Commonwealth Avenue Mall in Boston's Kenmore Square. Cut off from the more beautiful and statued side of the mall and Olmstead's Charlesgate Park by the Bowker Overpass, the mall's last parcel was the ideal spot to test functional art and plant a seed for future development. For three months, students, tourists, residents, and even the area's transient population coexisted within the tableau of a Louis XIV ballroom Glynn constructed from twenty-six pieces of cast concrete based on a ballroom designed by Stanford White.

The work created a backdrop for performances, grounding for a weekly meditation group, a visual punch for a housing protest, and a safe space for gathering, even deterring drug trafficking for its duration. But perhaps its two most lasting impacts were suggesting to future designers how the mall could be reimagined and bolstering the young nonprofit Charlesgate Alliance's mission to knit Charlesgate back together. In March 2022, the alliance was awarded a significant grant from the Commonwealth for engineering to remove two obstructing walls that bifurcate Olmstead's original design for the Emerald Necklace.

The more we involve the public in activating works of art, as *Public Trust* and *Open House* did, the more people feel connected to a larger public, and the more invested they become in challenging dominant narratives of a place. To that end, it is imperative that commissioners of temporary public artworks convey the duration of their projects as broadly as possible at both ends of the project's lifespan. The public often falls in love with art, especially when it represents their values or culture, and can be angered when it is removed without warning.

FIGURE 9.4. Liz Glynn's *Open House* in Kenmore Square, Boston, July–October 2018. Organized for Boston by Now + There. Originally commissioned by the Public Art Fund in cooperation with the artist and Paula Cooper Gallery, first presented at Doris C. Freedman Plaza in Central Park, New York. Image © Ryan C. McMahon.

Such was the case with the removal of *Roxbury Love*, Ricardo "Deme5" Gomez and Thomas "Kwest" Burns's temporary mural of 2014 depicting Nelson Mandela and the titular phrase that became a symbol of Black pride and Roxbury. On July 23, 2020, during the heat of the Black Lives Matter movement, the mural was demolished without warning by the Black-owned, Roxbury-based Cruz Companies who initially commissioned the project with the intent to replicate it, permanently, as part of their mixed-use development. Thinking they were doing right by their community by offering affordable housing, they found themselves portrayed in the news as the gentrifiers. While the mural is missed, the conversation about the permanency of art, which continued in news outlets and social media feeds throughout the summer of 2020, was arguably even more provocative, allowing Bostonians to air complex and independent thoughts. When temporary public art stirs up healthy debate, John Dewey's principles of "culture as an agent of self-realization and positive social change" are put into practice. A public is created.[10]

CHANGE STARTS WITH US

Public art, at its best and worst, is a form of practicing democracy. An artist has an idea. They test it with a commissioning agency. An engineer suggests changes. The fire department has questions. Hopefully, a funder supports it. Feedback sessions refine it. And, ultimately, the public defines it. A public art city where people and ideas freely circulate is not far off for Boston. We can encounter art—and one another—in active and inclusive shared spaces despite a globally isolating pandemic. When Boston is declared a public art city, we will embrace new forms of temporary and permanent public art that spark civic dialogue and inspire a shared sense of belonging. *The Embrace*—placed in a prominent location on the Boston Common honoring the life and legacy of Dr. Martin Luther King, Jr. and Coretta Scott King—was unveiled to great fanfare in early 2023 and moves us in the right direction (see chapter 7). The outcome: more artworks that challenge us to honor our diversity and wrestle with the complexities of Boston's public narratives, begetting more open minds, conversations, and spaces.

NOTES

1. "Percent for Art," City of Philadelphia Office of Arts, Culture and the Creative Economy, accessed April 4, 2023, https://www.creativephl.org/public-art/percent-for-art/#:~:text=The%20ground-breaking%20Percent%20for,art%20in%20the%20public%20landscape.
2. Mary Tinti, "Poll the Jury," in *A Companion to Public Art*, ed. Cher Krause Knight and Harriet F. Senie (Hoboken: John Wiley & Sons, 2016), 300–301.
3. Cher Krause Knight, "Public Art," in *Oxford Encyclopedia of Aesthetics*, 3rd ed., ed. Michael Kelly (Oxford: Oxford University Press, 2014), 212–16.
4. Patricia C. Phillips, "Temporality and Public Art," in *Critial Issues in Public Art: Content, Context, and Controversy*, ed. Harriet F. Senie and Sally Webster (Washington, D.C.: Smithsonian Institution, 1998), 295–304.
5. Phillips, "Temporality and Public Art," 304.
6. "Public Funding for the Arts Is Up" Axios, last modified March 15, 2022, https://www.axios.com/2022/03/17/public-funding-for-the-arts-is-up.
7. BAMS Fest mission, last modified June 16, 2022, https://www.bamsfest.org/whoweare.
8. The Environmental Justice Map Viewer is an interactive map that displays the 2020 environmental justice block groups, based upon three demographic criteria developed by the state's Executive Office of Energy and Environmental Affairs, available at https://mass-eoeea.maps.arcgis.com/apps/webappviewer/index.html?id=1d6f63e7762a48e5930de84ed4849212.
9. Knight, "Public Art," 314.
10. Mary Jane Jacob, "Audiences Are People Too," in *A Companion to Public Art*, ed. Cher Krause Knight and Harriet F. Senie (Hoboken: John Wiley & Sons, 2016), 252–53.

HEALTH

CHAPTER TEN

PUBLIC HEALTH

Planning to Reduce Traffic-Related Air Pollution in Boston Chinatown

A CONVERSATION BETWEEN DOUG BRUGGE, DAVID GAMBLE, LYDIA LOWE, MARIA PILAR BOTANA MARTINEZ, MARTHA ONDRAS, AND JEANETTE PANTOJA

This conversation brings together individuals interested in planning, air pollution, and Boston's Chinatown. Several of them have worked in the Community Assessment of Freeway Exposure and Health (CAFEH) studies of air pollution. Over many years the CAFEH research evolved from studying the problem of traffic-related air pollution to trying to do something to reduce exposure and risk. In this conversation the emphasis is on recent efforts to interject air pollution health concerns into community-led planning for development.

DG (DAVID GAMBLE): This book is a collection of conversations about ways in which the city of Boston, and the region in which it resides, could be improved in the future. Inspiration came out of some research I was doing a number of years ago about what makes cities unique and what projects, policies, and plans can be most transformative. Many of our problems are interrelated, so an underlying ambition about the book is really highlighting the interdisciplinary challenges of urban transformation. The chapters and conversations talk to one another.

We have concurrent crises, as you well know, and although public health wasn't previously in the forefront of most people's minds, with a global pandemic it certainly has become the most important. I knew Pilar previously from my architecture circles, and learned that she was looking at the intersection of public health and our physical environment, the buildings and spaces we inhabit. We thought about bringing together a number of people that are working in this domain and just having an open-ended conversation. I'd love if maybe each of you could just say a few words about your backgrounds and we could start.

PB (MARIA PILAR BOTANA MARTINEZ): David and I had a conversation about how necessary it is to incorporate a public health lens when talking about the future of cities, as the topics discussed in this book impact health, and public health was not part of the design conversation before the COVID-19 pandemic hit us. I am a PhD student in the [BU] School of Public Health, in the department of Environmental Health, and before starting this program, I worked in the field of architecture and urban planning for eighteen years. I came to public health because I wanted to understand how cities and buildings impact health. Buildings, parks, green and blue spaces, water, soil, air and noise pollution are present in cities and shape our health in different ways, and the level of research required to study those was not possible while working as a designer. Urban design and public health walk hand in hand, and everybody in this conversation we are having today believes so and does work in the Boston area that promotes better health outcomes through research and urban interventions. When brainstorming about who to join us, we first thought of bringing experts from different public health fields, like air quality, noise, climate change, et cetera, but struggled to find a cohesive theme. Rather, we decided to bring a group of researchers that have been working together toward the same goal. I thought about the work that the CAFEH team is doing focusing on ultrafine particles, that is being tackled through scientific research, advocacy, and planning.[1] So I'll now pass it to Martha Ondras, who inspired me to move into public health from a career in architecture.

MO (MARTHA ONDRAS): Thank you, Pilar. It's always interesting to hear what you're thinking. I have a long perspective on public health and urban design. Like Pilar, I've had a career as an architect and urban planner and then went into environmental health. Public health, I believe, is an extension of that. I have a masters from Tufts; I'm not going the PhD route. I'm not that brave. But I think there's a tremendous gap in architecture in terms of considering public health in a systematic way; it gets considered in an anecdotal way, and it needs to be more fully integrated in what we do.

I look at several points of contact. There's the built environment: what happens in buildings in terms of indoor air quality, design of buildings to encourage community and accessibility. I look at infrastructure, transportation, and mobility, access of communities to jobs and services and the wider region as a very important area of research. And I look at how neighborhood covariates affect the health of groups and individuals: walkability, green space, urban density, and noise. All of these things are very important aspects of public health, obviously access to health care and services as well, and agency, the ability to have a voice in what happens to your environment. So probably my first experience in this was working with people like Mel King in pre–Central Artery. Stopping the artery that was going to go through the heart of the city, and developing the Southwest Corridor and other areas of the city to be more of a community space.[2] That was a tremendous lesson in leadership and community engagement and how they affect the health of neighborhoods. One big unsolved issue is gentrification and affordability of the city, and I'd like to see more work in that area. Again, it's all very intersectional, and has to be done in concert with resilient climate adaptation.

LL (LYDIA LOWE): Hey everyone, I'm Lydia, and I'm actually a long-time community organizer who's the executive director of a community land trust in Chinatown. I'm interested in this conversation because all too often these (interdisciplinary) conversations are happening without much overlap. Everything is interconnected, and when we think about what we want for a healthy stable community, all of those aspects come into play. I'm happy to be a part of this conversation.

JP (JEANETTE PANTOJA): My background is mostly in housing and environmental justice advocacy work. I grew up and before grad school used to live in the Salinas Valley of California. Wonderful air quality . . . but we have a lot of issues related to poor drinking water quality, a lack of adequate wastewater infrastructure, substandard housing, and it's a predominantly farm worker and agricultural occupation–related population. And I was a student of David's at the GSD, and since then I'm kind of still working in that space. A lot of my work is related to housing and environmental health, but I would say that our work at MAPC (Metropolitan Area Planning Council), the public health department, is very intersectional.[3]

DB (DOUG BRUGGE): I guess that I'm sort of the person who's more narrowly focused at this point in my career. I have a PhD in biology, and a history of being more of an activist and politically active when I was younger, but the last twenty-seven years I've been an academic. First at Tufts University, and now more recently at the University of Connecticut. What I've tried to do is be an academic who engages with community partners around real-world issues. My focus has been environmental health because that's the one that made the most sense given my expertise and where I was starting from, and the deeper you go into it, the more you're locked into that frame of reference. So, as Pilar mentioned, I've played a leading role in the CAFEH studies, which have been a series of NIH grants and other funding, such as the Kresge Foundation, to do implementation work.[4]

I think it's both a strength and a weakness that research has to be very narrow and focused because that's the way it's framed, and I think there are technical limitations to doing so, especially NIH-funded research that's broad and holistic. But I would point, Lydia, to what you guys did on the R2A project with the health lens analysis, which Sharon at MAPC played a leading role in as well, where air pollution got integrated into the Chinatown master plan.[5] It didn't dominate it, it was just one piece among a lot of other issues. At many times that's what I say: I want traffic air pollution to be on the agenda, along with other issues that communities are concerned about. I think it's a little bit of a challenge because it's less tangible. You know, you can't see or smell it, and the health effects are incremental, and maybe years or even decades out, so it's a harder issue to make salient and tangible.

DG (DAVID GAMBLE): It would be great if we could talk specifically about the CAFEH's ambitions, and then how the issues that are raised in that research could be a model as the city continues to grow and change. Chinatown is one of those neighborhoods that is always under pressure from so many different directions. So, if one of you wants to talk about what that CAFEH endeavor meant, we can then try to speculate on how it might apply to issues in today's climate.

PB: Yes, Doug. It would be helpful to get some background on the work that CAFEH has been doing in Chinatown, what the different pieces of the CAFEH work are, and framing the public health concerns, scientific research, community engagement, intervention proposals, advocacy, and, most importantly, how it all started!

DB: CAFEH is a series of studies of traffic-related air pollution with a focus specifically on pollutants called ultrafine particles that are found in higher concentrations near highways and major roadways, such as those in and around Chinatown. These projects were conducted as community-based participatory research or community engaged research with community partners involved in all aspects of the research. Chinatown organizations have been partners in most of these projects. Initially, we were more focused on documenting air pollution near highways and its effects on health of near-highway residents, and increasingly we are looking at how we can mitigate those effects, reduce exposures, and show that reducing exposures has health benefits.

LL: I think over the past few years, because of Chinatown's involvement in the CAFEH project, we started to work with MAPC on a health lens analysis of Chinatown [which is a guided planning exercise that develops a new approach to address a problem], and as we thought of a health lens analysis, we thought of this as not one particular project but in terms of planning in general for Chinatown. The more we thought about the health lens, the more we realized that taking a health lens analysis was essentially looking at the community—you know, it encompassed everything, from an urban planning perspective and all those different boxes, whether you're talking about climate resiliency, whether you're talking about environmental justice, whether you're talking about housing, open space mobility, affordability, preservation, they're all connected. So, what happened was that through working on this health lens analysis it led to the development of a Chinatown master plan, which mirrored and ran parallel to the city of Boston's [neighborhood] PLAN: Downtown. And I think this process really showed me how important it is to think about the connections between public health. Of course, when we started it wasn't during the pandemic but it was when we ended.

The pandemic brought those public health issues even more to the forefront and made us realize how everything was connected to public health. So, when we looked at open space and mobility, clearly during the pandemic that's become so critical, that people have no open space to go outside their homes, and with everybody trapped inside their homes now, they really need that. And at the same time, whether you can enjoy that open space is related to many other issues around transportation and traffic, it's related to climate issues and heat islands, and the lack of greenery, and how we look at open space and how it gets used is really also related to gentrification and really figuring out how we create connections between the lower-income working-class residents that have always been in Chinatown, the immigrant working-class families, and the more upscale residents that are coming in. A healthy community is what everyone wants, and I just think that that framework is a very intersectional framework naturally. The interesting thing is an area that we actually did not intend to work on at all was the question of historic and cultural preservation, and yet through the dynamic discussion that happened, that emerged as a key strategy for Chinatown's resilience, and preservation, and future. So, it's kind of interesting how that evolved.

DG: So, the BPDA was running the downtown master plan, right? How did Chinatown as a sub-neighborhood nest in that border planning initiative?[6]

LL: Well, we actually did that very deliberately. Because the plan downtown did not actually include Chinatown, or it [only] included a section of it, we had begun advocating as a neighborhood because Chinatown had been the first neighborhood in Boston to have a neighborhood master plan in 1990. We felt that even though the community itself had been doing its own community planning, it was only somewhat effective because it wasn't officially recognized by the city. So, we began advocacy. We actually walked [then] Mayor Walsh through Chinatown, and ended the walk with asking to have a master plan, at which point he said, "Oh, we're doing this plan downtown, we'll roll you in," and we're kind of like "Is that a good thing or a bad thing?" But we discussed it within the Chinatown group and decided let's go for it, because we know it will really happen if we're part of "Plan Downtown," and we just need to be really organized around how we utilize that process.

So from the beginning, we organized ourselves, and by consensus we developed a slate of who we wanted from Chinatown to be part of "Plan Downtown," and all nominated ourselves together, got ourselves as a slate onto the "Plan Downtown" advisory committee, and really ran our process side by side in a way that utilized the information and discussions in "Plan Downtown," but gave detail, and it ended up being really successful, because in turn, we found out that it started drawing on some of the observation data and priorities that were coming out of our discussions. So, we found that that really worked out in a way that I think would not have happened through the "Plan Downtown" process itself, but because we from the community were really leading this parallel process, it worked. There are lessons there for participatory planning.

DB: I guess it is important to explain that the proposal that was funded included a health impact assessment, which requires an existing project proposal to assess.[7] We were at MAPC when this was discussed, and we soon realized that we had a problem because we were doing this both in

Somerville and in Chinatown, and in neither place was there a concrete target decision to make. It was much more of a formative, early stage process to think through ideas and develop them, and lead to a proposal rather than to evaluate a proposal and decide whether we were for it or against it. So, we shifted to the health lens analysis. I think it's sort of cool because I think it hasn't been used that much. There was a little bit of originality to taking that approach as well.

MO: As I recall, that was the main issue with the health impact assessment, it's kind of modeled on an environmental impact assessment, and again, that's the tool that ties regulatory and permitting power to a way of analyzing environmental issues. I think it was adapted to a health focus because it obviously had been very successful as a control on regulation. The health lens again, as Doug said, it's more diffuse, it's looking more generally at health impacts, but the challenge then is how do you tie it to something that enables policy or regulation? And I think what Lydia's described where it gets folded into a city plan, you know, those plans, if all goes well, become operative so that they get translated into policies, zoning, you know, all the places where we have levers to influence the built environment.

DG: So, my office (Gamble Associates) are urban design consultants for the BPDA in PLAN: East Boston, which followed the downtown master plan effort. It's been somewhat on hold since COVID-19 hit, although the city did a great deal of community engagement and evaluation of the existing conditions. Ambitions from the BPDA are that the neighborhood plan in East Boston—which has different issues than Chinatown—is going to result in some zoning changes and identification of areas where development and resiliency pressures really create a good deal of tension. What were some of the policy recommendations then in the work with Chinatown that affect public health?

LL: I think that one of the tensions here is that a lot of the city's, and particularly BPDA's, drive in these plans is to result in zoning amendments. When you talk about zoning amendments the goal is to up-zone. I think what came out of our own community planning process is that up-zoning is not what the community was looking for. The community has already been heavily impacted by an influx of luxury high-rise buildings, and what came out of the process was a strong advocacy effort by Chinatown to say, "If you're going to up-zone downtown Boston, we don't want to be a part of that, we want to be exempted or accepted, and we actually have some core streets that we want down-zoned." Whether ultimately that's what gets enacted into the zoning code, we're not sure. But we do think that "Plan Downtown" and BPDA have heard us, that there are some exceptions when they think about the blanket up-zoning of downtown and that there will be some exceptions in Chinatown. And I think that with the zoning issue, they have to look at resiliency and climate issues. Also, it really has a big impact in terms of how gentrification unfolds, because zoning is essentially the public creation of profit for developers and regulates what the values will be and how attractive certain areas will be to speculators. So, we're very sensitive to that. I think that's the real concern in East Boston, because we see East Boston as a neighborhood just following in the footsteps of Chinatown, but where the neighborhood may not have as many decades of organizing in dealing with development as Chinatown has.

DG: In Chinatown, there's so little room to grow. I mean, it must be one of the densest neighborhoods in the city, and density means something different now than it did a year ago.

DB: One issue with zoning and environmental impact assessment on new development is that actually air pollution is almost never considered in that process. For the health impacts they consider pedestrian injuries, they consider wind and shadow, they consider all kinds of things, but air pollution, locally generated traffic pollution especially, is not part of the assessment process. And we know from an environmental health perspective that particulate air pollution is, by an order of magnitude, the most serious environmental health hazard out there, and it's not on the list! I like what

FIGURE 10.1. Street level view in Chinatown. Image courtesy of Justine Wang.

Lydia and the others did with the Chinatown master plan because that issue is integrated holistically, it's embedded within the larger perspective. But if you look at an environmental impact assessment for a new development downtown, it wouldn't even be there. Not in any meaningful way, and not in ways that respect the most recent science, including our local research over the last fifteen years.

PB: And this gets tricky, because designers are not trained to look at scientific evidence. We are thinking about the visual aspect of the design, the building, we are not thinking about the air quality, and this information doesn't get to us that often. Recent residential developments in the Boston area are really trying to make buildings as sustainable as possible, but I don't think air quality is ever part of the conversation. And then you are specifically talking about ultrafine particles that affect people in buildings near highways; that's already so detailed, so scientific, that's just not part of the design conversation. Ultrafine particle mitigation is not in codes, so why will designers care? And frankly, as things are now, it is unfair to place the burden on the designers. Probably, a better approach is to codify what is now only in the form of recommendations. Designers and scientists need to talk more, too. Designers should be part of grant proposals, with fair fees, though, and then a bit of health education as part of the design curriculum is advisable too. And yet, I know that the CAFEH team was able to engage with some designers, and get them on board about incorporating air pollution mitigation in residential developments.

DB: And that's why we're counting on you, Pilar. You're going to be the person with an architecture degree and a PhD in environmental health. So, Martha, you're another example. We need more people that bridge that gap in my opinion. That's not specific to Chinatown, that's a much broader issue.

MO: Yeah, that's true everywhere, and there's some underlying issues. I just came off a session this morning about air pollution exposure assessment, and depending on where you live, the socioeconomic status, people living close to the road may be higher than people living further from the road, or it may be lower depending on the city or the region. Yet people with lower socioeconomic status are much more likely to be susceptible and vulnerable to health damage from air pollution. So the issues are not straightforward, and the quality of housing plays a great role. You can require the luxury developers to put in very high levels of filtration and triple pane windows, and so forth, and they're fine because they'll drive their Tesla into the garage and go into their well-cleaned apartment, but people who actually need the open space or send their kids to the school next to the Massachusetts Turnpike are the people that will actually be hurt. So, a lot of equity issues kind of get buried in the mud and you have to look into the details to find out what's happening to susceptible groups.

JP: I was just going to add that I know that this is a conversation about Boston, but something that we're seeing in a lot of our suburbs that's related is that the location of affordable housing in former industrial sites and near highways, and the health impacts of that is not even a consideration. Communities can be very reluctant to create affordable housing, but it's almost like we're accepting affordable housing at any cost. (See chapters 1 and 11.)

DB: Well, it also plays the other way. I don't know how far we want to go down this path, but I was involved in a case in Needham where they were building—and did build eventually—affordable housing right near Route 128, and I felt like what was going on is the people in the town didn't want affordable housing, and they were playing the environmental card. "You don't want to build housing there, that's polluted." So, it's very tricky. You have to sort of thread the needle, because you want to build affordable housing, but you don't want to put all of the low-income housing right near the highway where people are exposed. And I've come to the position, which I think has worked well in Chinatown, that we want affordable housing if that's the only place where we can get it is near the highway, but then let's build it with some protection. Let's negotiate with them to have better filtration in their ventilation systems, for example, so that there are protections. Martha, I thought you really encapsulated that brilliantly with the Tesla, coming up to the well-filtered apartments compared to someone living in subsidized housing where none of that is available. The politics of it are a little bit tricky, actually.

LL: Well, I was just going to say that it is really important to be having these conversations because of the impact of the pandemic, which, I think, is still really playing out. It's not completely clear where we're going to end up in a lot of different areas. So, it's essential to have very active participatory processes in thinking about these issues. Like I had said before, you know how people value open space so much more, so that's really spurred this new city investment in open space preservation and in helping communities create more open space. How is this going to affect downtown living? Will there still be such a demand as there has been? How does it affect the transportation and working patterns, and just the whole economy and where the economy is going? I think all of those things are a little bit in flux right now.

DG: Well, air quality seems like one of those things that people intuitively understand, but it seems difficult to communicate the impacts. You might be able to smell vehicular exhaust, but is that one of the challenges? Can one communicate these health care disparities in ways that the general population can easily understand? Even a brownfield may look like it's a totally benign landscape until you actually assess it. How is the public health profession trying to make these somewhat invisible particles more intelligible or easier to understand?

PB: You're talking about how do we communicate this [information] to the public, but also how we communicate it to developers and designers is also really important. I think that maybe a good and also bad outcome of the COVID-19 pandemic is that people are starting to listen about public health and taking it a little bit more seriously, although you have people that have been working in this field for decades. But still, if we talk about ultrafine particles, because they are invisible, and they don't smell either, it's very difficult to get designers interested, and they are not contemplated in codes, not part of the planning conversation. That is only starting to come to the surface. Whenever you have luxury developments where they want to do a sustainable building and they pursue something like LEED certification, or passive house, or WELL certification, then you have some constraints and guidelines to address air quality, but things like ultrafine particles are not even addressed at all.[8] So, you also need specific codes and regulations that regulate these pollutants. In my experience having that conversation with designers is difficult because it's not part of the design methodology, there is no space, or time, or fees to dedicate to health. How do you see this, Martha?

MO: I use the LEED certification as a model. There was nothing that gave building inspectors and designers an incentive or requirement to build sustainable buildings. And probably through two decades of hard work LEED became the standard rather than this crazy thing that nobody wanted to do. Now Boston and other cities require some level of LEED certification on buildings, and designers do it because (a) it's the law, they have to do it, so the owners are willing to pay for it, and (b), there are LEED sustainability consultants and architects who do it. It became a standard part of the practice today, but it wasn't always there. It wasn't magical, it took a lot of work by the U.S. Green Building Council and others. Look at the ADA, when I started in practice there was no ADA.[9] Accessibility was, "Well it's only a few people, and they probably won't come to my building anyways, so why bother." The ADA became the Access Board, and now it's an accepted thing, you have to do it because it's the law. I don't see why breathable air and other health measures couldn't become something you don't even ask about; you just do it.

DB: The other example that comes to my mind is smoking in indoor spaces. When I first came to Tufts there was still smoking in restaurants, and to me looking back it's a very strange thing. It seemed for a long time that nothing was going to change, then suddenly in a year or two, it just all changed and no one could imagine going into a restaurant where there was smoking allowed. It's almost a Malcom Gladwell "tipping point" kind of moment. It just all collapsed and changed to the opposite framework. Would you mind Pilar, if I shared your infographic?

Martha and Pilar were talking about the design community, but there's also an issue of just making the public and policy people aware of this issue. This is an infographic that Pilar worked with on with Sabrina Kurtz-Rossi, a professor at Tufts and colleague of mine, to try and boil down decades and hundreds of research papers to a few panels and simple words. (See the following page.) My point is that it's an attempt to make something that people are unaware about, that is technically complex, and make it accessible to a larger audience. And if we just have the words without Pilar's design skills, I don't think a bunch of panels with words on it would be nearly as compelling. And we just went over this this morning, and most of the feedback was quite positive. So, I think we've made some progress in that direction.

PB: So, this is interesting that you bring visualization to the conversation because that's one of the other elements about the intersection between public health and design. Designers are visual people; they think about how to communicate with visuals. So, these professionals also have the potential to facilitate the communication of scientific findings. It's very interesting for designers to consider how scientists evaluate something like an infographic, where you create a first version hoping to address these communication challenges, you have a script of what you want to communicate, you coordinate it with experts, you share it with the public and collect feedback, and then you refine the product. It's an interactive process. This design methodology is a bit more sound than what I typically see in a building or interior design process. I think this is good thing to consider as designers become more interested in public health. There are some people who are genuinely

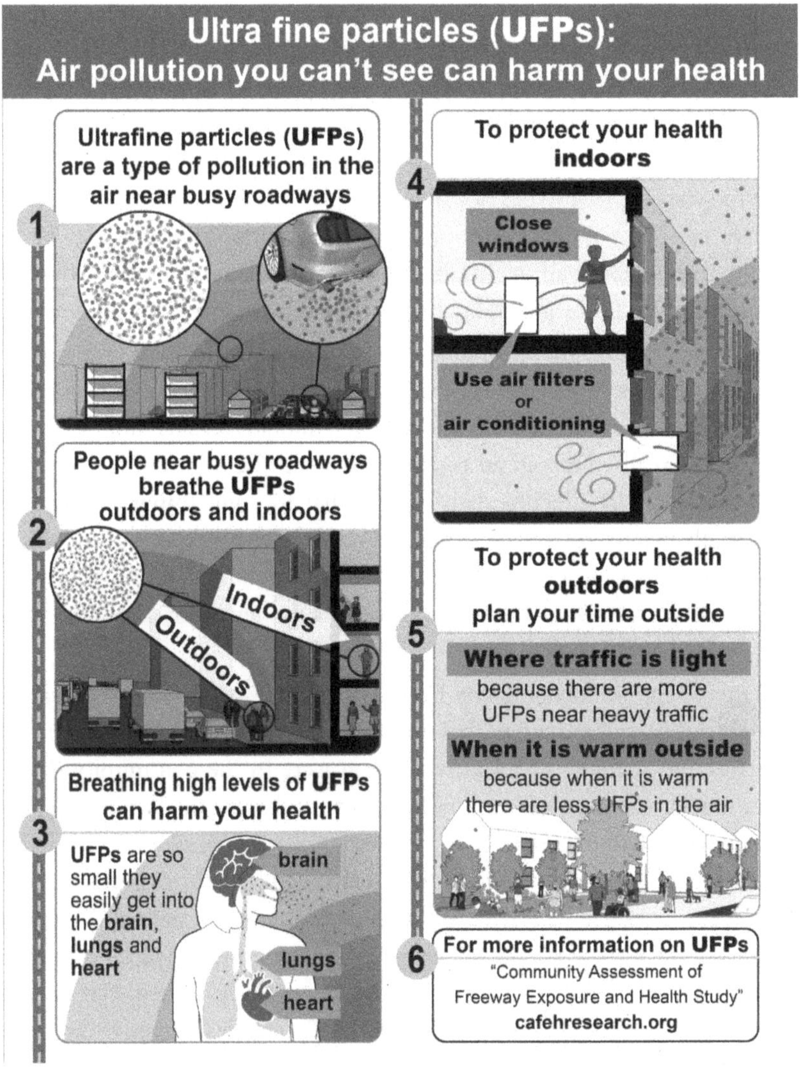

Ultra fine particles (UFPs):
Air pollution you can't see can harm your health
1
Ultrafine particles (UFPs) are a type of pollution in the air near busy roadways
2
People near busy roadways breathe UFPs outdoors and indoors
Indoors
Outdoors
3
Breathing high levels of UFPs can harm your health
UFPs are so small they easily get into the brain, lungs and heart
brain
lungs
heart
4
To protect your health indoors
Close windows
Use air filters or air conditioning
5
To protect your health outdoors plan your time outside
Where traffic is light
because there are more UFPs near heavy traffic
When it is warm outside
because when it is warm there are less UFPs in the air
6
For more information on UFPs
"Community Assessment of Freeway Exposure and Health Study"
cafehresearch.org

FIGURE 10.2. Information graphic about mitigating exposure to ultrafine particles in communities living near heavy traffic. Image courtesy of Pilar Botana Martinez.

interested in sustainability and health, but I still struggle thinking what is the adequate phase of the project and when is a good time to bring the topic of health into buildings? How can you get some advice and guidance when all these concerns are not part of a building's code or mandatory standards?

DG: The public is looking for ways to absorb dense, technical information in a manner that's easy to understand and absorb. Martha, you were talking about environmental impact assessments, which I'm more familiar with, or look at, say, transportation engineering impacts of a building, the things that get measured are level of service, throughputs for traffic, time signal delays, lots of heavy data things like that. (See chapter 4 on mobility.) They aren't really good metrics to understand mobility or livability. So, as it relates to public health, what types of data do people need to know? And Lydia, I'd be interested in your conversations with the community. There may be an intuitive sense about air quality, but how do you measure it specifically and communicate it to the general public in ways that are effective?

LL: I mean, I think that people are more interested in how it affects their own daily life and their own family. So, over time, for instance, we don't talk a lot about data in the CAFEH project, even though we're dealing with tons of data. It's really more about people understanding what the dangers are, how that might be affecting their family, what are some things they can do practically in terms of when to exercise and when to open your window and not open your window. Similarly, I think with mobility issues, open space issues, people are less interested in the data than they are in what it actually means for their lives.

One of the offshoots of the CAFEH project was a project to create a visual tool using computers that show people what's the condition based on land and temperature, and where you were in the community. There were visuals that showed you how bad it was at that particular time. People responded well to that.

MO: I've seen some pretty effective tools that combine the experiential, the personal experience with data. I've been working with a couple of student groups doing walk audits of neighborhoods where they have tools to map where the crossings are dangerous, or the sidewalk is broken, or cars parked across the sidewalk—the things that the traffic engineers need to know in order to prioritize fixes. I've seen some good work by the Boston group Speak for the Trees sending students out to map where there's good tree canopy and where there isn't and where there's a possibility of planting. So, these are microscale; they add up to data a policymaker or engineer can act on, and it's not abstract. It's what people went out and found out about their community.

JP: I've seen, similarly, data documenting thermal comfort on walking routes, documenting temperature. Melbourne, Australia, has this project called Cool Routes where they created an index on thermal comfort on their streets in order to provide people with access to an app where they could be like, "This is the most comfortable walking route for me in consideration of temperature."[10] Greater Phoenix has done community-led projects that are similar to that, there's Wicked Hot Boston, which has used community participatory research in order to document temperature in neighborhoods.[11] I think, as a planner, I definitely feel a certain mandate to combine data with storytelling, identifying ways to bring that narrative to a mother of a child that has asthma; you know, we don't have to present them with much data to convince them that the asthma that their child is experiencing is associated with particle pollution. If they live near a highway, it's a pretty simple link to make. So where do you find opportunities to provide folks with that experiential platform, and pair that with data? The *New York Times* recently did a really great story where they followed two children, I think, in New Delhi, and then they measured the air quality at various points throughout their day so that they could develop a graph of their air quality exposure throughout the day but also tell a story about how their differential levels of privilege either protected them from those air quality harms or exposed them.

MO: That was a really good story. I know the Health Effects Institute was involved in that in some small ways, and we need more of it, more people who are moved by that.

DB: I want to go back to what Lydia was talking about. The interactive map of ultrafine pollution in Chinatown. Caroline Wong headed up that project; it was published a few years ago. So, I think that's a very cool graphic. But Jeanette, I have felt for almost twenty years that the combination of stories and data is critical. The stories by themselves are anecdotal, they may or not be grounded in reality, but the data is dry and boring, and doesn't motivate people very much. So, when you have personalized stories that are connected to data that supports the claims and the concerns that are being raised, I think it really strengthens the case a lot. It's sort of hard with ultrafine particles, though. We study cardiovascular disease in adults. It's incremental risk over a lifetime; it's much harder to point to someone living near the highway who had a heart attack and say, "Was that because of their diet, or air pollution exposure, or a combination of a bunch of different things?" So, it's harder to have case examples and stories that illustrate the point.

DG: Jeanette, from a policy perspective at MAPC, the geography in which you're working is obviously well beyond a single neighborhood. So, how do you insert yourself, or how is public health part of the broader conversations about regional planning? I'm just curious about your role as a planner moving into public health. Did you gravitate into it or have you always been interested in this and MAPC is a good fit?

JP: Well, I started after undergrad doing environmental justice advocacy work in communities that had nitrate-contaminated drinking water because of farm fertilizer waste, and had poor housing conditions because a lot of people are living in old farm worker barracks. That's public health work. And then I moved into a position with the Building Healthy Communities Initiative in California, and that was my first exposure to "How do you organize around open space, environmental justice issues, housing, and really apply a public health lens to that work, or do it in order to achieve certain health outcomes?" And so that just helped me make the connection, and then at MAPC, it was an opportunity to continue working at that intersection. "How do we insert ourselves into these conversations regionally?" Well, for one, a lot of what our department does is focus on bolstering local public health department capacity. So in Massachusetts, public health is administered at the local level; California has county health departments. They're huge, they're well-resourced, even in a rural county, like the one I grew up [in], we had a lot of capacity at our local public health department and in fact they did a lot of planning work for smaller, rural municipalities.

That's not the case here in Massachusetts, where we're really feeling the strain of it now, where you have towns with a halftime public health nurse, one public health director, and maybe some community health worker staff that is per diem or part-time, and you're asking them to take on all this additional responsibility related to COVID-19. So, a lot of what we do is just try to bolster their capacity by being essentially the research arm for them, a technical assistance provider, facilitating spaces in which they can kind of collaborate together, ideally shared services. We're working on a shared epidemiologist position among some of our North Shore communities.

DG: One of the aspirations for these conversations is to launch this collection in neighborhoods where the confluence of issues is most pronounced. So, you could imagine if the Chinatown Community Center had a conversation with residents about affordability, public health, gentrification, and environmental justice. So, I'm just curious, asking you all, where do you think this conversation would be most effective, and how could we try to elevate the relationship between public health and some of these other categories I initially mentioned?

DB: I think the CAFEH work had really different experiences in Boston and Somerville. This is just my opinion, but it's based on experience and shared by others in our project. Somerville was a much easier municipal government to influence. So, if you get access into a few key people, and they buy into it, and the mayor has been on our side there for years, and his planning staff and so forth have come to look toward us. In Boston they're not opposed, but the Boston Public Health Commission, the Environment Department, BPDA, they're all huge, big separate entities, and if you make an inroad in the commission, it means nothing in the planning department. They're like countries separated by an ocean. So, I think it is one of the challenges that I don't know the answer to. Maybe Lydia and the planning process in Chinatown with their master plan seem to have some impact, so that's pretty cool, because I think that's hard to do, and I think it's because they spent decades learning how to navigate and influence the system in Boston. But it has been a lot easier in Somerville in terms of buy-in.

JP: I wouldn't rule out Boston, though. I think a lot of that intersectional thinking has been more led by some of the grassroots organizations, so it's interesting that you say, "The Boston Public Health Commission folks don't speak . . . ," that siloing is definitely real, but one thing we experienced this summer through that COVID-19-safe cooling program was, "Okay, public health folks, meet your environmental planning counterparts for the first time. You're going to have to work together because you have a shared problem that you need to fix." And a lot of the community groups were central to that. There was an example, I think Dorchester, where the Boston Public Health Commission worked with the Garrison Trotter Neighborhood Association and the Whittier Community Health Center, and the climate arm of the city of Boston to develop this project where they were working with the health center to screen patients for a need for an AC unit and then helping them access cooling, which is really new and really unique for the health sector here in the Boston area, definitely work we'd like to encourage further, but I think as devastating as COVID-19 has been, it's brought some folks together in ways that hasn't happened in the past.

DG: I'd like you all just to speculate about the implications of the pandemic looking ahead, and particularly as it relates to urban development. Honestly, I just wasn't even thinking about it as a theme [when this book began]; now it's one of the most important ones. So, as a culture, how do you think we're going to behave a generation from now? How much has this pandemic influenced how the public thinks about public health, how we use spaces, how we understand issues of density? Are you optimistic, or are you concerned about implications of the pandemic longer term in terms of how we live in cities?

FIGURES 10.3 and 10.4. Like nearly every city across the globe, COVID-19 shut down Boston for weeks at a time during the height of the pandemic, simultaneously calling into question both the benefits of density and its challenges. South Station and downtown, June 2020. Images © Peter Vanderwarker.

MO: I think part of it is an optimistic assessment that people are going to be more aware of health issues, and "How is the ventilation in this room I'm spending all day in?," that kind of thing. On the other hand, I think Americans tend to be very privatized, and find privatized solutions to things, and I think there's going to be a tendency toward that in terms of traffic, more people are going to want to drive because they don't want to be on public transportation that's full of other people. The arts suffer because people won't go to large gatherings like concerts. And again, it'll be tiered because some people are risk averse and will play it safe, and other people will not care and will go out in large groups. I'm not optimistic that any of the changes we're seeing will last long-term. People are talking about everyone moving out of the city; I think we're talking a 10 percent effect, not a 50 percent effect. People were saying that air pollution would go way, way down with COVID-19, and that didn't happen. It didn't happen partly because the goods movement traffic went up; people are getting more deliveries. And electric vehicles are not going to solve it either for us, because the non–tail pipe emissions are going to be a problem. I have mixed pessimism and optimism.

PB: I definitely worry about public transportation. Public transport was starting to get better, even if the city didn't have the all the money to truly address all issues, and we have good examples of great public transit in Europe, and then COVID-19 happens. Suddenly, public transportation becomes the transportation option for essential workers. It stopped being a place to have social interactions, to have conversations, it no longer was the sustainable commuting option for those that wanted to avoid driving. On the other hand, I want to think that people are now valuing more of the positive exposures in public health, like green and blue spaces. I hope people are thinking, "Oh, now I realize how nice it is to have a park near my home to walk, and connect with nature," so those thoughts were not in conversations before. There is a lot of research done on the health benefits of green and blue spaces, and that's something that will be interesting and not difficult to use as evidence for guiding designs for new public spaces. Which design features really matter, and which ones are there just for looks without any evidence backing it? I also see how environmental justice communities that lack those green spaces have been even more affected during the pandemic because these populations may live in smaller, crowded homes and they didn't have a place for relief. I know it's not Boston, but

Chelsea, Massachusetts, is an example of what I am talking about. It has few green spaces. It does have blue spaces, the Chelsea Creek waterfront, which is neglected; it's not accessible to the people. Lots of room for improvement. (Refer to the next chapter to learn how the city of Chelsea is striving to better connect its community to the waterfront.).

DG: Cautious optimism. Doug, what do you think?

DB: I agree, not just with the public transportation piece. Trains and public transportation in this country are so rudimentary compared to other places I've been, both in Asia and in Europe. It's really sad, and there's a potential for it to decline further, which worries me a lot. But let me take a different tack as an academic researcher: One of the things that struck me is that everyone's [now] got a huge education about epidemiology and infectious disease in public health. I think overall that's positive, but there's also a lot of backlash against it, and there's outright denial, but there's also frustration with the fact that research can't come up with definitive, clear, simple answers quickly. This has been my life; we deal with uncertainty and doubt, and questions, and even when you get to a really good study, like the ones we've published, there's still doubt. It's not like everything is resolved and figured out. So, I think there's frustration; I think there's also a backlash embedded partly in an opposition to "technocracy" in terms of educated professionals deciding everything and imposing it on the population in the interest of people. Maybe "benevolent" good interest, but it's not democratic, doesn't engage them and so forth. *I think there's some complexity, but it's helpful that public health and epidemiology are on people's lips in a way that they hadn't been ever in my lifetime.*

DG: That's really interesting, and as we talk about particles, my fire alarm is chirping, so there might be CO2 gases I'm not even realizing around here! I don't know if you can hear that, but Jeanette, you get the last word.

JP: So, something that's a little more prevalent in the housing field is just reflecting on the death toll within nursing homes, the comparatively better outcomes that we've seen in other types of senior living environments or affordable housing. I think there was already a trend in healthcare toward more community-based care, and I think that this is just going to continue that trend toward people wanting to stay at home as long as possible avoiding institutionalization. Telemedicine was this thing that healthcare said, "We've been working on it for twenty years, we can't make it happen" and with COVID-19 in a matter of months they were like "Okay, we're doing telehealth now." So, it's the ability to receive care at home, and the idea of home more than just a place. I think one place I struggle a lot is I have colleagues that really think of housing as (1) construction, (2) production of housing, and (3) production of affordable housing, and don't think of housing as a platform for well-being, like the ability to receive services in your home, or work on your health within your home. But related to that, we're seeing a lot of shortages in in-home care, because the healthcare economy is totally broken, workers are really poorly paid, they're not taken care of, they've seen high rates of COVID-19, and so, mostly women, mostly immigrant women, underpaid women that do that work. I'm a little bit skeptical that we will get there, just because of the inherent racism in how these things play out, that those professions will be valued and better paid, and we'll understand that in order to take care of ourselves we need to take care of the people doing this work as well.

NOTES

1. CAFEH serves as the larger umbrella for multiple, related community-based participatory research air pollution studies. The CAFEH partnership combines community and academic resources to advance scientific understanding of the health risks of highway pollution.
2. Karilyn Crockett's *People before Highways* documents exceptionally well the social, political, and environmental significance of local antihighway protests that led to portions of the interstate highway system being stopped through Boston and Cambridge Neighborhoods. Karilyn Crockett, *People before Highways: Boston Activists, Urban Planners, and a New Movement for City Making* (Amherst: University of Massachusetts Press, 2018).
3. GSD is the Graduate School of Design at Harvard University. With a mission to promote smart growth and regional collaboration, the Metropolitan Area Planning Council (MAPC) is the regional planning agency serving the people who live and work in the 101 cities and towns of metropolitan Boston.
4. The National Institutes of Health (NIH) is a part of the U.S. Department of Health and Human Services, the nation's medical research agency.
5. Research to Action (R2A) grants allow teams of researchers and their policy or practice partners to receive up to $80,000 to design and implement an applied research, translation, and dissemination project that focuses on a child well-being policy or practice question.
6. BPDA is the Boston Planning and Development Agency, previously known as the Boston Redevelopment Authority or BRA.
7. A health impact assessment is a tool that can help communities, decision makers, and practitioners make choices that improve public health through community design. It is a process that helps evaluate the potential health effects of a plan, project, or policy

before it is built or implemented. It brings potential positive and negative public health impacts and considerations to the decision-making process for plans, projects, and policies that fall outside traditional public health arenas, such as transportation and land use. A health impact assessment provides practical recommendations to increase positive health effects and minimize negative health effects.

8. Passive house is a voluntary standard for energy efficiency in a building, which reduces the building's ecological footprint. LEED (Leadership in Energy and Environmental Design) is an ecology-oriented building certification program run through the U.S. Green Building Council. The WELL building standard is a performance-based system for measuring, certifying, and monitoring features of the built environment that affect human health and well-being, through air, water, nourishment, light, fitness, comfort, and mind.
9. The Americans with Disability Act (ADA) became law in 1990. It is a civil rights law that prohibits discrimination against individuals with disabilities in all areas of public life, including jobs, schools, transportation, and all public and private places that are open to the general public. The purpose of the law is to make sure that people with disabilities have the same rights and opportunities as everyone else.
10. "Cool Routes," City of Melbourne, last accessed September 7, 2022, https://www.melbourne.vic.gov.au/parking-and-transport/streets-and-pedestrians/Pages/cool-routes.aspx.
11. The Museum of Science enlists the help of dozens of volunteers to map the hottest spots during Greater Boston area heat waves.

INDUSTRY

CHAPTER ELEVEN

PRODUCTIVE TENSIONS

Tactics for Negotiating Active Industry in the City

MARIE LAW ADAMS AND DAN ADAMS

Today's cities play an active role in generating material demands and are therefore intertwined with industrial practices. When industrial activities are displaced from cities and urban development conventions shroud us from our industrial footprints, we are left with no choice but to blindly participate with and perpetuate industrial systems that we are increasingly unfamiliar with and unaware of. How can we instead identify and foster complementary programmatic partnerships between industries and other urban systems or landscapes? How can industrial structures, landscapes, and operations be translated into local urban benefits? What new scenarios might such relationships create?

The widespread use of the term "postindustrial" to describe the contemporary American city (and increasingly cities throughout the globe) is reductive and misleading. Regardless of industrial heritage or lack thereof, all cities today are part of a globe-encompassing industrial milieu that includes sites of production and processing, transportation networks, and the boundless atmospheres that result from industrial operations. Our participation with industrial processes and their impacts saturates all forms of development, and correspondingly, instead of "post-," our contemporary condition is better described as a peri-industrial—a state of being fully encompassed or enclosed by our industrial footprint.

There is growing interest and capacity to measure the impacts that result from this condition. Yet both academic and professional design discourse almost exclusively considers industrial systems separate from the city without addressing how cities fundamentally negotiate their own active industrial footprints. This chapter explores the consequences that result from this lack of direct engagement, and introduces a variety of design tactics for negotiating active industry in the city.

CONTEMPORARY DISCOURSE

There are several tracks of architectural and urban design discourse that contend with industry today. But they do not interrogate how active industrial systems can be better designed into the public realm and everyday life of cities. This work can be categorized under four major themes.

1. The transformation of "post" industrial landscapes to new urban programs
   As manufacturing and logistics centers have been displaced from cities, designers have been engaged to reconsider what opportunities these former (often large) industrial tracts now afford. Example oft-cited projects include, in Boston, the Seaport District (no longer a seaport); in New York, the High Line (no longer a rail corridor); and globally, Parc de la Villette in Paris, HafenCity in Hamburg, Houtan Park in Shanghai, and countless others. This type of project is often referred to as reclamation of the postindustrial, implying that industry took land from the city that the city is now able to reclaim. This nomenclature, "post" and "reclaim," reflects a perception that industry and the city can be simply disassociated, and reinforces a collective mental separation between industry and the city, when, in fact, the industrial demands of these cities persist, simply further afield from the city.
2. The amplification of global infrastructure networks
   To remain connected to global centers of industry, cities depend on robust transportation and goods distribution networks. For example, a long-term ongoing project on the East Coast of the United States has been the ongoing dredging of federal navigation channels in port cities such as Miami, Jacksonville, Savannah, Charleston, Norfolk, Baltimore, New York, and Boston to match the new lock dimensions and draft of the expanded Panama Canal. These projects exemplify an approach of responding to increased material demands and expanding global networks by enlarging infrastructure to accommodate increased consumption. (Alternative approaches could be to reduce consumption or localize production.) While this is the largest ongoing construction project reshaping the submarine shorelines of the major East

Coast cities of the United States, these projects have neither significantly involved nor been influenced by the architecture and landscape architecture communities. Such projects, though located in cities, are engineered in service of global or regional infrastructure networks, and are not designed as situated urban architectures that productively participate with local urban conditions.

3. The mitigation of the accrued impacts of global industry

Major climatic events in the United States, such as Hurricane Katrina (2005) and Hurricane Sandy (2012), and more localized and common flooding events, such as the king tides in the Boston area, advanced discourse on developing architecture, landscapes, and infrastructure that can be resilient to the impacts of increased climatic extremes, such as storm surge events and coastal flooding, which result from industrial practices. Much of this work is focused on urban shorelines, where concepts for urban resilience to sea level rise and storm-surge events have been thoroughly promoted and are now beginning to be realized. In New York alone, in the short span from 2011 to 2014, three major and influential design exhibitions and competitions of international acclaim—Rising Currents, FAR ROC, and Rebuild by Design—were sponsored by organizations ranging from MoMA to the U.S. Department of Housing and Urban Development. These exhibitions and competitions have been highly influential in the design community on subsequent planning efforts, such as "Climate Ready Boston" commissioned by the city of Boston and published in 2016.[1]

The increasingly extreme character and destruction caused by forest fires, particularly in California, which is also linked to industrialization-born climate change, has similarly led to significant focus in landscape architecture on advancing better techniques of land management and development planning. A different, but related, topic of landscape remediation has focused on developing design strategies for risk abatement of contaminated landscapes to allow them to become reinhabited by new uses such as housing, office parks, shopping centers, parking lots, or parks. Both topics, resilience and remediation, address remnant shadows of industry after the fact and away from the source, but do not directly alter the relationship of the city to the active industrial operations on which it depends.

CONSEQUENCES

From the lack of innovation in the designed relationship between industry and the everyday life of cities, specific consequences can be observed.

Lost Metropolitan Consciousness

As cities grow, they become increasingly dependent on a globally distributed network of resource centers—a form of transportation-intensive global goods sprawl. From this increasing detachment, industry becomes "out of sight and out of mind." In the absence of productive frictions that would result from proximity, industries and cities become increasingly incongruent to each other across all scales and dimensions. (It should go without saying that if an industrial operation is so detrimental to the environment or human health that it must exist outside of populated areas, and depends on the finite capacities of the ocean and the atmosphere to dilute its impacts, then that industrial operation should be ceased. This chapter considers the vast majority of industrial operations, which if designed and maintained well, can coexist with urban life.)

In the constructed ecology of the city, one only needs to witness the everyday yet problematic activity of a tractor trailer transporting a cargo trailer—a module of regional transport—through a downtown, alongside cyclists and pedestrians, to realize that divergent evolution of cities and goods processing has made each detrimental to the other.

A shroud of mystery envelops the consumer objects of everyday life. Where did this come from? How did it get here? How is it made? What is it made of? This disconnect not only results from the diversification, decentralization, and advancement of industrial technologies but is also a symptom of conventional patterns of city-making that today disassociate seemingly incongruent programs and experience. Pretty, tame, dry, stable, quiet, and safe is designed away from ugly, smelly, leaky, shaky, loud, and dangerous. Yet these assessments are inherently married through urban chemistry, as raw iron is refined into the structure of buildings that eventually become scrap metal—just as byproducts of petroleum extraction become fertilizer that produces food that becomes human waste.

As cities become increasingly divorced or black-boxed from selected stages in a material lifecycle, metropolitan consciousness—the understanding of a collective environmental footprint—is diminished. This detachment propagates a type of myopia in which we are shielded from recognizing the industrial systems embedded in the materials of our everyday lives. Through design or coincidence, this condition prohibits choice. How can one choose whether or not to participate in an industrial system when they cannot even perceive that they are part of it? As our material processing capacities have pervaded everyday life (mined and processed silica, lithium, palladium, platinum, gold, copper, aluminum, and petroleums are baked into a mineral-based cake to make the cell phones carried every day in our pockets), it is incumbent on the designers of cities to make our participation in these material systems legible and understandable.

The detachment of urban life from the industrial systems that support it is reinforced by typical conventions of use-based zoning, which isolates and clusters industry away from other urban activities into dense singularly programmed districts (see chapter 2 in this volume). This is, or course, in cases when industry still exists in proximity to the city. In addition to diminishing the influences of industry on metropolitan consciousness, this clustering compounds other deleterious effects, such as propagating massive swaths of monofunctional, impermeable surfaces that make "soft" landscape systems–based methods of stormwater management nearly impossible, and excludes the types of productive frictions that make urban districts self-regulating.

Lost Urban Capacity

While the pattern of reclaiming postindustrial landscapes in cities for new uses such as parks and commercial development introduces recreation space and increases tax revenues, the productive industrial and infrastructural capacity of these landscapes, and therefore the city, is lost. For example, the industrial shoreline piers of Manhattan that once linked barges and ships to inland rail networks have been converted into residential towers and recreation space. The inland rail lines that stitched together vertical factories that processed and distributed goods into the city and the region have been eliminated, converted to passenger use or transformed into parks such as the High Line. Consequently, Manhattan's once dynamic goods distribution network has been reduced to total dependence on trucks. When compared to both rail- and sea-based infrastructure, trucks are less fuel efficient, more costly per ton hauled, and contribute significantly to congestion and infrastructural degradation of roads and bridges. While the resulting aesthetic of such landscapes might appear "greener," when considered as a broader network, the net footprint is an environmental negative as production and distribution move further afield from consumption. The increased gaps between production, distribution, and consumption are simply filled by trucking, and negative environmental impacts are absorbed into the atmosphere and ocean.

This urban development pattern is reinforced by locally biased equations for calculating "highest and best" uses that rarely account for a development's full regional footprint. Industries that network with distributed economies, like scrap metal yards, often have low direct employment and built square footage, and therefore low property tax and development value when analyzed through the singular lens of local city interests. Consequently, cities discourage such developments. However, when seen across a more regional perspective, a scrap metal yard adds tremendous infrastructural value, economic activity, and recycling capacity. Scale matters.

Lost Regional Service

Developments that displace industries to benefit an immediate neighborhood may be detrimental to a broader region. As mentioned by Sevtsuk earlier in this book, cities serve, and were often founded, as industrial hubs for processing goods for a broad region. Silos, mills, and docks, though located in a city, transship the goods of a regional network. Converting a dock to a park adds recreation space to the immediate neighborhood and eliminates infrastructural impacts in the city that were imposed by the region, but the inland communities that connected to this dock have to build new connections and infrastructure to replace that which was lost in the city. This again raises questions of scale and perception in characterizing and considering the valuation of infrastructural resources. For example, Does a rail line pass through a city? Or is a city located on a rail line? Alternatively, Is a harbor in a city? Or is a city located on a harbor?

Such subtleties in terminology are important and reflect conflicting considerations of scale and jurisdiction. For city authorities, the rail or the harbor is located within city boundaries, and therefore the infrastructure should be designed to meet the wants and needs of the city. This makes sense—local communities bear the burden of the most immediate and tangible impacts of regional infrastructure. In contrast, regional network planning prioritizes the unencumbered operation of regional infrastructure, wherein local variables or "obstacles" are to be avoided. This is legislatively validated by the financial history of such infrastructural projects. Rail, highway, and port development and maintenance have typically been funded over decades or centuries by state and federal investment. For example, the dredging of Boston Harbor was largely paid for by the federal government because the operations of the harbor serve the region, state, and nation—not just the city. The harbor is part of the shared "commonwealth" of Massachusetts such that even communities that are physically detached from the harbor infrastructure maintain a vested and inherited interest in its region-serving performance. However, in the public engagement process that often determines the fate of individual parcels on harbors, rails, highways, and other region-serving infrastructure, oftentimes only local abutters and interest parties are invited to participate in the planning process, or only local community members are invited to join community advisory committees. As such, individuals in the broader region who are affected are often entirely unaware that decisions being made in other jurisdictions are directly affecting their municipality and undermining investments that they contributed to through state and federal taxes.

As mentioned above, "reclamation" of postindustrial land implies that redevelopment into parks, housing, or institutions makes the landscape more conducive and accessible to urban life. However, this also is a question of scale. For instance, the conversion of piers from shipping infrastructure to residential real estate converts the waterfront landscape from a region-serving "resource" into a local real estate "commodity." Alternatively, the conversion of the same pier from private industrial port operations to a public park on one hand makes the landscape more publicly accessible to the local community; on the other hand, the broader regional community loses the public benefit that the industry—for example, seafood processing or scrap metal exporting—had served. How does an inland city export its scrap metal if the waterfront cities turn all their docks to parks? In such a transformation, the commonwealth of the region is reduced while a local community appears to benefit.

The contemporary lack of design for active industrial operations at the local scale of cities creates a stagnating paradox. Regions depend on industrial infrastructures in cities. Yet cities receive the infrastructural impacts of the region-serving industry, and often suffer from decreased property tax that could otherwise be accrued from higher real estate value uses. This is most pronounced in the performance of ports. If the industries are poorly designed, these infrastructural impacts become manifested as environmental burdens borne by the local host cities. Burdened cities enact measures to eliminate such industries from within their borders, while regions enact measures to maintain industry, and the urban landscape becomes trapped and stagnated by conflicting valuations of the infrastructural resource.

Mitigation is a development practice intended to break the stalemate between regional and local interests. Mitigation, as conventionally implemented, is often a one-time investment that is not integrated within the operations, specific impacts, or even local landscape of the industry. Consequently, while a city might receive specific tangible benefits from the arrival of the industry, the direct impacts of the industry on the city remain unnegotiated over time. Like zoning, mitigation often ignores industrial specificity and is instead based on generic metrics such as numbers of trucks, acreages of land, or dollar amounts of investment. This generic response can be attributed, at least in part, to the absence of designers from the development of industrial operations who are trained and knowledgeable in the operational differences in industrial typologies. For example, an ice plant for the fishing industry operates very differently, and has very different impacts and potentials for community partnerships, than an asphalt batching terminal, yet such radically different programs, even if both water dependent, often become generically categorized as industry and governed with the same urban regulations. Inevitably, generic mitigations that ignore these significant differences are perceived by industries as generic punishments and hindrances to their operations, which have the unintended consequence of discouraging industrial property improvements.

FIGURE 11.1. In Boston Harbor, the conflicting valuation of the harbor as a local or regional resource has created a development vacuum on much of the waterfront. In the absence of agreed valuations for waterfront resource lands, only temporary uses are permitted. As a result, a significant portion of Boston Harbor's waterfront is utilized as car parking (*midground*) despite its great value to both local industry (such as the jet fuel tanks, *background*) and ecology (such as the harbor seal, *foreground*) or recreation access (such as the pier from which the photo is taken), as seen in Chelsea, Massachusetts. Image courtesy of Landing Studio.

Lost Urban Heterogeneity

The displacement of industry from cities reduces not only infrastructural capacity but also spatial, socioeconomic, and cultural diversity. This contributes to the evolution of cities into service enclaves defined almost exclusively by housing, offices, shopping, and recreation. This loss of diversity is a reflection of the loss of diversity in economy and jobs. This is especially evident in many self-described postindustrial cities, like Boston, where economic disparity grows as job diversity shrinks. Such trajectories are antithetical to a sustainable, dynamic, and vibrant city. Routine industrial operations initiate a diversity of separate but interconnected jobs and tasks. A cargo ship approaching a dock triggers U.S. Coast Guard personnel for inspections; harbor pilots and tugboat operators pilot the ship to berth; ship chandlers gather supplies for the ship; water trucks arrive for deliveries; welders are called for repairs; new crew members arrive at the local airport to relieve shipmates; line handlers tie up the ship; longshoremen, machine greasers, and mechanics prepare dock equipment; security personnel arrive to guard gangway access; ship agents and lawyers pass cargo manifests; accountants process bills; and hundreds of truck drivers are alerted to transport the cargo.

At any given moment on a dock, one might see only a small number of workers, and such facilities might have a short list of full-time employees. However, like a "keystone species" in an ecological network, the removal of such operations from the city creates a cascading effect in which associated trades, archetypes, and personnel disappear from the urban ecosystem. Also, like ecosystems, there is a critical density required for the sustainability of these keystone operations and their support service industries. One marine dock cannot sustain a local ship repair facility, and one fishing boat cannot sustain an ice plant. As industrial activities like fishing are incrementally eliminated, support industries like ice plants become weakened. If the support industries inevitably collapse, then the interdependent network of direct and indirect industrial operations are likely to collapse with it. The global periindustrial condition absorbs the loss by shifting the resource network elsewhere. But at what cost? In this reductive process, the city becomes a monoculture while the energy-consuming footprint of goods delivery increases.

Conventions of use-based zoning segregate industry from other urban uses, tending to make each more homogenous and oblivious to the other. Likewise, many regional and national regulations for industries are calibrated to simple common denominators that neglect opportunities to develop points of productive overlap between cities and industrial operations. For example, marine industrial docks often actually require a security perimeter only during the small percentage of time when an international vessel is berthed. However, permanent fences are put in place, encircling entire terminals, to satisfy federal homeland security regulations. In such circumstances, the entire landscapes of docks, whether operated by public agencies or private industries, become "off-limits" whether or not operations with security or safety concerns are even occurring. Furthermore, industrial terminals often have specific areas where certain operations or materials may not be conducive to urban engagement, while other areas are innocuous. Broad-stroke definitions and regulations overwhelm and prohibit these particularities that could be grounds for resilient cross-pollinations of cultures and economies. For example, some small shipyards in Boston Harbor have now integrated accessory programs such as restaurants, housing, and art studios alongside ship-repair facilities and machine shops. Here, when there is a lull in ship repair, the economy of the shipyard is preserved by the rent from other programs. Such hybridizations are often prohibited by zoning, environmental, and security regulations enforced on industrial terminals.

TACTICS

The following are new design tactics to bring industry and the city into productive friction and greater engagement with one another. The global salt industry is used here as a medium to convey how the negotiation of industry with a city is achieved in multiple dimensions. The design tactics are specific and are not themselves inherently applicable to other situations. Rather, the repeatability lies in the translation of industry into particular actions and interfaces with the city that can be designed.

Plural Instead of Singular

As mentioned above, postindustrial reclamation replaces industrial use with new programs that relinquish industrial capacity. Instead of this "either-or" displacement, designs that tactically interweave "both-and" can preserve infrastructural capacity. Deicing salt stockpiles are seasonal landscapes, activated in the winter but relatively dormant in the summer. In these colder climates, outdoor recreation follows a nearly opposite seasonal cycle, where basketball, street hockey, and tennis courts are popularly used in the warm months and significantly less used in the winter. The PORT (Publicly Organized/Privately Owned Recreation Territory) in Boston Harbor was designed to forge a new programmatic partnership between salt operations and public recreation from this seasonal pattern. The PORT is a new shared-use landscape for salt operations in the winter and hardscape recreation space in the summer. Instead of the common practice of replacing industry with park space, this design overlays the two programs through seasonal coupling. Simple elements such as movable fences and portable basketball hoops are seasonally shifted by dock workers using dock machines. An area used for salt stockpiling and distribution in the fall and winter is used as recreation space in the spring and summer. The neighboring community directly participates with the cycle of the salt operations through changing access to the recreation landscape, fostering consciousness of the ebbs and flows of the industry, and interweaving patterns of city life and industrial operations in space and time.

FIGURE 11.2. Salt-pile basketball: the seasonal nature of the deicing salt industry allows this area to be used for basketball, a bike track, and event space in the summer, and to stockpile 100,000 tons of salt in the winter. By May 15 each year, salt is cleared off a portion of the dock, and the hard-scape recreation elements are repainted and restriped. This aligns well with the completion of the school year. Image courtesy of Landing Studio.

By creating such shared use of a landscape, new positive city-industry partnerships can develop, where programmatic isolation would typically prohibit productive partnerships. In the case of PORT, the recreational use of a portion of the salt dock gave rise to interests from a local theater company to use the landscape, site utilities, and the salt itself annually for outdoor theater. Now each year, in addition to opening the site for basketball, salt dock operators work with stage set designers to build salt stages for evening performances.

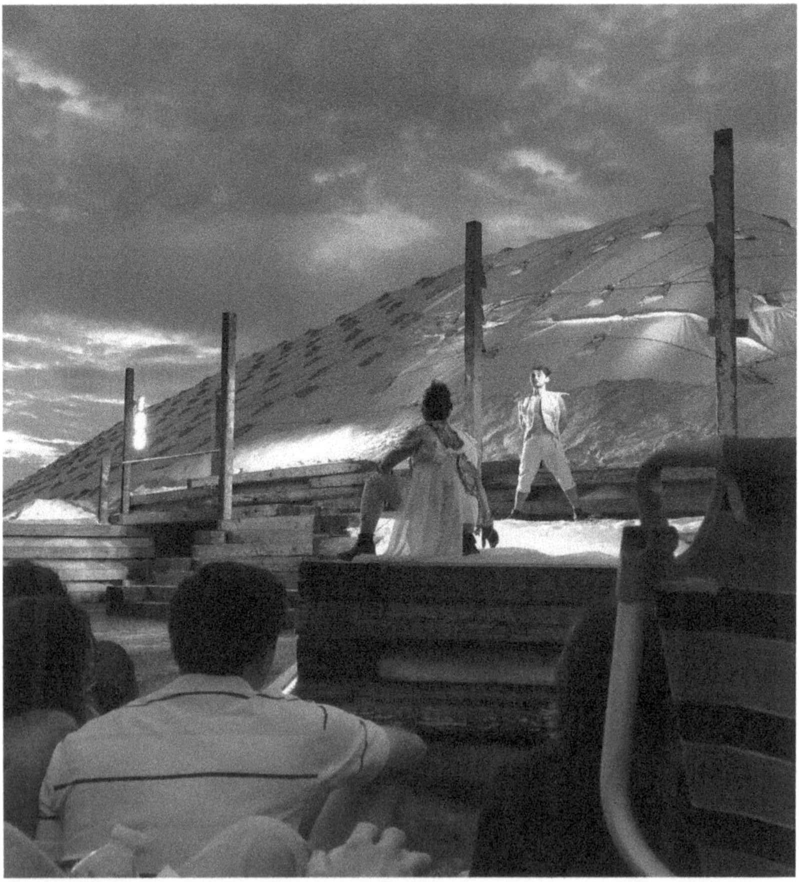

FIGURE 11.3. Salt stages jointly developed by a salt company and theater company to support performances. The first experiment in using the salt pile in these summer performances involved Hamlet's "To be or not to be" soliloquy in 2016. The stage was a simple salt pile built by dock workers. Two seasons later, in 2018, the stage set for *A Midsummer Night's Dream* was a more intricate design implemented jointly by salt dock workers, the Apollinaire Theatre Company, and a timber salvage contractor. Image courtesy of Landing Studio.

As a result of this partnership with the theater company, the salt dock operators continually upgraded PORT infrastructure, particularly electrical utilities for performance lighting. In the spring of 2020, these utilities, in concert with the strong community relations that have been forged between city and industry, supported the creation of a centralized food distribution hub to provide emergency relief during the COVID-19 pandemic. The industries' significant electrical capacity supported food refrigeration units. Large dock surfaces were utilized for truck deliveries, and the network of diverse trade workers, which is inherent to industrial operations, was called on to rapidly assemble a large-scale food distribution facility for the city.

Translation Instead of Mitigation

Conventional mitigation practices are intended to offset the impacts of industry. While the reduction of noxious impacts is vital, industries that

FIGURE 11.4. Food hub at a salt dock for providing emergency food relief to the city during the COVID-19 pandemic in 2020. A public access area of the salt dock and a portion of the dock itself and an adjacent parcel was repurposed as a central food storage, packing, and distribution hub for households in need. Approximately five thousand households received food from this distribution center beginning in June 2020 and continuing through January 2021. The food distribution hub takes advantage of the electrical utilities spliced off the main dock service, which were implemented to support summer theater uses described above, as well as the trucking, building, and material handling logistics know-how of salt dock workers. Image courtesy of Landing Studio.

serve the region also bring unique characteristics and capacities into local urban environments—such as an ability to easily move heavy things, process large quantities of unusual materials, or provide access to uncommonly large and robust landscapes or resources such as electricity. These unique traits can be farmed for new urban potentials.

In Staten Island, New York, the film and performance art festival called LUMEN organized by Staten Island Arts occurs biannually on a waterfront salt dock. The massive dock on one hand provides a uniquely robust landscape to support diverse media and installations (including fires, pyrotechnics, massive machines, and large group performances) that would be prohibitive at more conventional urban arts venues. On the other hand, the massive emptiness of the summertime terminal presents the challenge of an undifferentiated landscape that lacks any spatial framework to support artwork. To create such a framework, salt workers and machines were engaged to construct landscapes out of salt piles that support seating, climbing, podiums, digging, and projecting, and to create spaces that serve as galleries and stages. The material qualities of the salt are an important dimension of the design. For these events, only freshly evaporated sea salt is used. Such salt is "fluffy" to the touch, making it appealing to dig and climb in, in contrast to rock salts that are mined from underground deposits, where pressure has solidified the crystals into rock-hard granules. Freshly evaporated ocean salts are also bright white, which is good for projections and lighting. The unique capacity of the salt dock operators to rapidly move and sculpt landscapes, and the particular tactile qualities of the industrial product—salt—are translated into new urban capacity to facilitate art and installations. The LUMEN festival has become a new urban tradition, ongoing every other year since 2010.

Integration in Place of Isolation

Industries as a category of land use can be many things. Some industries, such as petroleum terminals, are difficult to make accessible to the public due to security and health concerns, while others are not. Similarly, within industrial landscapes, some areas pose environmental restrictions, while other areas do not. Instead of uniformly categorizing and separating industry from the city, the variable conditions of such operations can be evaluated to allow for varied degrees of urban and environmental engagement. *How can zoning be reimagined to allow for gradients of integration as opposed to sharp boundaries of isolation?*

FIGURES 11.5 and 11.6. Salt pile galleries: the salt dock, which moves large quantities of salt across a large landscape, becomes dormant in summer months, and is here translated into a summertime film and performance art festival. Salt and lighting are used to reshape the active industrial dock for temporary public access. These LUMEN events are each one night long, with attendance of five thousand to seven thousand visitors. Staten Island, New York. Images courtesy of Landing Studio.

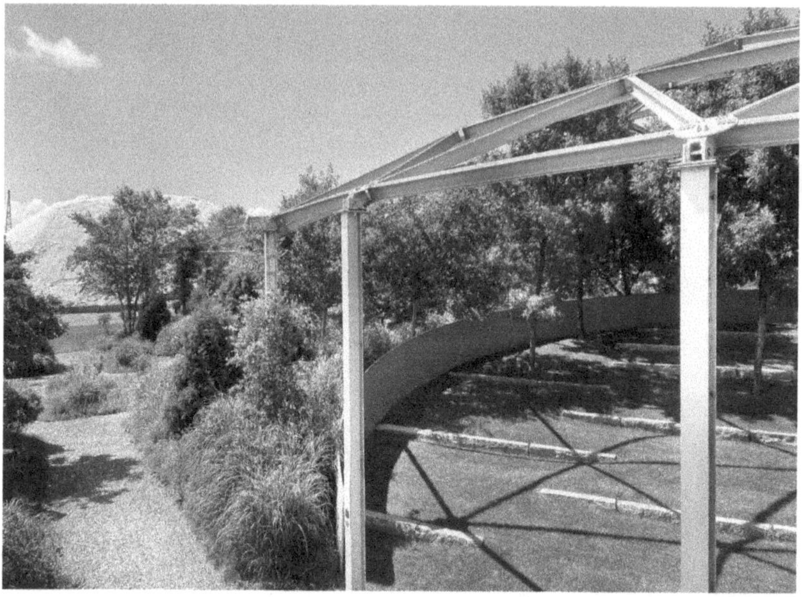

FIGURE 11.7. PORT public access area, within a salt dock, built above electrical and telecommunications utility easements, with a former oil tank transformed into an amphitheater and a truck loading rack as a new public viewing platform. Image courtesy of Landing Studio.

Public access, recreation, habitat, and natural infrastructure can be overlaid within maritime industrial salt docks by carefully dissecting the industrial operations and infrastructure. Just as industrial operations bring unique capacities to urban environments, they are subject to limitations that can be leveraged for new urban performance. The salt industry in particular handles massive quantities of tremendously heavy material with heavy machines. Such weight imposes restrictions on the operations of an industry. For example, stockpile and machine operation setbacks are established along waterfront bulkheads and subterranean utilities to prevent excessive loading of the relatively fragile subgrade infrastructure. Such setbacks become the "slack spaces" of operational use. Typically, such slack spaces are underutilized though still considered part of the industrial landscape. Instead of coarsely classifying the entire terminal for industrial use, the terminal is dissected and finely rezoned and new programs are inserted into areas where industry is otherwise restricted by weight.

For example, in Boston Harbor, subterranean utility lines that require constant access in case of emergency repair prevent material stockpiling on the surface. Through a strategy called "Parks over Pipes," small public access landscapes are developed over subterranean utility corridors such as potable water, telecommunications, and electric lines in order to reoccupy these zones that are otherwise limiting to industrial operations. The resulting fingers of public access are located within industrial terminals, creating public access and visibility in the heart of industrial operations. Likewise, along the steel bulkheads of the marine terminal, trucks are prohibited from regularly driving within eight feet of the shoreline bulkhead to avoid overloading the infrastructure. This setback provision creates an operational vacuum at the water's edge reoccupied with wildflower and grass habitat plantings.

Specific Instead of General

Industries and their operations can be dissected to identify specific points of friction as well as valuable points of overlap with the city. How can industrial operations be tuned to the specific cities of local urban environments through design?

In Boston Harbor, as with many waterfront communities, residential development traditionally occupied the uplands, while industry occupied the lowlands at the water's edge. This development pattern establishes a spatial relationship in which neighborhoods look out and down across

FIGURE 11.8. Light projections on salt piles: here lighting is designed not only to provide required foot candles for security and safety lighting to the industrial corridor but also to animate the kinetic salt pile landscape and create dialogue with urban context. Image courtesy of Landing Studio.

industrial landscapes and industrial operations become both a visible horizon and physical edge of the city. In the case of the salt industry, as with many dry bulk terminals, the industrial landscape is in a perpetual state of kinetic reconstruction as piles are built up and carved down in response to market and weather demands.

Beginning in 2005, at the seam between the industrial terminal and the adjacent urban neighborhood, the conventional street lighting along the industrial terminal was supplemented with changing projected light on the salt piles themselves. The light took the form of text and graphic patterns. As piles were carved away, the messages and patterns were variably distorted, erased, and resurrected on the horizon of the city in direct reflection of the transformation of the salt landscape and the dock's industrial activities. The lighting synchronized with and amplified the legibility of the industrial operations of the salt piles.

CONCLUSION

Cities are made vibrant and rich through the confluence of different people and diverse uses being accommodated through well-designed landscapes and architectures of negotiation. The tactics introduced here result from our own conjecture that the practice of displacing industry from the city has exacerbated negative environmental impacts from industrial activities at both global and local scales. Alternatively, we ask how cities can become better engaged through tactical architectural and urban design to directly negotiate the industrial systems they depend on, locally in real time. How can the inevitable conflicts of this interrelationship be translated into productive frictions through design?

NOTES

1. *Climate Ready Boston,* City of Boston, accessed October 30, 2022, https://www.boston.gov/sites/default/files/file/2019/12/02_20161206_executivesummary_digital.pdf.

CONCLUSION

DAVID GAMBLE

SET ASPIRATIONAL GOALS that redirect the use of public land toward affordable and middle-income housing with smaller unit sizes.

REFORMULATE DEVELOPMENT REGULATION to reduce land use friction and spread the benefits of growth.

COUPLE HOUSING AND TRANSPORTATION POLICIES to build public housing at scale near transit and invest boldly in rail and bus transportation to provide a dignified, car-free commuting experience.

DEVELOP NEW METRICS FOR TRANSPORTATION that advance multimodal streets to support mixed-use, infill development that deemphasize the car.

BREAK DOWN THE SILOS between institutional, nonprofit and private sectors to strengthen collaborative practices and increase social resilience in the face of disasters.

CULTIVATE A CIVIC CULTURE that aspires to urban excellence.

ADVANCE A PROGRESSIVE AGENDA that harnesses the organized power of communities of color to address systemic racism, economic justice, and spatial justice.

IMPLEMENT COMPELLING PILOT PROGRAMS and accountable actions that produce measurable transformations in Boston's racial culture.

EMBRACE PROVOCATIVE TEMPORARY PUBLIC ART that challenges our biases and reflects a diversity of opinions and cultures.

TIE POLICY AND REGULATORY CHANGES TO ASSESSMENTS of urban environments that improve public health and environmental justice.

INTRODUCE NEW DESIGN TACTICS to bring industry and the city into productive friction and greater engagement.

The challenges that the Greater Boston region faces require convergence of thought and action. We cannot address our affordability crisis unless a much greater amount of housing production takes hold. More housing density—which must include both a greater diversity of housing types and smaller unit sizes—needs to be geared toward our changing demographics and accessibility demands. Housing units must also be built on underutilized land close to public transportation, where connectivity between downtown and the suburbs or gateway cities is present. Such connections will languish without a massive investment in transit infrastructure. Granted, progress is being made. In August 2022, the Commonwealth of Massachusetts enacted legislation to increase density and affordable housing in "MBTA Communities" served by public transit which is moving in the right direction.[1]

The best way to actually address traffic congestion is counterintuitive, taking space *away* from cars that for far too long have splintered our neighborhoods and eroded our public realm. More space within the street right-of-way must be allotted for bikes, buses, and pedestrians, which will reduce, rather than induce, car traffic. Diminishing the number of single occupancy vehicles through "road diets" will cut harmful particulates that emanate from their exhaust, resulting in healthier outcomes for all, but especially for neighborhoods in the shadows of twentieth-century infrastructure.

More pedestrian-oriented and transit-rich districts that have a concentration of affordable housing in close proximity to parks and community amenities will lead to stronger commercial centers. Nevertheless, a tolerance for greater density will not come easily, as our parochial form of municipal government—together with an engaged citizenry—wields immense power to limit new development regardless of whether the positive benefits of that growth far outweigh the negative impacts. Is allowing an additional story (or two) onto the height of buildings along transit-rich corridors really worth the endless public debates? Removing our current patchwork of discretionary-based zoning and establishing clear, community-based visions tailored to our diverse neighborhoods can ease the tension and cultivate support for proactive planning and quality urban design that transcend individual properties.

Finally, we must leverage Greater Boston's enviable collection of institutional, not-for-profit, and private sectors to work more closely together on these complex, interdisciplinary challenges. Such wicked problems cannot be solved in isolation. Given our relatively modest size as a city, region, or state, relationships between partners can be tighter. We must channel our passion for strong municipal leadership and public participation into strategies that acknowledge our inequities and racism, creating more space for diversity and a greater tolerance for people different than ourselves.

Boston has much to be proud of, but there is much work to do. *Idea City* captures many our contemporary challenges and posits ways to overcome them. It's not that good ideas aren't being advanced by others. Our city and region is blessed with remarkable civic organizations, enviable institutions, and impressive leaders. What is keeping these ideas from having a bigger impact is that too often they aren't thinking long-term enough, fail to capture the imagination, and exist in isolation. Wicked problems are best resolved through intersectionality, so that as Boston approaches its four-hundred-year anniversary, it also approaches its promise to be a place that is truly more livable, equitable, resilient . . . and beautiful.

NOTES

1 The legislation for an MBTA Community was advanced by the Department of Housing and Community Development in consultation with the Massachusetts Department of Transportation and the MBTA. "The new law requires that an MBTA community must have at least one zoning district of reasonable size in which multi-family housing is permitted as of right and meets other criteria," such as a minimum gross density (15 units per acre); a location not more than a half mile from a commuter rail station, subway station, ferry terminal, or bus station; and a lack of age restriction and suitable for families with children ("Multi-Family Zoning Requirement for MBTA Communities," Mass.gov, https://www.mass.gov/info-details/multi-family-zoning-requirement-for-mbta-communities).

CONTRIBUTORS

DAN ADAMS is director and associate professor of the School of Architecture at Northeastern University and founding partner, with Marie Law Adams, of Landing Studio.

MARIE LAW ADAMS is an associate professor at the School of Architecture at Northeastern University and partner in Landing Studio with Dan Adams.

ALICE BROWN is an urban planner and chief of planning and policy at Boston Harbor Now.

DOUG BRUGGE is chair of the Department of Public Health Sciences at UConn Health.

MICHELLE DANILA P.E., PTOE is a licensed civil engineer that has redesigned streets and intersections throughout the United States that improve safety and mobility for all roadway users.

DAVID GAMBLE is an architect and urban planner and principal of Gamble Associates based in Cambridge, Massachusetts.

KATE GILBERT is an artist and executive director at Now + There, a Boston-based public art nonprofit.

REBECCA HERST is director of the Sustainable Solutions Lab at the University of Massachusetts Boston.

IMARI K. PARIS JEFFRIES is the executive director of King Boston, a trustee of the UMass System, and is currently pursuing his PhD through University of Massachusetts Boston.

JAMES JENNINGS, PHD, is professor emeritus of urban and environmental policy and planning at Tufts University.

MATTHEW J. KIEFER is lecturer at the Graduate School of Design at Harvard University and practices real estate development and land use law at Goulston & Storrs.

THEODORE C. LANDSMARK MEnvD, JD, PHD, is distinguished professor and director of the Kitty and Michael Dukakis Center for Urban and Regional Policy at Northeastern University and is on the board of directors of the Boston Planning and Development Agency.

MARIA ELENA LETONA, PHD, is executive director of Neighbor to Neighbor in Massachusetts.

RENÉE LOTH is an opinion columnist for the *Boston Globe* and former editor of *ArchitectureBoston* magazine, the quarterly journal of the Boston Society of Architects.

LYDIA LOWE is director of the Chinatown Community Land Trust.

ANNE-MARIE LUBENAU is a lecturer at Harvard's Graduate School of Design and former director of the Rudy Bruner Award for Urban Excellence.

MARIA PILAR BOTANA MARTINEZ is a PhD student at the Boston University School of Public Health, Department of Environmental Health. She has a background in architecture, urban planning, and design visualization.

ROSALYN NEGRÓN is an associate professor of anthropology at UMass Boston, a member of SSL's core team, a core faculty member in the Critical Ethnic and Community Studies program, and a research associate at the Gastón Institute for Latino Community Development and Public Policy.

MARTHA ONDRAS is a research fellow at the Health Effects Institute.

JEANETTE PANTOJA is a former public health planner at the Metropolitan Area Planning Council.

ANTONIO RACITI is an associate professor of community planning and ecological design in the Department of Urban Planning and Community Development at the University of Massachusetts Boston.

MARIE-FRANCES RIVERA is president of the Massachusetts Budget and Policy Center.

TAMARA ROY, AIA, is a principal at Stantec specializing in residential, academic, and mixed-use master planning projects, and an adjunct faculty member at the Massachusetts College of Art and Design.

ANDRES SEVTSUK is an associate professor of urban science and planning at the Massachusetts Institute of Technology, where he also directs the City Form Lab.

INDEX

Page references in *italics* refer to figures and photos.